DATE DUE

DE 1 '95			
DE 13 '99			
AP 2 6 '01			
AP 2 8 '03			

DEMCO 38-296

COLLABORATIVE LEARNING

Collaborative Learning

Higher Education, Interdependence, and the Authority of Knowledge

Kenneth A. Bruffee

The Johns Hopkins University Press

Baltimore and London

Library of Congress
Cataloging-in-Publication Data

Bruffee, Kenneth A.
Collaborative learning : higher education,
interdependence, and the authority of knowledge
/ Kenneth A. Bruffee.
p.   cm.
Includes bibliographical references (p.   ) and index.
ISBN 0-8018-4642-0 (alk. paper)
1. Group work in education—United States. 2. College
teaching—United States. 3. Team learning approach
in education—United States. 4. Education—United
States—Experimental methods.
I. Title.
LB1032.B76   1993
371.3'95—dc20   93-15073

A catalog record for this book
is available from the British Library.

Contents

Contents

Part 2
Higher Education, Interdependence,
and the Authority of Knowledge

Preface and Acknowledgments

This book is addressed to people who are college and university teachers and administrators, as I am. It is also addressed to people who are interested in higher education in ways that are not at all professional. Any college or university graduate, any parent of a college or university student, any parent of a child in high school headed for college could find what the book says about college and university education to be of direct and immediate interest.

What it says is that we should begin to think about college and university education in a way that is quite different from the way we have thought about it in the past. We should think of it as a process of cultural change. And we should think of college and university teachers as agents of cultural change. The book maintains that, to serve effectively as agents of cultural change, teachers have to organize students to learn collaboratively. And for collaborative learning to work, college and university teachers have to examine and revise longstanding assumptions that we all hold about what teachers do and why they do it.

The book defends this position in a broad range of ways. Chapter 1 begins with a fragment of autobiography that illustrates the issue. Chapter 11 analyzes a recent attempt to address it by highly respected scholars. In between, there are chapters about the day-to-day work and needs of students and teachers. There are chapters about things of concern to educational policy makers and administrators. Every chapter says or implies that in considering the changes recommended here the stakes in educational, cultural, and even economic terms are high.

The purpose of the book is to redirect the current debate about what we want college and university education to do for our children. Unless we redirect that debate, American higher education will enter the twenty-first century little different from what it was when it entered the twentieth.

My point of departure in writing the book was teaching writing and literature to college and university undergraduates. So throughout the book, perceptive readers cannot fail to notice that the writer is an English professor who has been foraging in other people's pastures: anthropology, philosophy, sociology, education, computer technology, the natural sciences, social group work, psychology, history—even law and medicine. People who normally graze these meadows and who naturally feel somewhat proprietary about them will find errors, oversimplifications, and possibly even (as Huckleberry Finn puts it) stretchers. I regret these transgressions and accept responsibility for them. But I have taken interdisciplinary risks because they seem to me unavoidable if we are ever to overcome the futile circularities of our current discussions of college and university education.

My interest in the nature of college and university education began in the sixties while I was a graduate student. As a young teacher troubled by the inadequacies of my own teaching, I sought help in the—as we called them then—"far out" educational ideas that were springing up in those days at every hand. I tried many of these ideas in my classrooms and talked with colleagues who had tried them. Some of the readers of this book may have been among our students. More often than not our students were disappointed with our experimentation, as in most cases we were too. None of those new educational ideas quite fulfilled their promise or my own youthful hope for deliverance. And I was puzzled by the fact that, in a way I couldn't quite put my finger on, most of them seemed uncomfortably similar.

In the early seventies, I had a chance to explore pedagogical innovation in colleges and universities somewhat more thoroughly. At that time, Richard Ohmann, at my alma mater Wesleyan University, was the editor of the professional journal *College English.* He kindly invited me to review the diverse innovative—or seemingly innovative—educational ideas of the day, some of which I discuss in Chapter 4. Since they represented many of the very ideas I had been looking into, the task compelled me finally to come to terms with my discomfort.

In that way I discovered what had appealed to me in these attempts to rehabilitate undergraduate teaching. They all raised the issue of the teacher's authority in college and university classrooms. I also discovered what troubled me about them. Most of them addressed that issue by trying to "give" students authority over their own knowledge, a gift that most students (in their wisdom) rejected as spurious. I surmised at the time that the failure of most attempts to revitalize college and university teaching was related somehow to the fact that they tried to change the way teachers exercise authority, without changing in any significant way the nature of that authority.

That guess led to study in areas far from my own academic background. First, I spent some valuable time at the Columbia University Graduate School of Social Work studying social group work with the late William Schwartz and acquiring a bit of the remarkable body of knowledge and expertise that that discipline provides. As I had hoped, social group work gave me many of the basic tools I needed to pursue my interest in classroom social organization. And yet, in trying to understand the nature of teachers' classroom authority, I still found myself feeling that there was a piece missing. Eventually it dawned on me that the significant changes I was looking for in the way college and university teachers understood their authority depended on their understanding of what knowledge is.

So I trotted off to school once again, this time to learn what I could about epistemology, a word I could barely pronounce, much less understand. I began by pestering (and dismaying) my kind, indulgent, and knowledgeable colleagues in the Brooklyn College Department of Philosophy. No doubt in self-defense, one of them suggested that perhaps I should take a course in theory of knowledge. I found just what I needed in a basic graduate course at the New School taught by the infinitely patient and helpful Reuben Abel. In that course I managed more or less to bend my mind around the traditional epistemological understanding of knowledge. I also first encountered Richard Rorty's *Philosophy and the Mirror of Nature.* Only when I had taken in, to the best of my ability, the nonfoundational social constructionist understanding of knowledge, in large part by reading not only Rorty but Stanley Fish, Clifford Geertz, Bruno Latour, and others, did the pieces finally fall into place. Along the way, I had adopted Edwin Mason's phrase "collaborative learning" as a useful umbrella to cover alternatives that did not evade what I had learned to regard as the key issue: the authority of knowledge and its implications for the authority of teachers.

In short, for two decades I educated myself in public. At each stage, everything I wrote was informed by what I had learned up to then, but uninformed by the thought and research that led to what I wrote later. I had no systematic knowledge of social group work until about 1976, no systematic knowledge of epistemology until about 1980. In articles published during the period 1981–1985 I tried to make practical, disciplinary sense of the (to me) shockingly new and different understanding of knowledge called social construction. In 1986, in a bibliographical article addressed to disciplinary colleagues, I pulled together what I had been reading. Only in 1989, when I began to write this book and address a larger audience, did I begin to understand under the rubric of nonfoundational thought the relationship that pertained among the three elements that concerned me—classroom teaching, social group work, and our understanding of knowledge.

To reach that point I had to reevaluate and recontextualize everything I had written up to that time, some of it as long ago as 1972. I pulled out the bits that still made sense, and I developed and synthesized ideas that now seemed implied in them: peer tutoring and institutional change, college and university teaching as a profession, teaching science, using microcomputers in education, the poststructuralist critique of cognitive thought, and poststructuralist attempts to change college and university teaching. To my mind, the book's originality, if any, lies in that synthesis.

If that seems like a tortuous route to a relatively simple conclusion, I can confirm that it often felt that way. My conclusion turned out to be simple, because it is a version of the old saw that teachers teach the way they were taught. My version is that the way college and university teachers have been taught to think about what they know and how they know it drives the way they teach it. So teachers can change the way they teach only by changing what they think about what they know and about how they know it.

Two collaborative occasions served as a matrix for writing the book. One was the series of events described in Chapter 1. The other was an institute in peer tutoring and collaborative learning that I organized in 1979–81, supported by the Fund for the Improvement of Postsecondary Education (FIPSE). That institute, two summers stretched to four by Marcia Silver's prudent management of limited resources and a contribution from Carol Stanger's follow-up FIPSE grant, is an experience that I remain enormously grateful for. Perhaps the single most important contribution to the institute was Alex Gitterman's. In teaching the institute's seminars in social group work, Alex opened a door to knowledge and expertise without which, it seems to many of us now, college and university education cannot go forward. As Harvey Kail has remarked, it was a life-changing experience. Everyone who participated in the institute, furthermore, contributed directly or indirectly to this book, and with great justification they can feel that its publication is the result of a collaborative effort.

I especially want to thank those who have contributed to the endeavor directly. FIPSE's support for the institute came about through the intervention of Alison Bernstein, my first program officer there, and through continued help from her successor Richard Hendrix and their colleague Russell Garth.

The happiest product of the institute, from my personal point of view, has been a group of friends and colleagues who have, on their own initiative, maintained contact during the intervening years as a sort of "invisible college." To that far-flung but perdurable community I am proud to belong. Most active recently have been Peter Hawkes, Mara Holt, Harvey Kail, Ronald Maxwell, and John Trimbur. Others, each of whom has made a distinctive and important contribution, have been Marian Arkin, Mary Anne Feola, Paul Connolly, Bene Scanlon Cox, Luisa Fels, and Carol Stanger.

For reading the manuscript of this book in early versions and for commenting on it so usefully I am especially indebted to Paul Connolly, Mara Holt, Harvey Kail, and John Trimbur. Others who have read all or part of the book in various states of disrepair, and who have helped make it clearer, more accurate, and more sensible, are Uldis Blukis, Benzion Chanowitz, Anne Ruggles Gere, Leon Gortler, David Leveson, Ted Marchese, Michael G. Murray, and Richard Pizer. Each of these readers has raised helpful questions about some or all of what I say here. In addition, Wilfried W. Daehnick and Brian Schwartz provided facts I needed about physics and physicists. Sheila Tobias put me on to Arnold Arons's excellent book about teaching physics. And Karen Campbell and Marisa Giannini helped prepare the manuscript in early stages.

I am grateful to Eric Steinberg for his patient lunchtime discussions of epistemology and Elmer Sprague for withholding all but gentle laughter on my account more than once. I am most grateful also to Myra Kogen for encouraging me to submit my quaking self in the spring of 1990 to a faculty seminar on the material that has become Part Two of the book. The seminar participants included Stanley Aronowitz, Louis Asekoff, George Cunningham, Dion Farquhar, Tucker Farley, the late George Fried, Myra Kogen, Thomas Mermall, Paul Montagna, Ruth Rosenberg, Stanley Salthe, Paolo Spedicato, Elmer Sprague, and Robert Viscusi. All were members of a study group sponsored by the Brooklyn College Ethyle R. Wolfe Institute for the Humanities, under Viscusi's inspired direction—a confederation of colleagues that has met monthly for more than a decade. I am indebted to the Wolfe Institute also for the Faculty Research Fellowship that gave me time to complete the book.

I am grateful to members of the faculty of Worcester Polytechnic Institute for listening gracefully to some of Chapter 9 and letting me get off campus with less egg on my face than I had feared; to Peter Elbow, Robert Lyons, Donald McQuade, Elaine Maimon, Sondra Perl, the late Mina Shaughnessy, Richard Sterling, Harvey Wiener, and the late Robert L. Hess for encouragement, challenge, and good conversation over the years; and to William Rau and Barbara Sherman Heyl for clearing up the mystery of why, until recently, the social sciences have been so slow to embrace collaborative learning. To William B. Coley I have been indebted for help and encouragement longer than either of us would care to admit. I am grateful also to my editor at the Johns Hopkins University Press, Jacqueline Wehmueller, for her intelligent, sympathetic response to the book, and to my eagle-eyed copy editor, Jeanne Pinault, for making the book more consistently readable.

Some parts of the book have been published before but in different form and synthesized in different ways. Other material was originally written to be delivered on a variety of occasions as addresses to a variety of audiences. Most of the book is entirely new. I thank the following publishers for allowing me to adapt for the present purpose parts of essays that originally appeared in their pages: Association for Educational Communications and Technology for "CLTV: Collaborative Learning Television," *Educational Communications and Technology Journal* 30 (Spring 1982): 26–40; Association of American Colleges for "The Brooklyn Plan: Attaining Intellectual Growth through Peer-Group Tutoring," *Liberal Education* 64 (1978): 447–68, as well as "Liberal Education and the Social Justification of Belief," *Liberal Education* 68 (Summer 1982): 95–114, "The Structure of Knowledge and the Future of Liberal Education," *Liberal Education* 67 (Fall 1981): 177–86, and "Liberal Education, Scholarly Community, and the Authority of Knowledge," *Liberal Education* 71 (Fall 1985): 231–39 (reprinted from *Interpreting the Humanities*, published by Woodrow Wilson Foundation, Princeton, N.J., 1985); Brown University Press for "Peer Tutoring: A Conceptual Background," *Proceedings of the Brown University Conference on Peer Tutoring*, Providence, Rhode Island, November 2–3, 1984: 1–20; City University of New York Instructional Resource Center for "On Not Listening in Order to Hear: Collaborative Learning and the Rewards of Classroom Research," *Journal of Basic Writing* 7 (1988): 3–12; HarperCollins Publishers, for parts of the "Introduction" to *A Short Course in Writing*, 3rd ed. 1985; National Collegiate Honors Council for "Knowledge, Communities, Collaborative Learning, and Honors Education," *Forum for Honors* 18 (1988): 9–20; National Council of Teachers of English for "Peer-Tutoring Writing Centers," in *Basic Writing: A Collection of Essays for Teachers, Researchers, and Administrators*, eds. Lawrence N. Kasden and Daniel Hoeber, as well as "The Way Out: A Critical Survey of Innovations in College Teaching," *College English* 33 (1972): 457–86, "Collaborative Learning and 'The Conversation of Mankind,'" *College English* 46 (November 1984): 635–52 (abridged in *Collaborative Learning: A Sourcebook for Higher Education*, ed. Anne S. Goodsell, Michelle R. Maher, and Vincent Tinto, University Park, Pa.: National Center on Postsecondary Teaching, Learning, and Assessment, 1992), "Social Construction, Language, and the Authority of Knowledge: A Bibliographical Essay," *College English* 48 (December 1986): 773–90, my contributions to "Comment and Response," *College English* 48 (January 1986): 76–78, and to "Comment and Response," *College English* 49 (1987): 707–16, and "Writing and Reading as Collaborative or Social Acts: The Argument from Kuhn and Vygotsky," in *The Writer's Mind: Writing as a Mode of Thinking*, ed. Janice N. Hays, et al., 1983; and Pennsylvania State University Writing Center for "Peer Tutors as Agents of Change," *Proceedings of the Seventh Annual National Conference on Peer Tutoring in Writing*, Pennsylvania State University, University Park, Pennsylvania, October 26–28, 1990: 1–8. Chapter 9 of this book originally appeared in slightly different form in *Change* (Fall 1992).

COLLABORATIVE LEARNING

Introduction

This book is about an underdeveloped, underused, and frequently misunderstood kind of college and university teaching and about its implications for college and university education. In collaborative learning students work on focused but open-ended tasks. They discuss issues in small consensus groups, plan and carry out long-term projects in research teams, tutor one another, analyze and work problems together, puzzle out difficult lab instructions together, read aloud to one another what they have written, and help one another edit and revise research reports and term papers.

Collaborative learning gives students practice in working together when the stakes are relatively low, so that they can work effectively together later when the stakes are high. They learn to depend on one another rather than depending exclusively on the authority of the teacher. They learn to construct knowledge as it is constructed in the academic disciplines and professions—the knowledge communities that students aspire to join when they attend colleges and universities. And they learn the craft of interdependence.

The craft of interdependence is not new to most college and university students. Many of them already know they will need it when they go to work in the "real" world of government, industry, business, finance, and the professions, where collaboration, consultation, and teamwork are increasingly the norm, not the exception. So some students prepare themselves for collaborating productively after they graduate by organizing themselves whenever they can to collaborate at school. They play ball; they plan dances, parties, and protest marches; they publish newspapers, run charitable programs, and organize self-help groups.

Interdependence is the rule in most colleges and universities, too, of course, for faculty and administrators as well as students. Everybody is on some council, committee, or task force. Everybody collaborates everywhere, in fact, except where it counts educationally. Most students do not collaborate in their classes. If they do, they may pay a stiff price. As a result, most college and university students get no experience in applying the craft of interdependence to thinking about substantive issues and to making reliable decisions.

Colleges and universities do not cultivate the craft of interdependence among students educationally, because traditional college and university teaching has little use for collaboration, does not teach it, distrusts it, and often penalizes it. Only in rare instances have college and university teachers overcome or suppressed this distrust in favor of the benefits of constructive interdependence.

A conspicuous example is a new, justly celebrated, and closely watched program in graduate education: the New Pathways program at Harvard Medical School. What makes the program collaborative is both the way it organizes students to work together and the kind of tasks it asks them to work together on. New Pathways excuses a portion of each entering class from the traditional first year curriculum—upwards of eight hours of lecture a day, five days a week. It subdivides them into consensus groups of six to eight, gives them a diagnostic problem with clinical and scientific ramifications, and allows them six weeks to come up with a solution. Each group has a faculty mentor and access to all of Harvard Medical School's extraordinary resources. But the problem is theirs and theirs alone to solve—collaboratively.[1]

New Pathways does not foster cooperation among students to help them jump through hoops of well-defined subject matter using well-defined methods. It is not another way to produce physicians who are good at answering exam questions. Harvard's traditional medical curriculum does that superlatively well. Its goal is to respond to the perception by the general public that our hospitals and clinics are staffed by physicians who must have been wonderfully adept at taking exams but can't "doctor." And its goal is to respond to the perception by many in the medical profession itself that although traditional medical education stuffs young physicians full of facts, it leaves their diagnostic judgment rudimentary and does not develop their ability to interact socially, with either colleagues or patients, over complex, demanding, perhaps life-and-death issues.

Diagnostic judgment and collaborative skills are the capacities that the New Pathways program tries to develop in young physicians. Indeed, the larger educational importance of collaborative learning is that it makes capable intellectual interdependence an integral part of college and university education. In any college or university today, mature, effective interdependence—that is, social maturity integrated with intellectual maturity—may be the most important lesson students should be asked to learn.

Students cannot learn this lesson if college and university teachers continue to teach the way most of them teach today. College and university teachers teach the way they do because they understand knowledge to be a certain kind of thing. Changing college and university teaching depends on changing teachers' understanding of what knowledge is.

Most of us, including most college and university teachers, assume a foundational (or cognitive) understanding of knowledge. Knowledge is an entity that we transfer from one head to another—for example, from a teacher's head to a student's or from a staff member's head to the head of the boss. Collaborative learning assumes instead that knowledge is a consensus among the members of a community of knowledgeable peers—something people construct by talking together and reaching agreement.

This is the understanding of knowledge that Thomas Kuhn describes on the final page of his seminal book *The Structure of Scientific Revolutions,* when he says that knowledge is "intrinsically the common property of a group or else nothing at all."[2] Understanding knowledge in this way goes by an ungainly name: nonfoundational social construction. This term is useful in talking about the future of college and university education, because it helps explain the authority of college and university teachers. It is also useful in talking about collaborative learning, because it helps explain what collaborative learning is and how it works.

Collaborative learning is a reacculturative process that helps students become members of knowledge communities whose common property is different from the common property of the knowledge communities they already belong to. It extrapolates from Kuhn's conclusion that to understand knowledge we have to know "the special characteristics of the groups that create and use it."[3] We gain access to the common property of one or another community by reacculturating ourselves so as to acquire the special characteristics of its members. The most important of these special characteristics is fluency in the language that constitutes the community, the language in which community members construct the knowledge that is their common property.

This book describes college and university education, therefore, as a process by which students become members, to one degree or another, of the knowledge communities to which their teachers belong, and it describes collaborative learning as a necessary part of that process. The job of college and university teachers is to represent the knowledge communities of which they are members in a way that will most effectively reacculturate potential new members. College and university teachers help students cross the boundaries that divide members of

3

disciplinary communities from those who want to join them: biologists from biology students, sociologists from sociology students, philosophers from philosophy students.

The most effective way to help students cross these boundaries is not, however, direct influence, apprenticeship, or what is sometimes called "collaboration" between students and teachers. College and university teachers tend to overrate somewhat their direct influence on students, and as long ago as 1962, Theodore Newcomb cited research that contradicted the traditional assumption that there is some "magic" about it. There is no evidence that intellectual development varies "—other things equal—with frequency of student-teacher contact." Newcomb argued instead that college and university teachers have their greatest influence indirectly, when they establish conditions in which students "spend a good deal of time together—particularly . . . without a sense of constraint—jointly [creating] norms, concerning their common interests, by which each of them is influenced."[4]

To effect this indirect influence, collaborative learning provides teachers with an important tool: transition communities or support groups that students can rely on as they go through the risky process of becoming new members of the knowledge communities they are trying to join. In transition communities students can achieve together what John Dewey calls the ideal aim of education: the "power of self-control" as they develop the ability and confidence to exercise the craft of interdependence.[5] First, they learn to vest authority and trust, tentatively and for short periods of time, in other members of their transition group. Then, with more confidence, they learn to vest authority and trust in the larger community that comprises the class as a whole. Finally, they learn to vest authority and trust in themselves as individuals who have internalized the language, values, and mores of the still larger community, the community of knowledgeable peers, that the teacher represents and that they have been striving to join.

Collaboration in education is not something new under the sun. The recent history of collaborative learning begins in Britain in the late 1960s. The case for a kind of educational innovation that institutionalizes classroom organization of the type explored in this book was first made in 1970 by the British educator Edwin Mason. Mason was writing about British comprehensive and grammar schools, not about American colleges and universities. But he states the case against traditional education in familiar terms: "We are directly teaching mistrust of humanity wherever we make the young compete for esteem," because we encourage the "license we have allowed ourselves in the antisocial use of our aggression," license that the world can no longer afford.[6]

Justifying a call for "a moratorium on the development and application of learning theories while we explore collaboration instead and see whether better learning results from a change of approach," Mason writes,

> I cannot think of any part or moment of life in which we are not reacting to the presence of other people, or carrying over into relationship with everything else, what we have learned (by no means all of it consciously) from collaborating with other people while exploring the world with them. It is not only to move mountains that [we] collaborate; we collaborate to pass the time pleasantly and, if we make love well, to make love, and it does not exclude conflict.[7]

Although Mason deserves a great deal of credit for calling attention again to the value of collaborative learning in the late twentieth century, collaboration in education has a much longer history. In America its principles are traceable, as Mara Holt has shown, to profoundly American sources. De Tocqueville noticed that the tendency to voluntary association is a distinctively American trait. And interdependence appears with an educational goal in the autonomous learning groups that, as Anne Ruggles Gere has pointed out, Benjamin Franklin invented to promote his own informal education.

In eighteenth- and twentieth-century America, autonomous peer groups were the only educational resource available to women and to most working men. In the 1920s and 1930s, interest in educational peer influence continued to flourish. In the forties and fifties it nearly died out. Then in the 1960s, interest revived, encouraged in part by the growth of self-help mutual-aid groups, by the systematic study of social group work, and especially by the impetus, experience, and expertise gained in support groups developed by the women's movement. In the 1970s and early eighties, collaborative learning languished once again, this time in part because, as William Rau and Barbara Sherman Heyl have shown, sociologists tended to associate it unfairly and inaccurately with managerial manipulation of workers.

At all times and in all of its manifestations, collaborative learning has "worked" by mobilizing to educational ends the informal cooperation typical of student life. Uri Treisman's award-winning program organizing minority students to work collaboratively in math and science at Berkeley confirms the position taken twenty-five years ago by James S. Coleman in *Youth: Transition to Adulthood*. Discussing the social, political, and economic assimilation of American youth into adult roles, the Coleman report suggests that it is through collaborative activities that adolescents are most effectively drawn into active participation in academic and other constructive activities.

Coleman was advancing the position Theodore Newcomb had taken as early as 1962. Newcomb reported research demonstrating that the single most powerful force in undergraduate education is peer-group influence. And like William Perry, who observed in 1970 that the "mores" of college and university education had "not kept up with" the radical change in our conception of knowledge and learning that has occurred during this century, Newcomb remarks with a note of impatience that "as an educator, I consider it deplorable that some of the kinds of changes that I think should be occurring in contemporary American colleges are not, apparently, occurring."[8]

In American colleges, large and small, Newcomb and his colleagues show, undergraduate peer groups effect most of the changes that students undergo in values and attitude—especially those related to social development and self-understanding—and yet colleges and universities waste that valuable resource. To achieve academic objectives requires a consciously organized process, what Newcomb calls mobilizing peer-group influence around intellectual concerns: taking advantage of the nature and extent of college and university students' influence on one another to help them recognize "new facts or widened perspectives" and "better mediate and reinforce the academic and intellectual influences which colleges are presumably capable of exerting."[9] Collaborative learning claims to achieve these ends by providing the essential conditions for mobilizing peer-group influence that Newcomb foresaw, in order to lead students to the heart of the intellectual process.

Recent work on the effects of peer-group influence in education confirms this early research, but has concentrated mostly on primary and secondary school education. The work of Robert Slavin, Shlomo Sharan, and David and Roger Johnson, for example, has abundantly demonstrated how "teamwork" among school children can help overcome racial and ethnic bias. It has also shown that children learn better through collaborative group work than in classrooms that are highly competitive, hierarchical, and individualized.

Research on collaborative learning in college and university education that assumes an understanding of knowledge appropriate to collaborative learning has hardly begun. What little there is tends to suppose (or, more likely, perhaps, to hope) that collaboration in learning will not change in any troubling way *what* students learn. It is merely a method, as the subtitle of a recent contribution to the literature has it, of "increasing college faculty instructional productivity": more bang for the buck.[10] Lack of appropriate research is due in large measure to the tendency of educational research projects to be dominated by the foundational (usually referred to as "cognitive") understanding of the nature and authority of knowledge. As I show in Chapter 10, because of these foundational assumptions, even the best educational research is foundationally biased in concept and result.

Research on collaborative learning tends in particular to leave unquestioned the coherence of such concepts as "situated cognition," in which social relations affect "cognition" as its "environment" or "context." It tends to distort the collaborative process itself in a foundational direction, confusing, for example, collaboration among peers (students) and cooperation between non-peers (students and teachers), classifying both as a form of hierarchical relationship between apprentice and master. And it tends to explain its results incoherently, masking its explanatory limitations with educationist bombast ("enriched learning," "rich engagements," "robust understanding").

To earn its educational keep, any shift from a foundational to a nonfoundational understanding of knowledge has to do more than affect research. It has to change what goes on in college and university classrooms. Edwin Mason approaches this central institutional issue in his last chapter. "Redesigning an educational system," he says, "is a relatively easy exercise. Changing one's own teaching, especially when it has been acclaimed as successful by all the old standards, is very much harder."[11]

The reason that college and university education is so hard to change where it counts most is that most teachers tend to oversimplify or ignore the issue of their authority as teachers. Collaborative learning brings to the surface the relationship between the authority of knowledge and the authority of teachers. By challenging the traditional, foundational understanding of the authority of knowledge, collaborative learning helps college and university teachers begin thinking in quite a different way about what it means to teach.

This change may not always be a comfortable experience for teachers, at least at first. Exercising a different kind of authority can make teachers ask themselves if they are still exercising authority at all. When they have successfully organized students to learn with one another instead of isolating themselves or competing against one another, teachers sometimes ask themselves if they can possibly be fulfilling their responsibility to their discipline and doing the job that their institution pays them to do. Their supervisor, their students, and their students' parents may find themselves asking the same question. Are teachers who organize their students to learn collaboratively still "really teaching" at all?[12]

In this book I try to demonstrate that the nonfoundational social constructionist understanding of knowledge can help answer questions like these. I argue that the nature and source of the authority of college and university teachers, not curriculum or students' intellectual and emotional development, is the central issue in college and university education in our time. Behind every public debate about college curriculum today lie comfortably unchallenged traditional assumptions. For example, although former Secretary of Education William Bennett, Allan Bloom, E. D. Hirsch, and members of the National Association of Scholars differ widely from their adversaries in academic organizations such as the Modern Language Association and the American Council of Learned Societies on questions of what and whom college and university teachers should be teaching, and why, both sides make the *same* assumptions about the authority of knowledge and thus the authority of teachers. When we become fully aware of how deeply and irremediably these traditional assumptions have been challenged by twentieth-century thought, we see that a potentially more serious, and perhaps more rancorous and divisive, educational debate lies in wait for us.

It is time to begin that debate, because the authority of knowledge and the way it plays out in college and university education is not just an academic issue. It is, for everyone concerned, a concrete and personal one. It is related, for example, to the way our children behave in college and the sort of fellow citizens and professionals they are likely to become after they graduate. In the long run it is related to our productivity as a nation. For a decade or more, reports on the state of American higher education have complained that many undergraduates tend to be authority-dependent, passive, irresponsible, overly competitive, and suspicious of their peers. Similar complaints have been made about students in professional training, especially those preparing for professions, such as medicine and law, that require them to interact constructively with other human beings. These complaints will persist as long as we fail to understand interdependence and constructive human interaction as part and parcel of knowledge and learning.

My assumption is not, however, that nonfoundational social constructionist thought is a "theoretical rationale" that "grounds" the practice of collaborative learning. Nonfoundational social construction and collaborative learning are related in a way that is entirely different from the foundational relation between theory and practice. They are related by virtue of their common assumption that knowledge is a socially constructed, sociolinguistic entity and that learning is inherently an interdependent, sociolinguistic process.

The nonfoundational understanding of knowledge provides a language with which to redescribe and talk coherently about college and university education as an enterprise engaged in promoting change. It assumes that we construct and maintain knowledge not by examining the world but by negotiating with one another in communities of knowledgeable peers. Similarly, collaborative learning assumes that learning occurs among persons, not between persons and things. I have assumed in this book that the central issue for college and university education today is the educational significance of this understanding of knowledge, undifferentiated as to subject matter or type, and the nature of the authority of college and university teachers that such an understanding of knowledge implies. The book shows how education can more effectively mobilize peer-group influence around intellectual concerns if we understand knowledge to be a social construct and learning a social process.

This book aspires to offer, therefore, a set of terms and assumptions for talking about knowledge, learning, and teaching, and about college and university education in general, that does not fudge that central issue. The most important of these are listed and defined, and their significance briefly discussed, in a glossary at the end of the book.

Collaborative learning is not a universal educational cure-all, and it does not make obsolete such time-tested pedagogical activities as lecture, drill, and recitation. There are times in every college and university course when the best thing teachers can do is tell students something, make them repeat something, or ask them to respond to questions. What this book contends is that if we understand knowledge as a social construct rather than a cognitive entity, then lecturing, drilling, and leading recitations are appropriate and effective only within the context of structured conversation among students: collaborative learning. Collaborative learning is not just another arrow in a teacher's quiver of pedagogical tricks. It requires teachers to subordinate and transform traditional teaching methods.

As for the likelihood that the proposals I make here will have any effect on college and university education in the near future, I am not holding my breath. But I take some comfort in Nicholas Jardine's view that educational change can affect the state of knowledge and professional practice to the degree that it is part of a more general process of cultural change.[13] Collaborative learning applies, legitimizes, and establishes in college and university education practices that are in fact already familiar and well established in American educational, political, and social life. This familiarity accounts for the alacrity with which one form of collaborative learning, peer tutoring (discussed in Chapter 5), has been adopted by American colleges and universities over the past twenty years. Other forms of collaborative learning will be educationally persuasive, pervasive, and effectual to the degree to which they are, as Jardine puts it, appropriated or grafted on to existing practice. For educational change of the sort advocated here to achieve maximum effectiveness, the academic and professional disciplines, college and universities as a whole, and the general public must come to regard collaborative learning as analogous to, adaptable to, or in harmony with ways of doing things that they are already familiar with, find useful, and depend on.

The book is divided into two parts. Part 1 discusses the implications of nonfoundational social constructionist thought for college and university teaching. It explains what collaborative learning is, how it works, and why. Part 2 reconsiders other topics related to college and university education in light of nonfoundational social constructionist thought and the interdependence it implies. Three related assumptions are central to both parts. One is that, understood nonfoundationally, knowledge is a social construct. The second is that students need to learn interdependently in order to become effectively interdependent at work and as citizens. And the third is that interdependence, the authority of knowledge, and the authority of college and university teachers are integrally related.

Chapters 1 to 6, Part 1, outline several aspects of collaborative learning, based on my own twenty years of tinkering with it and on the experience of several colleagues around the country with whom I had the privilege to work during that time. Chapter 1 describes the experience in which I first became aware of the change in our understanding of knowledge and learning that was in fact already well under way around me. Chapter 2 explains the principles of a common model of collaborative learning, classroom consensus groups. Chapter 3 outlines the role that the educationally most important displaced form of conversation, writing, plays in collaborative learning and, conversely, the role that collaborative learning can play in teaching students to write well.

Chapter 4 works through many of the pedagogical issues generated by collaborative learning as college and university teachers confront them in classroom teaching and suggests the changes in attitude that are necessary if institutional response to these issues is to be more than cosmetic. Chapter 5 discusses one way in which institutions can initiate these changes in attitude and thereby begin to institutionalize collaborative learning in college and university education: through the influence of peer tutors. Chapter 6 explores the implications of collaborative learning and the nonfoundational understanding of knowledge for modern advances in education technology, in particular television and microcomputers.

Readers interested primarily in considering the relationship between nonfoundational social constructionist thought and somewhat broader issues in college and university education might consider beginning with Part 2. Chapter 7 says that the nonfoundational understanding of knowledge implies that college and university education involves interdependence in the form of constructive conversation, or collaboration, at the boundaries of knowledge communities. Chapter 8 explains some of the professional implications of the nonfoundational understanding of knowledge for college and university teachers as members of communities of knowledgeable peers. Chapter 9 discusses the benefits of teaching science in colleges and universities as a tradition of pragmatic, interpretive thought, benefits that include returning undergraduate science courses to their rightful place in the liberal arts curriculum.

Chapter 10 shows how foundational (that is, stereotypically cognitive) thinking has negatively affected not only the education provided by colleges and universities but also some of the research done there. Chapter 11 describes and evaluates some attempts by eminent college and university teachers to come to terms educationally with the nonfoundational understanding of knowledge and learning. And Chapter 12 sketches an undergraduate curriculum that attempts to institutionalize in a more or less systematic way a nonfoundational understanding of knowledge.

Part 1

Collaborative Learning:
What It Is and What It's About

CHAPTER ONE

Collaboration, Conversation, and Reacculturation

Once upon a time, many years ago, a time when the youngest faculty member at most colleges and universities today had not yet entered puberty, a young assistant professor at one of those colleges was assigned a task that was in those days de rigueur for low level English Department types. He was asked to become Director of Freshman English. Feeling flattered, having a modicum of interest in teaching writing, but lacking even the most rudimentary sense of caution, and in any case not having a great deal of choice in the matter, he agreed. The year was 1971. The college was Brooklyn College. The young assistant professor was me. And at the City University of New York, of which Brooklyn College is a constituent campus, 1970 turned out to be the first year of open admissions.

In open admissions, some 20,000 new students, many of them lacking the basic skills of reading, writing and mathematics needed for college work, entered the City University of New York. These new students challenged the university's faculty in ways that often far exceeded the experience, training, and expectations of scholars and scientists bred in the quiet intensity of library carrels and research labs. To most of us it felt like a rout.

My job as the new Freshman Comp Director was to organize, more or less from scratch, a program of courses in writing at all levels, remedial to advanced, that would meet the needs of those new students, teach freshman composition and a literature survey course, teach my English Department colleagues how to teach remedial writing and freshman composition to the college's new unprepared students, and manage upwards of 108 composition instructors teaching some 160-odd sections each term.

I don't mind admitting I was soon desperate. I thought wistfully about that manuscript sitting half-finished on a shelf in my study, a truly splendid book of literary criticism about the great monuments of modern fiction, and my pellucid lecture notes on Wordsworth and the English

Romantics yellowing away in a drawer, unthumbed, unreferred to, unapplauded.

In my state of confusion and despair, it occurred to me that there must be other people in my shoes on other City University campuses—CCNY, Hunter, Queens, somewhere. Surely they must be coping better than I. I had never heard of any of them, and they had never heard of me. But surely someone in this anonymous crowd would help me understand and accomplish the seemingly impossible task I had committed myself to. I called them up. They all claimed that they too were desperate. Warily, we agreed to get together for a beer.

They did help me, as it turned out, but not quite the way I had expected. I thought I would ask some questions and they would provide the answers. But it wasn't long before we were all startled to discover not just that none of us had any answers, but that none of us even knew the right questions.

It bears witness to our collective state of mind that we found this appalling discovery refreshing and provocative. The tedium of petty college and university administration had unaccountably coughed up an intellectual challenge. We decided to meet again and talk some more. We began converging Saturday mornings on a mutually convenient Manhattan coffee shop. We also met several times at a wonderful soup shop that had just opened on Fifth Avenue called La Potagerie. We had a pretty good time. To focus our discussions in the midst of all this medium-high living, we decided to give ourselves some reading assignments. We chose several books and articles that one or another of us had run across in some context or other and that seemed to offer some help in looking at the needs of our students, if possible in a larger than merely academic context.

Working together in this way, we gradually began to make some striking discoveries about our students, ourselves, and our profession. In fact, what we found out about our students was not unlike what we found out about ourselves and our profession.

One of the first things we read together was Sennett and Cobb's *The Hidden Injuries of Class*, a book that talks about families of blue-collar workers living in and around Boston. These families had a lot in common with the family I had grown up in and, as we eventually learned from one another, with the family life many of us in the group had experienced. They also had a good deal in common with the families of the students we were now teaching. One of the first and most important things that Sennett and Cobb suggested to us was that teaching writing to open-admissions students might raise issues that were more profound than simply how to "correct errors." Teaching writing might in fact involve an issue that seemed altogether beyond our professional training and expertise to understand: acculturation.

It began to dawn on us, in short, as we read and talked about what we read, that our students, however poorly prepared academically, did not come to us as blank slates. They arrived in our classes already deeply acculturated, already full-fledged, competent members (as we were, too) of some community or other. In fact, they were already members of several interrelated communities (as we were, too).

If that was the case, we concluded, then in the first instance the way our students talked and wrote, and even the way they behaved in class, did not involve "errors" at all. They talked, wrote, and behaved in a manner that was perfectly correct and acceptable within the community they were currently members of. The way they talked, wrote, and behaved was "incorrect" and unacceptable, we found ourselves saying, only in a community that they were not—or were not yet—members of. The community that the students were not yet members of and were asking to join by virtue of committing themselves to attend college was of course the (to them) alien community of the "literate" and the "college educated." In a word, us.

Beginning to describe our students in this new way, we also began to talk about our job as their teachers in a new way, a way that differed strikingly from the way we were in the habit of talking about college and university teaching. If how our students talked, wrote, and behaved was not in the first instance a matter of "error," we began to say, then perhaps our job as teachers was not in the first instance to "correct" them. We recognized, of course, that what the community of the "literate" and the "liberally educated" regarded as correct and incorrect talk, writing, and behavior remained an issue. But what we were now saying was that in the first instance our job as teachers was to find ways to begin and to sustain a much more difficult, painful, and problematical process than "correcting errors" in our students' talk, writing, and behavior. Our job as teachers, we were saying, was to find out how, in some way and in some measure, to reacculturate the students who had placed themselves in our charge.

The way my colleagues and I were beginning to talk about college and university education was not only new to us, it was entirely different from the way our disciplinary colleagues on our home campuses still talked about it. Increasingly, we found, they failed to understand what we were saying. As a result, we felt less and less comfortable with those at home and abroad to whose professional company, values, and goals we had committed ourselves as graduate students. It seemed like a pretty risky situation to most of us, and would have seemed even riskier except for our realization that we were feeling more and more comfortable with one another. In short, we began to be aware that the change in the way we talked about what we were doing signaled a cultural change in ourselves, about which we were deeply ambivalent.

In fact, I would say now, the change in the way we talked about college and university education was more than a signal of change. Change in the way we talked was the cultural change itself that we were undergoing. The language we had begun to use literally constituted the small transition community of which we were now increasingly devoted members. Learning, as we were experiencing it, was not just inextricably related to that new social relationship among us. It was identical with it and inseparable from it. To paraphrase Richard Rorty's account of learning, it was not a shift inside us that now suited us to enter new relationships with reality and with other people. Learning *was* that shift in our language-constituted relations with others.

To further this process of cultural change we were experiencing, another text we assigned ourselves was Paulo Freire's *Pedagogy of the Oppressed.* This book is about teaching reading and writing to the illiterate poor in Brazil, and it has an unmistakably Marxist slant. Now, I don't think anyone in our group would have called us Marxists. Observing us lunching on parmentier and Perrier water at La Potagerie, no outsider would be ineluctably driven to that conclusion. For the most part we shared a bias that was fairly typical of the early-nineteen seventies academics that we were: a bias that was mostly white, mostly male, and solidly American middle-class.

Despite that bias, however, we were fully aware that there was a sense in which many of our students were forced to pursue postsecondary education, largely through economic pressure, by a society that paid workers better who were literate in the standard dialect of English than those who were not literate in it. A job at the telephone company turned up as a point of reference, and a high proportion of those who even today fail the New York Telephone Company employee entrance exams suggests that that was not a wholly unrealistic criterion. And one thing we learned from Freire was that our middle-class American goal of establishing literacy in the standard dialect was shared by at least one person whose basic political assumptions differed quite a bit from our own.

Stirred by these concerns, our discussion of Freire began by addressing the troubling key word in his title, the term "oppressed." I think we all found it somewhat melodramatic as applied to open-admissions students. But we had to admit also, without casting aspersions as to the source of that condition, that to say that our students existed in a state of "oppression" was not entirely inappropriate. Sennett and Cobb had taught us that our students had been acculturated to talk to and deal effectively only with people in their own crowd, their own neighborhood, perhaps only in their own family or ethnic group.

Their worlds were closed by walls of words. To be acculturated to those perfectly valid and coherent but entirely local communities alone had severely limited their freedom. It had prepared them for social, political, and economic relations of only the narrowest sort. It had closed them out of relations with other communities, including the broader, highly diverse, integrated American (or for that matter, international) community at large represented in a perhaps minor but (from their point of view) not insignificant way by a job at the New York Telephone Company.

One result of this exclusively local acculturation appeared to be that many of our students could not discover their own buried potential and could not achieve the more economically viable and vocationally satisfying lives they aspired to. We suspected (given our middle-class, professional, liberal-humanistic bias) that our students' acculturation also prevented them from living lives that were intellectually, emotionally, and aesthetically fulfilling. We realized furthermore that this was not exclusively an "open admissions" problem. Parochialism of undergraduate experience and thought is a problem that, on William Perry's testimony, is not unknown even among undergraduates at Harvard College.

So, although we knew that what Freire meant by the key word in his title, "oppressed," was not exactly what we meant by it, to the extent that our more liberal sense of the word did correspond with Freire's intent, it led us in a useful direction. In order to make any positive impression at all on the students we were encountering in our classes, it was clear that we too needed a pedagogy of the "oppressed," even in our more pallid sense of it.

The pedagogy that Freire offered turned out, furthermore, to be something we had come across before in our reading and would come across again, used to accomplish a similar end. The feminist movement of the sixties and seventies, for example, had used this pedagogy to help women change their attitudes toward themselves and to reconstruct their role in society. Kurt Lewin had used it to help people accept dietary changes caused by food scarcities during World War II and to liberate children and adolescents who had been raised as Hitler Youth. A pedagogy that could relieve or overcome "oppression" in many relevant senses, we began to see, would inevitably be a pedagogy of reacculturation: a pedagogy of cultural change.

Freire, in fact, went well beyond leading us toward considering the possibility that a pedagogy of reacculturation could meet our needs. He and others also told us something about what a pedagogy of reacculturation might be, and how it might work. We learned first that reacculturation is at best extremely difficult to accomplish. It is probably next to impossible to accomplish individually, reacculturation fantasies such as *The Taming of the Shrew* and *Pygmalion* notwithstanding.

What does seem just possible to accomplish is for people to reacculturate themselves by working together. That is, there does exist a way in which we seem able to sever, weaken, or renegotiate our ties to one or more of the communities we belong to and at the same time gain membership in another community. We can do that if, and it seems in most cases only if, we work collaboratively. What we have to do, it appears, is to organize or join a temporary transition or support group on the way to our goal, as we undergo the trials of changing allegiance from one community to another. The agenda of this transition group is to provide an arena for conversation and to sustain us while we learn the language, mores, and values of the community we are trying to join.

In short, this pedagogy of reacculturation had been right under our noses all along. What we had been doing ourselves was exactly that. We ourselves were engaged in the complex, tortuous, wearing, collaborative process of reacculturation. Faced with a situation that seemed alien to us and which our training as conventional academic humanists, library mice, and English-teacher types did not prepare us to cope with, we had in self-defense recognized the degree of affinity that existed among us, on that basis formed a transition group, and assigned ourselves tasks to do collaboratively. We read. We met regularly. We treated ourselves well and had a good time. We got to know one another. We talked. We wrote, and we read one another's writing. We even managed to get some of it into print.

We learned a lot from reading, of course. That was because reading is one way to join new communities, the ones represented by the authors of the texts we read. By reading, we acquire fluency in the language of the text and make it our own. Library stacks from this perspective are not a repository; they are a crowd. Conversely, we make the authors we have read members of our own community. Our little discussion group had, in effect, adopted Sennett and Cobb and Freire into membership.

But although we learned a lot from what we read, we learned a lot more from what we said to one another about what we read. Each of us began to change, and we discovered that the most powerful force changing us was our influence on one another. In the process we became a new community. It was a knowledge community in which its members talked about college and university education as quintessentially reacculturative and talked about reacculturation as quintessentially collaborative.

Not everyone has gone through an experience of boundary conversation and collaborative reacculturation quite as extensive and long-lived as the one in the tale I have just told. But the essence of it will be familiar to anyone who has been in a mutual-aid self-help support group devoted to a special interest or disability. Groups of this sort concentrate on solving or dealing with a formidable problem. They constitute in many cases a transition community between small, isolated communities of despair (such as alcoholics or families of alcoholics, those who take care of cancer victims or victims of Alzheimer's disease, battered women, and so on) and a larger community of more confident, more knowledgeable, more competent, and a good deal less lonely people who can cope. Group members distribute knowledge and authority among themselves, taking it upon themselves to help each other in times of threat and calamity to find the will and the way.

The essence of collaboration will even be familiar to those who have worked with an intelligent, compatible committee or task force on an interesting, demanding project. People in groups of this sort assume one another's will to do the job. They concentrate instead on a way to get the job done. One person gets an idea, stumbles around with it a bit, and then sketches it out. Another says, wait a minute—that makes me think of . . . A third says, but look, if we change this or add that . . . People who take part in a collaborative enterprise such as this exceed, with a little help from their friends, what no one of them alone could have learned, accomplished, or endured.

Collaboration will be familiar, too, to lawyers, journalists, accountants, science and technical writers, and others who have ever asked colleagues to read a manuscript of theirs or who have ever "done an edit" (as my wife the lawyer puts it) on something a colleague has written. Constructive readers of that sort read a draft, scribble some notes in the margins, maybe write a page or two of comments congratulating the writer on a good start, suggest a few changes, and mention one or two issues to be thought through a bit further. Then the two of them, reader and writer, sit down together and talk the draft over before the writer goes back to work on it.

If I am right that experiences of this kind are familiar to many people, then few are likely to be strangers to reacculturation by means of collaboration. When shopkeeper A asks shopkeeper B to take a look at the way she has rearranged the floor of her shop, and A agrees to do it, they become an autonomous collaborative group of two with the task of revising and developing the product of one of its members. The collaboration is worthwhile for both of them for two reasons. As members of the same, concentric, or overlapping communities of interest and expertise, they speak much the same language. And as members of different communities or subgroups, they look in upon each other's communities with the uncommitted eyes of outsiders. Both know in general what it takes to display wares in an attractive way, but shopkeeper B doesn't know much about handling the particular line of goods that A is selling. B will understand and agree with some of what A has done with her store but will raise questions about other things. Challenged, A will translate unfamiliar terms and ideas into language that B can more or less understand and accept. They will come to terms, reach a consensus.

The same sort of thing happens when anyone, even a college or university student, works collaboratively. With material his students generated in a course he taught collaboratively some years ago, John Trimbur shows what happens in such a collaborative group.[1] The assignment was to read a Studs Terkel interview with a former Ku Klux Klan leader who had reversed his position, coming in the end to agree with Martin Luther King. While the students were reading, thinking, and discussing, they were to keep a personal log. Trimbur first asked them to discuss the piece in small, task-oriented groups of the sort I describe in Chapter 2. Then he asked them to go home and write an essay explaining that change, all the while keeping track of their thinking and their class discussion in their logs. He tells the rest of the story this way.

> One woman wrote in her log that at first she couldn't think of anything to say [about the Terkel interview]. She found the assignment difficult because she did not want to "judge" the guy. She went on quite a while in this entry to say how in her family she had been brought up not to "judge" other people.

Notice that the student herself (I'll call her Mary) attributes her difficulty in discussing the subject to the way she had been acculturated in the first place: the way "in her family she had been brought up." Mary's teacher was asking her to talk about something beyond the boundaries of the knowledge community she belonged to. Trimbur continues:

> Then, in a log entry written a few days later, she wrote again about the class hour when we discussed the Terkel piece and the writing assign-

ment. What she remembered now was something that another woman in the class had said about "conversion." She found herself "talking it over" with that woman in her mind, and as she talked it over she began to connect the idea of conversion with the story of Saint Paul in the Bible. Making this connection was a dramatic event for her, as the entry describes it. "Dramatic" is not too strong a word for the experience, because it actively involved an imagined conversation with a classmate. Once that event occurred she felt ready to write and interested in what she had to say.

One thing this passage tells us is that change—reacculturation, learning—began for Mary when she engaged in conversation with a peer at the boundary between the community she was brought up in and the community her classmate was brought up in. Her classmate shared part of her cultural background, the religious part, but did not share another part of it, the antijudgmental part. In this conversation, Mary's peer provided the new word that allowed her to talk about the topic she had been assigned. She interposed, helping her to "translate" a word she was familiar with (*conversion*) from a strictly religious context to a secular one. Then she internalized this boundary conversation with her peer and continued it on her own, in her imagination, as thought.

After direct conversation ended for Mary, collaboration continued indirectly, because direct conversation had provided the language she needed in order to "talk to herself"—that is, think—productively in a new way. As it had for my colleagues and me, boundary conversation had given Mary the means for crossing that boundary. It gave her the terms with which to renegotiate her relationship with two communities, the one she was brought up in and the one she was entering by virtue of her college education.

Another thing the passage tells us is that at the same time that conversation, external and internalized, changed Mary's opinion, it also changed her feelings about the topic, about the conversation, and about herself. It made her feel "ready to write and interested in what she had to say." Her early acculturation into one community (being "brought up not to 'judge' people") made her reject the whole idea being presented in the Terkel interview. Conversation changed this attitude to a willingness to entertain the idea. It also let her formulate a new opinion and want to write about it.

In recording that change and its educational consequences, this student has recorded the crucial step in educational collaboration, the first step we take whenever we set out to join a larger, more inclusive community of knowledgeable peers. That step is to overcome resistance to change that evidences itself as ambivalence about engaging in conversation at the boundaries of the knowledge communities that we already belong to. As Roberto Unger tells us, we are drawn to one another and distrust one another at the same time. We want to get to know one another, but we are disinclined to talk with strangers. We continue to resist and feel uncomfortable with one another, until we find terms that we feel are translatable, terms that we know are appropriate and acceptable in the community we currently belong to and that we can also displace in acceptable and appropriate ways into the community we are tempted to join. In Mary's case, the term that served this purpose was "conversion." In the case of my City University colleagues and me, the same purpose was served by terms such as "culture," "reacculturate," and "oppressed."

This transitional process of translation, this willingness to learn the elements of new languages and gain new expertise, is the most important skill in the craft of interdependence. It is a willingness to become members of communities we have not belonged to before, by engaging in constructive conversation with others whose background and needs are similar to our own but also different. Reacculturative conversation of the sort exemplified in the tale that begins this chapter combines the power of mutual-aid self-help groups with the power of successfully collaborative intellectual work. It integrates the will and the way. And as we shall see in Chapter 2, in this process of arriving at consensus, dissent may also play an important, sometimes even decisive, role.

To be able to engage in constructive, reacculturative conversation, however, requires willingness to grant authority to peers, courage to accept the authority granted to one by peers, and skill in the craft of interdependence. This book takes the position that a good college or university education fosters that willingness, courage, and skill, but that many college and university educations today, widely regarded as very good indeed, do not in fact foster them.

Understanding the importance of conversation to college and university education began in the late 1950s with M.L.J. Abercrombie's research on educating medical students at University Hospital, University of London. Abercrombie showed that her medical students learned the key element in successful medical practice, diagnosis—that is, medical judgment—more quickly and accurately when they worked collaboratively in small groups than when they worked alone.

A close look at Abercrombie's results in light of Mary's experience is revealing. Abercrombie began her work by observing the scene that most of us think is typical of medical education: the group of medical students with a teaching physician on "rounds," hovering over a ward bed to diagnose a patient. She changed that scene by making a slight but crucial difference in the way it is usually played out. Instead of asking each individual member of the group of medical students to diagnose the patient on his or her own, Abercrombie asked the whole group to examine the patient together, discuss the case as a group, and arrive at a consensus: a single diagnosis that they could all agree on.

The result, that students who learned diagnosis collaboratively acquired better medical judgment faster than individual students who worked alone, showed that learning diagnostic judgment is not an individual process but a social, interdependent one. It occurs on an axis drawn not between individuals and things but among people. Students learn judgment best in groups, Abercrombie inferred, because they tend to talk each other out of their unshared biases and presuppositions. That is, the differences among them push them into socially justifying their beliefs or, failing that, into acknowledging that their beliefs are socially unjustifiable and abandoning them.

This is also the message of Uri Treisman's work at the Berkeley campus of the University of California, for which he has won the Dana prize and a MacArthur Fellowship. On that polyglot, multiethnic campus, Treisman, who is a mathematician, was puzzled by the fact that students in some ethnic groups did significantly better at math and science than students in other ethnic groups. In particular, Asian-American students at Berkeley tended to excel, whereas African-American and Hispanic students tended not to.

To find out why, Treisman devised an elegantly simple experiment. He followed the Asian-American students around campus to see how they did it. What he discovered was that they were continually engaged in conversation about their work. They moved in packs, ate together, studied together, went to classes together. In contrast, the African-American and Hispanic students Treisman watched were largely isolated from one another. They seldom studied or talked together about their work.

Treisman surmised that this was the crucial difference between the academic success level of these two groups of students. So he set out to change the way in which Berkeley's remedial math and science program was organized. He brought the African-American and Hispanic students together, gave them a place to study collaboratively, showed them how to work together effectively, and insisted that they work collaboratively on a regular basis. Lo and behold, many of Treisman's "remedial" students soon became B and A students. Conversation, Treisman discovered, is of such vital importance to learning that, with it, any of us has a shot at doing whatever we want to do. Without it, none of us stands a chance.

Institutionalized educational collaboration in whatever form, however, is never unproblematical. It almost always involves an attempt on the teacher's part to reacculturate students at several levels. Reacculturation extends beyond initiation into a disciplinary community of mathematicians, sociologists, or classicists to initiation into a community of willingly collaborative peers. A class must somehow manage to constitute itself as a community with its own particular mores, goals, linguistic history, and language.

This process is not always easy, because students do not always work effectively as collaborative peers, especially at first. There are several reasons for this. First, given most students' almost exclusive experience of traditional classroom authority, many have to learn, sometimes against considerable resistance, to grant authority not to the teacher alone but to a peer ("What right has he got . . . ?") instead of the teacher. They also have to learn, sometimes against considerable resistance, to accept the authority given them by a peer ("What right have I got . . . ?") and to exercise that authority judiciously and helpfully in the interest of a peer.

Any teacher who has asked students to criticize one another's work without preparing them to do it has seen resistance of both kinds. Students' first reaction to being asked to comment on another student's work is almost invariably to interpret it as an invitation to rat on a friend: mutual criticism as a form of treason. If the teacher does manage somehow to break through this refusal to comment on another student's work except in the blandest terms, the alternative reaction goes to the opposite extreme: almost vile excoriation. At first students refuse to admit that they see anything wrong with a fellow student's work. Then they refuse to admit that there is anything of value in it at all. They become, as a student once put it to me, either teddy bears or sharks. Both responses are typical of group solidarity, which tends to enforce loyalty and mutual defense and to scapegoat some members of the group, ejecting them and closing ranks against them. Needless to say, neither response is likely to develop the craft of interdependence and lead to mature judgment.

These typically solidarian responses show that most college and university students have thoroughly internalized long-prevailing academic prohibitions against collaboration. Traditionally, after all, collaboration skates dangerously close to the supreme academic sin, plagiarism. Furthermore, most college and university students are confirmed in the habit of identifying the authority of knowledge in a classroom exclusively with the teacher's authority. As a result, they often do not believe that a request to collaborate is genuine, and they do not always know what might be in it for them if they did collaborate.

Of course, even in a collaborative classroom, authority does begin in most cases (as it should) with the institutional representative or agent, the teacher. Mary and her classmates did not read and discuss Studs Terkel on their own initiative. Their teacher asked them to do it. Furthermore, most students start most semesters in most classrooms as strangers. They do not begin, as shopkeepers A and B did, as trusted neighbors, colleagues, or friends. They begin with the wariness of one another that my City University colleagues and I began with. And, semesters being short, students do not have the kind of time that we had to get to know and trust one another. It is therefore not surprising that some students may not be overly eager at first to collaborate, and that a few may remain skeptical.

But the experience of skillfully managed classroom collaboration can help move students toward incorporating into their intellectual work much of what they have learned about working interdependently in their many collaborative experiences outside class. For students who are inexperienced in collaboration, a series of modestly challenging tasks can, over time, give them a chance to discover the value, interest, and often in fact the excitement that they can derive from interpreting tasks on their own and inventing or adapting a language with which to negotiate the consensus that they need in order to get the work done. With the instructor for the moment out of the way and the chain of hierarchical institutional authority for the moment broken, most students enjoy the freedom to reinvent in class the collaborative peership that most of them are quite familiar with in their everyday lives. Chapter 2 will illustrate with one kind of collaborative learning how the process works.

CHAPTER TWO

Consensus Groups:
A Basic Model of Classroom Collaboration

One model of collaborative learning, although by no means the only one, is classroom consensus groups. In consensus groups people work collaboratively on a limited but open-ended task, negotiating among themselves what they think and know in order to arrive at some kind of consensus or agreement, including, sometimes, agreement to disagree. In organizing these groups, teachers typically do four things:

- They divide a large group—the class—into small groups.
- They provide a task, usually designed (and, preferably, tested) ahead of time, for the small groups to work on.
- They reconvene the larger group into plenary session to hear reports from the small groups and negotiate agreement among the group as a whole.
- They evaluate the quality of student work, first as referee, then as judge.

Organizing small consensus groups is not hard to do. But satisfactory results require college and university teachers to behave in their classrooms in ways that strike many who are used to traditional teaching as at best unusual. The nitty-gritty of this process of social organization can look trivial on the page. But it adds up to fairly sophisticated expertise that includes some familiarity with the research on "group dynamics," some forethought, some sensitivity to social situations and relationships, a somewhat better-than-average understanding of what is being taught, and self-control.

This chapter describes what happens in a typical consensus-group class and outlines some of the relevant research. It explains what goes into designing a good collaborative learning task. It explains how teachers draw a collaborative class back together to develop a consensus of the whole. And it explains how they evaluate students' individual contributions to the class's conversation through the students' writing.

A Basic Model of Classroom Collaboration

A collaborative class using consensus groups goes something like this:

After explaining what's going to happen, the teacher divides students into groups of five or six. This usually means that the teacher acts a bit like a social director at a vacation resort or summer camp, counting students off, wading in to help them rearrange chairs, separating groups to minimize noise from other conversations, and encouraging group members to draw close enough together to hear one another over the din and to make the group more likely to cohere.

Then the teacher gives students a sheet with a task and instructions on it. An alternative is to pick out a passage of text as it appears in a book that all the students have at hand and write questions and instructions on the blackboard. (Later in this chapter I will explain what is distinctive about collaborative learning tasks and offer suggestions for designing them.)

Once students are settled in their groups, teachers ask them to introduce themselves (if necessary) and decide on a recorder, a member of the group who will take notes on the group's discussion and report on the consensus the group has reached when the work is over. As the small-group work starts, the teacher backs off. Emphatically, the teacher does not "sit in" on consensus groups, hover over them, or otherwise monitor them. Doing that inevitably destroys peer relations among students and encourages the tendency of well-schooled students to focus on the teacher's authority and interests.

If a teacher's goal is productive collaboration among peers, closely monitoring student small-group discussion is self-defeating. That is because the message that teachers deliver when they monitor student small-group discussion is a foundational message: that students should first and foremost be striving to use the language of the teacher's discipline, the teacher's own community of knowledgeable peers. This is a foundational message because it reinforces dependence on the teacher's authority and unquestioning reliance on the authority of what the teacher knows. Students fear that they will "get it wrong." Teachers fear that discussion will "get out of hand"—that is, go in some direction that the teacher has not anticipated and thereby cast doubt on the teacher's classroom authority and the authority of the teacher's knowledge.

While students are at work, the teacher's main responsibility is keeping time. Time is a nonrenewable natural resource. The teacher's job is to conserve it. The length of time that students spend on a task depends on the complexity of the task and on how accustomed students are to working together. Depending on how much time is available, the teacher sets a time limit for the work or simply asks each group at some point how much more time they think they will need. When most groups have completed the task, the teacher asks the recorder in each group to report and, acting as recorder for the class as a whole, writes out the results on the blackboard or asks the recorders to write their results on the board themselves. If most groups have been able to complete only part of the task, the task the teacher has assigned was too long or complex for the time available. Recorders report on the part the group has been able to complete and leave the rest for another time.

When the small-group work is finished, the teacher referees a plenary discussion in which the class as a whole analyzes, compares, and synthesizes the groups' decisions, negotiating toward an acceptable consensus. Here, the teacher serves as recorder for the class as a whole, not only writing out and revising the consensus as the discussion proceeds, but also pointing out gaps, inconsistencies, and incoherence. Finally (as we shall see later in this chapter), the teacher compares the class's consensus with the current consensus in the knowledge community that the teacher represents.

Throughout this process—group work toward local consensus plus reports, followed by plenary discussion toward plenary consensus—alert teachers will expect some awkwardness at first. During the small-group work, teachers and students alike may have to adjust to the noise produced by several excited conversations going on at once in the same room. Classroom noise is partly a matter of room size and sound-absorbing materials. Sensitivity to classroom noise is largely a matter of expectation. Teachers who normally think that students should sit quietly and take notes or speak only after they have raised their hands find that the din of conversation in a smoothly running collaborative classroom takes a lot of getting used to. Most college and university teachers and students have not experienced classes where active, articulate students are the norm. They decidedly are the norm within the protective security of collaborative consensus groups. With experience, some teachers even become so acutely sensitive to the register of sounds generated by consensus group conversation that they can tell by the tone of the din whether or not things are going well.

Teachers and students alike may also be disturbed at first by what they feel as the chaos of collaborative classes. This feeling of chaos is also a matter of expectation. As Chapter 4 explains, classroom social interaction of the sort that goes on in collaborative learning is rare in the classrooms that most college and university teachers are used to. Traditional teaching places teachers at the center of the action and makes teachers the center of attention. Conversation goes on between the teacher and each individual student in the room. Traditional lecturers seem to be speaking to a socially coherent group of people. Actually they are speaking one to one, to an aggregate set of isolated individuals among whom there are no necessary social relations at all. Even when discussion among students in the class does occur, it tends to be a performance for the teacher's benefit, just as the teacher is performing for the students' benefit.

In place of this traditional pattern of one-to-one social relations, collaborative learning substitutes a pattern in which the primary focus of students' action and attention is each other. Teachers teach for the most part indirectly, through reorganizing students socially and designing appropriate tasks. Students converse among themselves with the teacher standing by on the sidelines, for the time being mostly ignored. Once consensus-group collaborative learning finally "takes" in a class, even when teachers lecture and conduct drills and recitations (as they almost inevitably must do once in a while), the negotiated understanding among the students changes the lecturer's position relative to the class. Teachers no longer lecture to a set of aggregated individuals. The fact that the students have become a transition community of people who know one another well means that whatever the teacher says takes its place in the context of an ongoing conversation among the students to which the teacher is not entirely privy. Empowered by their conversation, students are less likely to be wowed into passivity by whizbang lectures. They are more likely to question actively and synthesize what the teacher has to say.

So, both in organizing consensus groups and in lecturing to classes in which students have worked together collaboratively, teachers used to traditional classroom organization may at first feel that a collaborative learning class is desperately out of control—that is, out of the teacher's control. It may well be out of control if the collaboration is successful, but from the point of view of nonfoundational teaching it is comfortably and productively so. And the teacher's initial feeling of lost control tends to dissipate as students and teachers alike understand and accept the unaccustomed social structure of collaborative learning.

Much of the research on the negotiations that go on in collaborative learning consensus groups was done in the 1950s and 1960s, although in recent years there has been some resurgence in this research. Because to date most research has studied "decision-making groups" in businesses, government, and the military, some of it is only marginally related to college and university teaching. The relevant work is nevertheless important to collaborative learning, and awareness of it can be

Collaborative Learning

useful to teachers organizing consensus groups. It has mainly to do with group composition (effective group size relative to the type of task and the effects of heterogeneity and homogeneity), the quality of decisions made (number of options considered or variables accounted for), the phases of work through which groups pass in negotiating decisions (openings, transitions, endings; resistance to authority, internalization of authority), barriers to effective group decision making (authority-dependency problems, effects of reticent and dominating personalities), the nature of consensus, and the effects and fate of dissent.[1]

Studies suggest that the optimum size for decision-making groups (such as classroom consensus groups) is five. More than five will not change the social dynamics much but will dilute the experience, negligibly in groups of six but significantly in groups of seven and eight, and almost totally in groups of nine, ten, and more. Fewer than five in a group will change the dynamics in fairly obvious ways. Groups of four tend to subdivide into two pairs; groups of three tend to subdivide into a pair and an "other"; and groups of two (called "dyads") tend to sustain levels of stress sharply higher than those of any other group size. In contrast to consensus or decision-making groups, however, working groups (students doing research projects together for several days, weeks, or months, for example) seem to be most successful with three members. Long-term working groups larger than three often become logistically cumbersome.

Degree of heterogeneity or homogeneity is another issue in group composition. In general, heterogeneous decision-making groups work best because, as we saw in Chapter 1, differences tend to encourage the mutual challenging and cancellation of unshared biases and presuppositions that Abercrombie observed. Groups that are socially or ethnically too homogeneous (everyone from the same home town, neighborhood, family, or fraternity; close friends, teammates, clique members) tend to agree too soon, since they have an investment in maintaining the belief that their differences on basic issues are minimal. There is not enough articulated dissent or resistance to consensus to invigorate the conversation. Worse, homogeneous groups tend to find the differences that do arise difficult to endure and are quick to paper them over. On the other hand, members of decision-making groups that are too heterogeneous may have no basis for arriving at a consensus—or no means for doing so: they find that they cannot "come to terms" because they "don't speak the same language."

This inability to come to terms can be literally the case in some highly diverse student populations in which many people are struggling with English as a second language. Too much heterogeneity can also occur

32

when the different languages in question are community dialects of standard English (ethnic, regional, or neighborhood) that students bring with them to class. But difficulty in coming to terms does not of course afflict only students. Lawyers, physicians, accountants, and members of the academic disciplines have "community dialects," too. For example, ask a group composed of otherwise cooperative, well-disposed faculty members from a half-dozen different disciplines (say, biology, art, mathematics, English literature, cultural anthropology, and history) to arrive at a consensus on the definition and proper use of the word "natural," and the only resulting agreement is likely to be an agreement to disagree.

Some of the most troublesome differences that teachers organizing consensus groups may encounter are ethnic differences, often masked by stereotyping (including self-stereotyping) or by superficial conformity. Difficulties arise because collaborative learning requires students to do things that their ethnic background may not have taught them to do or that it actively disposes them not to do.

Some ethnic groups (indeed, some families) accustom people to negotiating decisions that affect all members of the group. Students with this kind of background tend to be comfortable with collaborative learning and know how to go about it. In other ethnic groups (and families), decisions are made autocratically by one person or by a small in-group. Negotiation is unknown. Dissent is forbidden and punished. Students with this kind of background tend to feel uncomfortable in collaborative learning, don't know how to do it, and resist it.

In still other cases—typically among adolescents—the pressure to maintain the coherence of cliques or gangs can curtail participation in other relationships, such as working collaboratively in classroom consensus groups. Classroom collaboration on tasks that excite interest can threaten clique values and, by cutting across clique loyalties, weaken them.

On the average, most students take well to collaborative learning, but many still have something to learn about it. Many students working together in small groups go through a fairly predictable process of adaptation in which they relate to each other differently at different times during their collaboration. Studies of people working together tend to identify two such "phases of work," dependence and interdependence, and two "major events" that challenge people's preconceptions, one at the beginning of each phase.[2]

Each phase of work displays a characteristic source of disruptive stress. In the first phase, the source of stress is stereotyped attitudes toward authority that people bring with them into a group. *Authority* here refers to feelings about the way power is distributed in the group: who makes

33

the decisions and how those decisions are enforced. The major event that precipitates an authority crisis in consensus groups is withdrawal of the acknowledged external authority. It may happen in collaborative learning, for example, if the teacher leaves the room.

The second source of stress comes into play in the second phase, as the group develops interdependence. It is the stereotyped attitudes toward intimacy that people bring with them into a group. *Intimacy* here means how people normally get along with their peers. The event that precipitates an intimacy crisis is being asked as peers to exercise authority with regard to one another. In collaborative learning, typically, it happens when the teacher asks students to evaluate one another's work.

Teachers organizing consensus groups have to keep all these variables in mind—degree of heterogeneity, group size, ethnic background, phases of work, and so on. When collaborative learning "just doesn't work," any number of forces may be in play. The first few times students work together at the beginning of a term the principal agenda may have to be, for some students, learning how to negotiate effectively. For others, it may be feeling comfortable negotiating at all. Sometimes, when teachers find that some students need to learn how to work together productively, they may have to teach them what they need to know through role playing or modeling. Very occasionally, teachers may have to suggest some basic rules for respecting others in conversation. Some students may have to be told explicitly not to interrupt when others are talking, to maintain dissent firmly but not obstreperously if they continue to believe in it, and to expect that negotiation and consensus building may involve compromise—giving up something you want in order to get something else you need or want more.

Students may also resist consensus group work or other kinds of collaborative learning simply because social engagement can be hard work. It calls upon a range of abilities that many college and university students may not yet have developed fully or refined: tact, responsive listening, willingness to compromise, and skill in negotiation. But it is usually a lot better for teachers to assume until they find out otherwise that their students have learned at least some rudimentary skills of the craft of interdependence and are socially mature enough to work together productively. Most college and university students, whatever their age and background, have had a lot more informal experience working collaboratively than most teachers give them credit for. Only when ethnic background, personal incompatibility, or social immaturity gets in the way of working on the task will it help for teachers to call attention to the process as opposed to the task. Even then, usually, the best way to do it is to turn the way the group is working together—the way people are helping or not helping get the task done—into a task like any other task for the group to work on collaboratively.

Partly because of the many variables involved in successful collaboration, many teachers find that, over time, changing the makeup of consensus groups from class hour to class hour tends to ease classroom tensions. Change in group makeup helps students enlarge their acquaintance, escape aversions and entrenched enmities, dissolve entrapment in cliques, and acquire new interests and abilities by working with a variety of student peers. In any case, the teacher's goal is to create a collaborative class as a whole, not an aggregate of loosely federated mini-classes coherent in themselves but unrelated to all the others.

On this issue of regularly changing the composition of consensus groups, as in the other practical matters, there is room for disagreement among teachers who have had experience with collaborative learning. Peter Hawkes argues, for example, that social coherence among students working in small groups may be time-consuming to achieve, and achieving it may be demanding and complex for the students involved. In that case, keeping students in the same small groups all term may be more efficient than mixing them up from class to class. A teacher's decision on this score may be in part a function of institutional conditions such as size, composition of the student body, whether students are in residence or commute, and so on.

Besides composing students into consensus groups, teachers who organize collaborative learning also set the tasks that students work on together. Designing effective exercises, problems, or tasks for people to undertake collaboratively requires forethought and practice. Tasks may be questions to be answered by arriving at a consensus, or they may be problems to be solved to the satisfaction of all members of the group. A closed-ended question with a yes-or-no answer is in most cases of little value, although an open-ended task that requires groups to agree on a rationale for a yes-or-no answer can be very valuable indeed. That is, collaborative learning tasks do not ask, Yes or no? But they may ask, Why yes or why no?

In general, collaborative learning tasks differ significantly from textbook, problem-set tasks, which are usually foundational in nature. Foundational tasks are what Richard Rorty calls "jigsaw puzzles." They have a predetermined right answer that students must arrive at by a predetermined acceptable method. Their solution requires, as Rorty puts it, a tidy "inferential process . . . starting with premises formulated in the old vocabularies," the accepted disciplinary languages and method, lead-

35

ing to the discovery of "a reality behind the appearances, . . . an un-distorted view of the whole picture with which to replace myopic views of its parts."[3]

In contrast, collaborative learning tasks are nonfoundational, con-structive, tool-making tasks. They do not presuppose either one right answer or one acceptable method for arriving at it. As Chapter 4 suggests, these tasks draw students into an untidy, conversational, constructive process in which, because they do not yet know "the old vocabularies," they create new ones by adapting the languages they already know. The result is not an undistorted view of a reality presumed to lie behind appearances. The result is a social construct that students have arrived at by their own devices and according to their own lights.

Foundational and nonfoundational tasks are, of course, alike in some ways. Usually both are unambiguous about initial procedures and start-ing points. But unlike foundational tasks, nonfoundational tasks are ambiguous about methods and goals. That is, they tell students how to begin, but they are designed so that neither teacher nor students can predict with much accuracy where the discussion will go from there.

A nonfoundational, tool-making task may look at first like a foun-dational task, a jigsaw puzzle. It may look as if it requires students to fit together old vocabularies in order to discover "the right answer." But even if it has this traditional appearance, a nonfoundational task is de-signed so that, as students work through it, it turns into an eccentric, ill-fitting puzzle. They may find out that there are not enough pieces included in the task to complete the puzzle, so that they have to hunt up or invent some. Or they may find that some of the pieces are the wrong shape for the holes they seem intended for. In some cases, there may be too many pieces, so that students have to select among them. Or the pieces of the puzzle may turn out to be inappropriate, so that students have to translate them, changing their shape in order to make them fit.

In practical terms, therefore, there are two basic types of nonfoun-dational tasks that can be used in consensus-group collaborative learning. The purpose of both is to generate focused discussion directed toward consensus. They are both "open-ended," but in different ways.

One kind of collaborative learning task, which we might call Type A, asks a question to which there is no clear and ready answer. The purpose of this kind of task is to generate talk about the kinds of consensus that students might reach in response to the question asked. The instructions tell groups to arrive at a consensus that completes the task in a way that satisfies most members of the group and to discuss the possible reasons for differences of opinion among members of the group or dissent from the group's consensus.

An example of a Type A task, one that I have sometimes used in demonstrating collaborative learning, is to ask people working in consensus groups to consider a key sentence of the Declaration of Independence:

> We hold these Truths to be self-evident, that all men are created equal, that they are endowed by their Creator with certain unalienable Rights, that among these are Life, Liberty, and the pursuit of Happiness.

The instructions for this task ask people to reach a consensus on the definition of several words in the sentence (such as *truths, self-evident, created equal, unalienable rights, life, liberty,* and *happiness*) and to write, collaboratively, a sentence that paraphrases the passage in their own words. What makes this task a nonfoundational, constructive, tool-making exercise and not a foundational jigsaw-puzzle task is that several crucial terms in the sentence are, to say the least, somewhat vague, while other terms, most notoriously the reference to "men," contradict popularly held current views.

The other kind of collaborative learning task, which we might call Type B, asks a question and does provide an answer to it—an answer that is accepted by the prevailing consensus in the disciplinary community that the teacher represents. The instructions tell groups to arrive at a consensus about how (or why) the larger community may have reached that answer.

The purpose of this kind of task is to generate talk about what the small group would have to do to reach the consensus reached by the larger community. The task might pose a textbook problem in mathematics or the natural sciences, give the accepted answer to that problem, and ask the group to explain two or more ways to reach that answer. Or it might quote an authoritative scholar's interpretation of a poem or historical event and ask the group to explain how they suppose the critic arrived at that interpretation.

Peter Hawkes has described one example of a Type B task. In teaching *Huckleberry Finn,* he points out that the way the novel ends—by humiliating the runaway slave, Jim—seems inconsistent with earlier passages in which Huck and Jim become reconciled as human beings. He asks students working in groups to arrive at a consensus in response to the major questions that critics discuss: how do they explain "Huck's 'forgetting' what he learned about Jim on the raft," whether they think the ending "undercuts all the meaning developed in the main body of the novel," and how they think the novel should end (what the "right ending" would be).[4]

So far, the task differs little from a Type A task. What turns it into a Type B task is that Hawkes then asks students to compare the positions they have taken with "positions staked out by various critics." He introduces them to the critical opinions of major writers on the novel, such as Ernest Hemingway, Lionel Trilling, and T. S. Eliot. The students may then discover that some of the positions they have taken correspond to positions that the critics have taken. When they do not correspond, the students' task is to try to determine how a critic might have arrived at such a position. In the process, the students have joined a conversation that has gone on among members of the community that the teacher represents, rather than being merely outsiders looking in. They are not talking about literary criticism. They are being literary critics.

Mathematics, the sciences, and technical subjects also offer opportunities for both Type A and Type B collaborative learning tasks. In an introductory college or university physics course, a Type A task might ask students to address the question, How do we think about things we can't touch and don't have an instrument to measure, such as quarks and supernova? Arnold B. Arons exemplifies a Type B task, in which the teacher provides minimum guidance by asking questions and eliciting suggestions. In introducing the laws of inertia, for example, Arons places a 50-pound block of dry ice on a level glass plate and asks students, working in groups, to answer questions such as, How does the block behave once it is moving? What action on our part is necessary to make the object move faster and faster, that is, accelerate continuously? Suppose the block is moving: what actions change the *direction* of its motion? and so on. Questions such as these are designed to help students "notice systematic changes," "impose systematic alterations on a configuration and predict or interpret the resulting effects," and "invent interesting and fruitful configurations of their own." Like Abercrombie's medical students, it is up to these physics students, working in small groups, to "suggest, try, argue, and interpret in their own words, carefully avoiding any, so far undefined, technical vocabulary."[5]

Both kinds of open-ended, collaborative learning tasks have a consistent, long-run educational purpose and a clear, short-run criterion for success. The purpose in both cases is to help students organized collaboratively to work without further help from the teacher toward membership in the discourse community that the teacher represents. The criterion for success is that students have created the tools they need to solve the somewhat eccentric puzzle that the task presented them with.

A Basic Model of Classroom Collaboration

Besides being appropriately nonfoundational and constructive in design, the degree of difficulty of consensus-group collaborative learning tasks should be appropriate to the students in the class and to the point in the course that the class has reached. When a task is too easy, students get bored. There is not enough to talk about, the conversation is trivial and unchallenging, and the groups solve the problem too quickly. If a task is too hard, it stymies students from the start and throws them back into dependency on the teacher's authority. Then both students and the teacher have no choice but to rely once again on direct instruction. This reversion to type puts the whole process at risk. Effective consensus group tasks engage the collective labor and judgment of the group and keep students' interest focused long enough and sharply enough for the job to get done. They therefore fall within a band of complexity and difficulty defined by each class's collective "zone of proximal development."

"Zone of proximal development" is a term invented by the Russian psychologist L. S. Vygotsky to refer to understanding that lies just beyond current knowledge and ability: what we cannot learn on our own at the moment, but can learn with a little help from our friends. For any of us individually, the "zone" of what we are capable of learning next, between what we already know and what we can't make sense of for love nor money, can often be somewhat narrow: what I am ready to understand working alone may be fairly limited. But in a heterogeneous group that includes diverse experience, talent, and ability, people's "zones of proximal development" overlap. The distance between what the group as a whole already knows and what its members as a whole can't make sense of for love nor money—the area of what as a whole they can learn next—is likely to be fairly broad. As a result, I may be ready to understand a good deal more as a member of a working group than I would be ready to understand by myself alone.[6]

One thing that students learn in consensus group collaboration, therefore, is that they can accomplish the task at hand by analogizing, generalizing, or extending what they know—the knowledge and abilities they have acquired in other social, conceptual, or practical contexts—so as to complement other people's strengths and limitations in unexpected ways. Teachers design collaborative learning tasks to help students transform the knowledge that everyone brings to class and apply it to the new problems and conditions imposed by the task.

For example, suppose the task were to examine the political or sociological problems involved in installing a new sewer system without killing business on Main Street. In that case, what one student knew about how to address a complex audience (learned, say, working in a factory job trying to talk simultaneously to the boss, the shop steward, and fellow workers) might enlighten another student who could provide expertise in efficient work planning and division of labor (learned in dividing household tasks equitably among several children in order to gain time for work or study or in assigning responsibilities to a television production team).

Or if the task were to understand a love poem by John Donne, a student who was a dictionary or encyclopedia freak might rustle up definitions and background; another who has learned to read aloud effectively in a speech class or on the campus radio station might provide insights through emphasis and tone of voice; still another might call upon an unusual wealth of personal experience in affairs of the heart. What one person knew about how to put together a carburetor, a banjo, or a sales campaign might complement what another knew about the personal tensions among people on a basketball team, in a church vestry, or on a construction crew. In examining the effects of inertia on a block of dry ice, students may be able to bring to bear what they have learned rowing a boat, biking, driving, or moving their luggage into the dorm.

The teacher's job is to design tasks that help people discover and take advantage of group heterogeneity and thus, by expanding the group's collective "zone of proximal development," to increase the potential learning power of every individual in the group. In order to help students discover these collective resources, tasks often include an element of "polling" sometime early in the process. After one student in each group reads the whole task aloud (to get the issue as a whole "on the table" and break the ice), the task requires each person in the group to give his or her off-the-cuff definition of key words in the passage being discussed. Later tasks may include an element of writing and collaborative editing. Typically, toward the end of a group-work period the group asks its recorder to read aloud a draft of the report. Listening to its recorder rehearse the report to be given to the class as a whole, the group then suggests ways to make it more complete and represent more accurately the group's discussion and consensus.

The way that task design can foster constructive conversation may be illustrated by my own experience a number of years ago in a freshman course intended to introduce undergraduates to reading fiction. The goal was to acquaint students with a few well-known stories in a standard anthology, help them interpret those stories in a relatively sophisticated way, and introduce them to some basic critical issues. In planning the course and in devising collaborative tasks for it, I returned to the tried-and-true source of critical principles, Aristotle's *Poetics*. I followed the Aristotelian emphasis on "action" or "plot" as first in importance among the elements of fiction, followed closely by "character."

I divided the analytical tasks for collaborative work into a set of questions that focused the students' attention on these aspects of several short stories I had assigned. The students dealt collaboratively with one task each class hour. The first task asked them to identify the central action in one of the stories (What "happens" in the story?) and its central character (Who does it? or, To whom is it done?). The second task asked students to identify the story's central action and central character as generic "types" (action: falling in love, the end of a career; character: ingenue, old man). The third task was to explain how the story distinguishes the central action and central character from that "type." That is, it asked what expectations the story raised and how the story met, fulfilled, frustrated, or changed those expectations.

What I learned from posing these deceptively simple, apparently unsophisticated generic questions to the consensus groups I organized in that class is that even relatively naive, untutored students can be trusted to generate many important disciplinary (in this case, literary-critical) problems and even some classic solutions. Of course, the better prepared students are, the more complex and sophisticated the resulting consensus may be.

But even when students start such a set of tasks from scratch, their first and persisting problem, as Abercrombie discovered, is to unearth the presuppositions and biases that each of them brings to the task and to resolve conflicts between them resulting from those presuppositions and biases. Being required to arrive at a position that the whole group can "live with" can hurl students headlong into the knottiest and most sophisticated issues of almost any discipline. It can therefore lead to a firmer and more sophisticated grasp of subject matter. That's what happened in the course I have just described. Eventually, the students began to understand this particular set of short stories in considerable depth. They also began to read fiction in general with greater understanding and talk and write more effectively about it.

There is no foolproof method for devising consensus tasks. I have written plenty of tasks that I believed would work perfectly and wound up revising every one of them again and again. I have nevertheless found that the following set of principles, devised by Peter Hawkes, covers the basic issues in collaborative learning task design.[7]

1. **Head every worksheet with the same general instructions.** This eliminates the time groups may spend interpreting new directions. One heading that works well is this:

Instructions.

Once the groups have been formed, please introduce yourselves to each other. Then agree on one person to record the views expressed in the group, including both the decisions the group makes collaboratively and significant dissent. The recorder will speak for the group. For each question, decide on one answer that represents a consensus among the members of the group.

2. If the task asks students to discuss a written passage (a primary, secondary, or student-written text), in the first instruction following the general instructions **ask one member in each group to read the whole task aloud.** To encourage participation, the person reading the task aloud should not be the recorder.

3. Because arriving at a consensus can be time consuming, **make the material to be analyzed short.** A single short paragraph or even just a sentence or two is plenty—often more than enough—for a thirty- or forty-minute discussion.

4. For the same reason, **limit the number of questions that the task asks students to address.** In most cases one question is enough. More than two or three can be overwhelming.

5. **Make the questions short and simple.** Conversation leads students in most cases into as much profundity and complexity as they can handle and in some cases more than the teacher bargained for.

6. **Make the questions concrete and clearly expressed.** Otherwise, students are stymied and throw the questions back. That is, the task becomes figuring out the terms of the question and the teacher's intent, not dealing with the substantive issue.

7. **Sequence the questions within each task, and sequence tasks from class to class and week to week.** The general direction should be from low-involvement, nonthreatening questions and tasks to high-demand questions and tasks.

For example, a task might begin by asking students to explain to one another their first impressions of a topic, problem, or text, or to survey how each student in the group would define key terms (that is, do some "polling"). Then it might ask an analytical question. Finally, the task might ask a broad question that requires students to synthesize the material and their answers in order to climb a few rungs on the abstraction ladder. A whole semester of tasks could be developed on this general sequence.

8. **Ask questions that have more than one answer.** Different responses ensure that recorders' reports do not become repetitive and will provide issues for debate. In a composition course, for example, "What's wrong with sentence five?" is less effective than "How would you improve the weakest sentence in this essay?" If the task is to analyze material drawn from a subject matter textbook, the questions should go beyond "What does it say?" to "What does it assume?"

9. In some tasks **ask controversial questions.** Some of these can be based on issues raised by prominent authorities in the field but not yet satisfactorily resolved. After the groups have made their decisions and the class has discussed them, the teacher can read aloud some of the published controversy for comparison and further discussion.

10. In some tasks **ask students to analyze short passages concretely.** These passages can be typed out or reproduced from the printed page, or the task can refer to a page in a book that everyone brings to class. Make the questions directing students' analysis pointed: ask about specific words and phrases, what they mean, their relation to other specific words and phrases, their significance in the whole passage, and so on.

11. **Whenever the task asks students to generalize, ask them to support their generalizations with particulars.** For example, if the task is to evaluate a student essay, also ask the groups to specify, say, three examples from the essay that support their opinion. If the task is to discuss a substantive issue, don't just ask "What are the implications of the passage?" Ask "Where exactly—with which words—does the passage imply what you think it implies?"

Teachers have to be prepared for the fact that faulty tasks often provide an occasion for students to draw the teacher into the small-group discussion. Even under the best conditions and with the best-designed tasks, traditional dependence on a teacher's authority exerts a powerful undertow on students and teachers alike. It sometimes leads to "performance" questions—requests for information or clarification made in the belief that the student role demands it. These apparently innocent requests take the form of "What does X mean?" or "How are we supposed to do Y?" Teachers handle questions like these best by turning them back to the students to decide in group discussion what they think X means or how they think they should do Y, and then go on with the task.

For example, sometimes a task turns out to be ambiguous in a way that the teacher hadn't noticed or fails to supply a basic item of information. When that happens, in addition to apologizing, teachers can redirect students' appeal for help or information in several ways. One way is to ask if any group has found the necessary information, in the textbook or elsewhere, or has discovered a way to clarify the ambiguity or work around it. Another is to provide the whole class with the necessary information or clarification. A third is to ask the groups to stop discussing the question asked in the task and begin discussing instead how they would go about getting the information they need in order to answer the question, or how they would debug the task.

The payoff for teachers who turn questions back to consensus groups in this way is that the teacher is likely to get an unusually precise (and sometimes dismaying) estimate of just how much students really understand so far about the course material, in contrast to an estimate of the native student ability to parrot answers. This new awareness has been known to undermine college or university teachers' previously unquestioned belief in the imperative of "coverage," because it tends to explore the tacit but widely held notion that (as Elaine Mamion has aphoristically put it) "I know I've taught it, because I've heard myself say it." Asking students to question the task can sometimes also sow healthy, unanticipated doubts in the minds of the most self-confident college and university teachers about their own grasp of the subject matter and the universality of some of their discipline's least questioned, most authoritative truths.

The third responsibility taken on by teachers who organize consensus groups, or any other kind of collaborative learning, for that matter, is to evaluate the quality of students' work, both individual and collaborative. Teachers fulfill this responsibility in two ways, or rather, during two phases of the process: as referees while the work is going on and as judges after the work is over.

Every social relation that involves differences of opinion requires a referee. Someone has to represent, not the interests of one party or another, but the values and mores of the larger community that has a stake in the peaceable, profitable outcome of negotiations that go on in the subcommunities it encompasses. Even in sandlot baseball games, kids know the importance of nominating someone in the group to call strikes, balls, and outs. In jury trials, defense and prosecution lawyers represent the defendant and the state, respectively. The jury represents the local community of the defendant's peers. The judge referees, representing the legal system as a whole: the larger community that includes all of us who agree to live by the rule of law.

Consensus-group collaborative learning also needs a referee. Whenever small groups of students negotiate toward consensus, there are, within groups and among them, both resolvable differences of opinion and unresolvable dissent. When students disagree on the main point of a paragraph because they understand a key word differently, for example, they may be able to resolve their difference by resorting to a dictionary. But if two factions in the discussion disagree because they are making different assumptions, based, say, on ethnic, gender, or class differences, the disagreement may not be so easy to resolve. One faction may dissent from the consensus being forged by the other members of the group and refuse to be budged. In this case, the group agrees to disagree. That is its consensus. That agreement (and an account of what led to it) is what its recorder reports in the plenary session.

Throughout this stage of the process, teachers typically remain uninvolved in any direct way. Once the small-group work is over, however, teachers become more actively and directly involved, not by taking sides but as referees who organize and moderate a plenary discussion based on the reports delivered to the class as a whole by the groups' reporters. Whether or not they understand every aspect of their agreements and differences, most student consensus groups will be prepared, and usually eager, to maintain their position against different positions arrived at by other groups. The teacher's role in plenary discussion is to help the class synthesize reports of the groups' work and draft a synthesis that draws together major points in those reports, if possible helping to construct a consensus that represents the views of the whole class.

Here dissent becomes especially important. In collaborative learning, teachers should make it clear that dissent is welcome and actively encourage recorders to mention in their reports dissenting views that were expressed during the group's discussion. By a "dissenting view" I do not mean only a hard-line, entrenched position. I mean any opinion or view expressed by anyone in any group, anytime during the discussion, perhaps only in passing, perhaps incompletely formulated, that could not be completely assimilated into the group consensus.

Dissent is important in collaborative learning for at least two reasons. First, it may frequently happen that dissent in one group turns out to be the essence of another group's consensus. A split opinion within or between groups may be just what is needed to disrupt complacent or trivial decisions arrived at by the rest of the class. It can also happen, even more strikingly, that one lonely voice of dissent in a class can eventually, in the course of plenary discussion, turn the whole class around, leading it out of a quandary and toward a more satisfactory consensus of the whole or toward a more correct or acceptable view— that is, toward the view that is currently regarded as correct or acceptable by the teacher's disciplinary community.

Another reason for ferreting out dissent is that part of the point of collaborative learning is to teach the craft of interdependence to students who face a world in which diversity is increasingly evident, tenacious, and threatening. Plenary discussions may therefore explore the sources of dissent in ethnic, gender, class, and other "background" differences. Part of the lesson in that case, as John Trimbur has argued, is that understanding why people dissent can be as important to reaching accord as understanding the dissenting opinion itself.

In order to achieve a larger consensus of the class as a whole when the issue is divided, teachers direct student energies in the plenary discussion toward debating two (or more) sides of the issue. The debate ends when the differing parties arrive at a position that satisfies the whole class, or when they agree to disagree and understand the reasons for their disagreement. Occasionally, of course, a lone dissenter or small faction of dissenters will hold out against the class as a whole, taking a position that would not be regarded as correct or acceptable by the teacher's discipline. In that case, wise teachers trust the negotiating process over time either to bring the dissenters within the boundaries of what is currently regarded as acceptable, or (rarely, but also possible) to move the teacher's own and the discipline's current view of what is acceptable in the direction of the dissenters' position.

The teacher's role changes once again once the class reaches a plenary consensus—some sort of agreement that most members of the class as a whole can "live with," including perhaps, for some members, an agreement to disagree. At this stage in the process teachers act for the first time directly and overtly as representatives of the larger community they are members of and that their students hope to join. That community may be a disciplinary one, a community of mathematicians, historians, chemists, sociologists, or whatever, depending on the course and teacher's field of expertise. Or it may be the larger community of those who write, and who expect to read, standard written English organized in certain conventional ways. In speaking for the community at large at this stage of collaborative work, teachers are in the educationally fortunate position of not having to label the consensus formed by the class as merely right or wrong. Rather, the teacher's role is to tell the class whether or not its consensus corresponds to or differs from the prevailing consensus of the larger community.

If the class consensus is more or less the same as the consensus of the larger community, in most cases that's that. Next task. But if the consensus reached by the class differs from the consensus of the larger community in a significant way, then the issue becomes "Why?" To answer that question, teachers usually send the class back to small-group discussion. The task is to examine the process of consensus making itself. How did the class arrive at its consensus? How do the students suppose that the larger community arrived at a consensus so different from their own? In what ways do those two processes differ?

Here the teacher's job, although quite a bit different from the job of a baseball umpire, still looks a lot like the job of a judge in a court of law. Umpires do not explain their decisions to players. But judges often explain their decisions in terms of precedents: the existence of similar decisions in other cases, arrived at by other members of the judge's community of knowledgeable peers. That is, they show that their views are consistent with the views of the community they represent. When they do that, judges are acting a lot like college and university teachers who organize collaborative learning.

Teachers do not tell students what the "right" answer is in consensus-group collaborative learning, because the assumption is that no answer may be absolutely right. Every "right" answer represents a consensus for the time being of a certain community of knowledgeable peers: mathematicians, historians, chemists, sociologists, or whatever—or perhaps only some mathematicians, historians, chemists, sociologists, or whatever. The nature of the answer depends on the nature of the reasoning conversation that goes on in differently constituted communities. And the authority of the answer depends upon the size of the community that has constructed it and the community's credibility among other, related knowledge communities. Once the teacher has shown the class the relation between its own process of negotiation and the negotiations that go on in larger, professional communities, it is poised to take an important step beyond reliance upon external authority toward learning more about the process by which ideas, values, and standards are constructed, established, and maintained by communities of knowledgeable peers.

Comparing the class consensus with that of the larger community is one way to evaluate students' work. The other way is by judging the work that students do individually, based on their collaborative work. That is, teachers evaluate the degree to which students have internalized the language of the conversation that has gone on both in small-group discussion and in the plenary discussions. In this capacity, college and university teachers do not usually judge the quality of students' social behavior in class or how effectively they work with each other in collaborative groups, although (rarely) they may find it appropriate to do that. They evaluate the quality of students' contributions to the class's conversation in its displaced form, writing.

Writing enters the collaborative process at several points. In the first place, conversation in consensus groups prepares students to write better on the topic at hand by giving them an opportunity to rehearse and internalize appropriate language. Recorders write reports, and the groups they represent help edit them. Teachers can ask students to write their own essays or reports on the basis of consensus group conversation, or to revise what they have already written based on it. And (as Chapter 3 explains in detail) teachers can ask consensus groups to undertake tasks that increase students' ability to talk effectively with one another about writing itself and to help one another revise. As a result, after students have begun to acquire language appropriate to peer evaluation—that is, as they begin to learn how to talk effectively with one another about writing—teachers can ask students to begin writing peer reviews of one another's writing and then evaluate the helpfulness, incisiveness, and tact of their remarks.

But in the end, it is the writing that students produce individually as a result of this process that counts in evaluating them. It is with their writing, after all, that students apply for official membership in the communities—of chemists, lawyers, sociologists, classicists, whatever— that are larger, more inclusive and authoritative than any plenary classroom group, reaching well beyond the confines of any one college or university campus.

One reason for judging the quality of students' written contributions to the working conversation among peers is that, as agents of the institution, teachers must satisfy the college or university's grading requirements in order to maintain institutional records. A more important reason is that judging the quality of students' output helps students understand the responsibility they accept when they join a community of knowledgeable peers. The process fosters in students the responsibility to contribute to that community, to respect the community's values and standards, to help meet the needs of other members of the community, and to produce on time the work they have contracted to produce. When students join the community of those who write standard English organized in conventional ways, for example, they accept responsibility on terms agreed to by that community for the writing and reading that they do. They write so that others in the community can understand what they have written. And they read one another's work carefully enough so that if they were to report on what they have read, the writer would agree that that indeed was what was intended.

In this chapter we have followed a class of college or university students discussing an appropriately limited issue through a series of nested consensus groups: small groups, the class as a whole, and the disciplinary community that the teacher represents. Each group in the series constructs knowledge in conversation with knowledgeable peers. That is, the knowledge that group members wind up with was not "given" to them directly by the teacher. They constructed it in the course of doing the task that the teacher supplied. So at first their new knowledge, the knowledge they have constructed, does not have the same degree of authority—or "clout"—as the knowledge that teachers "give" students in a traditional class. There, the authority of knowledge is understood to vary according to the preparation of the teacher. In a class organized for collaborative learning, authority of knowledge varies according to the size and complexity of the groups of students that, with the teacher's guidance, construct it. In the sequence we have followed, the knowledge constructed by small consensus groups has less authority than the knowledge that, based on the reports of those groups, the class as a whole constructs. The knowledge that the class as a whole constructs has this greater authority not only because the class is larger than the small groups, but also because it contains the small groups nested within it.

The knowledge constructed by each small consensus group has only the authority of a group of five students. Nevertheless, the authority of these small groups is greater than the authority of any individual student in the group before the group reached consensus. Small groups increase the authority of their knowledge when they compare their results with the consensus that other groups have arrived at and negotiate a consensus of the class as a whole (of, say, twenty-five students). In that way they increase the authority of the knowledge they have constructed from that of one student to that of twenty-five.

The final step in constructing knowledge and increasing its authority occurs when the class as a whole compares its consensus on the limited issue addressed in the task with the consensus on that issue of the immeasurably larger and more complex disciplinary or linguistic community (such as chemists, historians, or writers of standard English) that the teacher represents. If the two match, the authority of the knowledge that the students have constructed increases once again. The small knowledge community of the class as a whole, with its still smaller discussion groups nested in it, has itself become nested, on one issue, within that much larger community. The students in the class have joined, with respect to that issue, the community that they aspired to join by taking the course.

An example of the process would be the way a class might analyze the key sentence in the Declaration of Independence. Four or five small groups might arrive at quite different definitions of, say, the term "unalienable Rights." These definitions would be the knowledge (or "understanding") that each group constructed and would have the authority implicit in a consensus arrived at among five people. The teacher would ask the class as a whole, after hearing reports from each group, to work toward a single consensus, acknowledging differences. That consensus would then be the understanding of the term that the class as a whole has constructed. It might be similar to some of the definitions constructed by the small groups, or, as a result of further discussion, it might be quite different. It would have greater authority than the definition arrived at by any one student or any one small group: it would have the authority implicit in an agreement among twenty-five people as opposed to just one or five.

Finally, the teacher might ask the class, perhaps working again in small groups, to compare the whole-class consensus with relevant passages from Supreme Court decisions that, speaking for a still larger community, define which benefits or privileges American citizens enjoy by "inalienable right" and which ones may be limited or eliminated entirely. The Court's understanding of the term would of course have a lot more authority than the class's understanding of it. And if the class's consensus matches the Court's, the knowledge the class constructed would have the authority of the whole community that the Court represents, the community of American citizens, in which the class-community is nested. If its consensus does not match that larger community's consensus, the teacher asks students to return to small-group discussion. Their task now is not to decide why their consensus was "wrong." Their task is to try to reconstruct the reasoning by which the Justices of the Court might have arrived at a different consensus and compare it with the reasoning by which the class arrived at theirs.

As we shall see in Chapter 7, this process models the collaborative process by which the authority of all knowledge increases, assuming that all knowledge is socially constructed. Communities of knowledgeable peers construct knowledge in an ongoing negotiation to consensus that involves increasingly larger and more complex communities of knowledgeable peers, a conversation in which, as Richard Rorty says in

Philosophy and the Mirror of Nature, community members socially justify their beliefs to one another.

In describing knowledge in this nonfoundational way, Rorty generalizes Thomas Kuhn's description, in *The Structure of Scientific Revolutions,* of the way scientists construct scientific knowledge, a description that in their two-year study of the Salk Institute, *Laboratory Life: The Social Construction of Scientific Facts,* Bruno Latour and Steve Woolgar corroborate. Scientists, they say, construct knowledge in conversation about their work over lab benches and in hallways and offices and by revising what they think in the course of that conversation. This is the conversation of "conjoined intelligence . . . made by confluent, simultaneously raised human voices, explaining things to each other" that Lewis Thomas hears on the beach at the Woods Hole Marine Biological Laboratory in *Lives of a Cell.*[8]

But constructive conversation among members of communities of knowledgeable peers takes different forms. Community members engage in direct, face-to-face conversation: they talk, as college and university students do in small consensus-group discussion and as scientists do on the beach at Woods Hole. More importantly, Latour and Woolgar show, they engage in indirect, displaced conversation: they write to each other. In the next chapter we will discuss the important role that writing plays in the craft of interdependence.

CHAPTER THREE

Writing and Collaboration

Collaborative learning models the conversation by which communities of knowledgeable peers construct knowledge. Such a community can be as large as all English- (or Urdu-) speaking people or as small as a family or a half-dozen world authorities on sea urchins. All of these communities are constituted by people talking with one another. Most of them are also constituted by people writing to one another. That is why writing lies at the center of collaborative learning as one of the most important elements in the craft of interdependence. There is no more important skill to learn in acquiring the craft of interdependence than learning to write effectively.

As we noticed briefly at the end of Chapter 2, writing is central even to the construction of scientific knowledge. In *Laboratory Life: The Social Construction of Scientific Facts*, Bruno Latour and Steve Woolgar show that scientists construct scientific knowledge through conversation, and that the most important kind of conversation scientists engage in is indirect, that is, displaced into writing. Scientists, they tell us, are "compulsive and almost manic writers." Conversation among scientists illustrates, furthermore, how we construct knowledge in every field and walk of life.[1]

The view of scientists as writers in displaced, indirect conversation with one another contradicts most people's conception of scientists day and night alone in their labs, tinkering with their experimental equipment. Of course scientists spend some of their time in labs working alone. But even in the lab, Latour and Woolgar tell us, scientists "spend the greatest part of their day coding, marking, altering, correcting, reading, and writing." A scientific lab, they say, is "a hive of writing activity."

Scientific knowledge results from scientists' interpretive translation of their research data and direct conversation about it—that is, their transformation and displacement of it—into draft after draft of argumentative essays reporting their research.[2] Even the data they work with are written. Scientists gather it from the instruments they use, instruments that Latour and Woolgar call "inscription devices" because they "transform pieces of matter into written documents . . . a figure or a diagram" which scientists use directly in constructing an argument. Scientists write and rewrite these arguments in order to support an interpretation of the data their inscription devices have provided, an interpretation that seems, for the moment, to explain the data in an appropriate and convincing way. "The construction of scientific facts," Latour and Woolgar tells us, is "a process of generating *texts* whose fate (status, value, utility, facticity) depends on their subsequent interpretation" by other scientists.[3] Publication in a professional journal is only one stage in this writing process. Conversation, direct and indirect, goes on among a relatively few scientists, long before publication, and it continues after publication among many more, when scientists elsewhere who read published reports of research join the conversation.

In generating texts—in writing—scientists do what all writers do who write in an active, engaged community of knowledgeable peers. They carry on a "meticulous sorting of weak connections between existing ideas" by willingly subjecting themselves to mutual criticism. They read and reread, check and recheck, revise and re-revise their own and each other's written material. It goes without saying that social scientists and humanists, lawyers, doctors, and accountants construct knowledge in much the same way, writing to one another in an active, engaged community of knowledgeable peers.[4]

One purpose of collaborative learning is to give college and university students opportunities to experience this reacculturative, conversational process, direct and indirect, by which not only scientists, but also doctors, lawyers, mathematicians, sociologists, classicists, and other bearers of intellectual tradition construct knowledge in the language of their communities of knowledgeable peers. It is the same reacculturative process that my colleagues and I experienced, and that the student we called Mary undertook, as I described it in Chapter 1. It is because writing is so important to this process, as we saw in Chapter 2, that the principal way teachers evaluate students in collaborative learning is by evaluating their indirect, displaced, written contributions to class conversation. Writing is not ancillary to teaching with collaborative learning, as it is to traditional teaching. It is central.

There are, of course, many ways to teach writing.[5] This chapter describes how college and university teachers can teach writing in a collaborative way that is consistent with the role that writing plays in constructing knowledge and consistent also with the collaborative nature of writing itself.

Most of us are not in the habit of thinking about writing nonfoundationally as a collaborative process, a distanced or displaced conversation among peers in which we construct knowledge. We tend to think of writing foundationally as a private, solitary, "expressive" act in which language is a conduit from solitary mind to solitary mind. Through language we "communicate" our privately generated, unique thoughts to one another. When each solitary reader in the socially unrelated aggregate reads what we write, what happens, we suppose, is that another mind "absorbs" the thoughts we express in writing. Our goal is to distinguish our own distinct, individual point of view from other people's points of view and demonstrate our individual authority. Our readers are adversaries whom we try to "win" to our view by persuading them to agree with us, sympathize with us, or do what we want them to do. Their presumed goal as readers is "winning," too, by doubting what we say and by countering our arguments, thus resisting agreement with us unless we manage to overwhelm them with our persuasive power.

What has led us to misunderstand writing in this way is the solitude most of us usually require for one aspect of writing—inscription, putting pen to paper or fingers to keys—combined with our awareness that there are a fortunate few writers who, because they have thoroughly internalized their community's conversational conventions and vocabulary, give the impression of being able to write without engaging in conversation. These range from a minority of practiced journalists, who seem to provide edited copy off the top of their heads, to Milton, who while blind dictated *Paradise Lost* to his amanuenses, and Shakespeare, who is reputed never to have blotted a line.

Once we understand writing in a nonfoundational way as a social, collaborative, constructive conversational act, however, what we think we are doing when we write changes dramatically. The individualist, expressive, contentious, foundational story we have been telling ourselves about writing seems motivated by socially dubious (perhaps even socially immature) self-aggrandizement. As a peculiar and in some cases harmful by-product, when we write we may well distinguish ourselves and enhance our individuality. But in understanding writing as a collaborative, conversational process, we understand that what we are actually trying to do is the very opposite. When we write we play the "language games" of the communities that we (and, we assume, our readers) belong to.

That is, we exercise our fluency in the linguistic and paralinguistic symbol systems that constitute those communities. We use a language that is neither a private means of expression nor a transparent, objective medium of exchange, but a community construct. It constitutes, defines, and maintains the knowledge community that fashions it. We write either to maintain our membership in communities we are already members of, to invite and help other people to join communities we are members of, or to make ourselves acceptable to communities we are not yet members of. Our goal in writing (and reading) is to celebrate our own current acculturation, or else to reacculturate ourselves, reacculturate others, or reacculturate both ourselves and others at the same time. That is why writing and reading are such profoundly human, profoundly civilizing acts. By reading and writing (as we shall see in Chapter 7), we take part in what Michael Oakeshott calls "the conversation of mankind."

So a written text is a bit like a pueblo, one of those traditional Navaho adobe villages piled high, story upon story against the cloudless skies of the American Southwest. Both are constructions whose origins are lost in time. The architect in charge is no one person. The architect is the community consensus. Together, decade after decade, in some places century after century, community members made the adobe bricks from local clay and built the village with them. Together, today, the community continues to adapt and reconstruct its domain. Even linguistically, the community of people (*el pueblo*) is indistinguishable from the adobe structures (*el pueblo*) in which it lives.

Similarly, when we write we adapt and reconstruct the existing communities that we have inherited by renovating the inherited linguistic material that constitutes them. The indirect, displaced conversation between writers and readers does not get under way at all except by virtue of a complex web of agreements already in place. From the beginning writer and reader agree about what counts as a meaningful question and what counts as a fair or unfair answer to it. Agreements of this sort constitute the community, the peer group that "speaks our language," within which and to the members of which we write and read.

Because language is a social artifact, intrinsically collaborative and constructive, not even the bitterest politician's polemic or the cleverest lawyer's courtroom brief is written only to "win" or merely to defeat an alien antagonist. Likewise, not even the most intimate diary entry is entirely the expression of a wholly unique self. Every time we write, we try to construct, reconstruct, or conserve knowledge by justifying our beliefs to each other socially. We judge what we write, and other people judge it, according to the assumptions, goals, values, rules, and conventions of these communities.

So we write political polemic, courtroom briefs, and diary entries all for the same reason: to affirm the social nature of writer and reader and their constructive collaboration. We write to affirm an abiding social, collaborative, and constructive relationship among those immediately concerned and, in the largest sense, among us all: our membership in a common human community.

To achieve these goals when we write, we are continually making judgments, large and small, each one affecting all the others: what to write about, what to say about it, how to say it, how to begin, what word to use, how to phrase this sentence, where to put the comma. Writing is one dad-dratted decision after another. And learning to make knowledgeable, discerning, reliable decisions in any activity is, as Abercrombie demonstrated, something we learn best collaboratively.

The analogy between Abercrombie's experiment in teaching medical students the art of diagnosis—medical judgment—and teaching writing is apt, because there can be as much riding on decisions made when we write as on diagnostic decisions. It is not just that cautionary notes in travel brochures and on detergent and medicine bottles, architects' specifications, even instructions for taking care of your car, can impinge on health and welfare. Latour and Woolgar's study implies that writing decisions and medical decisions are one and the same. What the diagnostician writes is what the diagnosis is. Nothing is a symptom until it is construed (that is, constructed) as a symptom. Diagnosticians construct their judgments in the language of their community of knowledgeable peers. They don't diagnose an illness and then decide what to call it. They diagnose it *by* deciding what to call it.[6]

But in addition to this basic similarity between these two kinds of judgment, writing and medical diagnosis, there is also a significant difference between them. A pair of consulting physicians trying to construct a diagnosis can easily distinguish the patients they are talking about from the language they are using to talk about them. They can easily maintain an illusion of objectivity, therefore, by referring to a commonly accepted, before-the-fact, highly systematic taxonomy of symptoms formulated in that language and apply them to unique, entirely unsystematic complaints and physical changes.

But when we write, we cannot so easily distinguish the "patient" we are talking about, a bit of language (a word, a sentence, a paragraph), from the language we are using to talk about it. We find ourselves talking about the "the" in that sentence, or the " 'the' " in this one. To use language to identify what's wrong in a confusing sentence and decide what to do about it, say, is to enter an infinitely regressive hall of mirrors in which we construct a judgment with the same, or nearly the same, linguistic symbol system in which the sentence itself is constructed. In writing, we are always pulling ourselves up by our own bootstraps.

Before-the-fact objectivity ("what the dictionary says," the "rules" of grammar) is more illusory even than in medical diagnosis. There are only the conventions of grammar and usage subscribed to by one or another community of "literate" peers that we happen to belong to.

To write is to use the writer's socially constructed authority to socially construct the authority of the text being written. To say therefore that, in writing a medical diagnosis, writing decisions and medical decisions are one in the same and that what the diagnostician writes is what the diagnosis is, is to say that when we think about which word to use next, or its proper form, or how to begin the next paragraph, we are talking to our (socially constructed) selves, and to (socially constructed) others, about the (socially constructed) subject about which we are making a (socially constructed) judgment. So we have to be aware (awareness being a socially constructed state of mind) of how we are using our (socially constructed) language to make that judgment.

That is why writing can sometimes feel as awkward, and on occasion turn out as badly, as cutting your own hair looking in a mirror. The complex decisions we have to make when we write are complicated even further by the fact that we write to suit our goals, interests, and knowledge of as many as three communities of readers. One of these is the community (or the several overlapping and nested communities) that we are already members of. Another may be the community (or several communities) that we hope to join. And the third is the enormous community of communities whose "language game" is standard written English, the community that demands that our writing be acceptably correct as well as unified, coherent, and stylistically appropriate according to that standard.

Thinking of writing as social, collaborative, and constructive tells us a good deal about how college and university teachers (and textbooks) should be teaching writing and expecting students to learn it. One implication is that, as much as they might like to, college and university teachers (and textbook writers) cannot *tell* students how to write. Instead, because writing is itself a displaced form of conversation, teachers have to find ways for students to learn to engage in constructive conversation with one another about writing.

The value of constructive conversation among students about writing depends on several assumptions. First, students can only write about what they can talk about with each other, and also, in most cases, they can only write about what they have already talked about with each other. Second, students can write effectively only to people they have been and continue to be, directly or indirectly, in conversation with. And third, students' writing can only be as clear, incisive, and effective as their conversation is, both their conversation about the topic they are writing on and their conversation about writing itself.

Based on these assumptions, a writing teacher's first goal is to give students opportunities to talk with their peers about what they are writing. Students' conversation with their teachers is obviously of value. But for students, talking with their teachers is talking with members of another community. Conversation with members of other communities is always somewhat mannered and strained, something of a performance. Learning to converse constructively with peers about writing is at least equally important. for student writers because, as we shall see William Perry's informants reveal (in Chapter 10), conversation with people we regard as our peers—our equals, members of our own community—is almost always the most productive kind of conversation. So students have to converse with their peers about writing both directly and indirectly. They have to talk with one another face-to-face about writing. They have to write to each other about writing.

Another implication of understanding writing as social, collaborative, and constructive is that students have to learn how to converse with one another about every step in writing: finding a topic; deciding what to say about it; developing material to defend or explain what they say; reading, describing, and evaluating what they have written; and re-writing. The short-range purpose of this conversation is to improve students' writing here and now. Its long-range purpose is to help students internalize conversation about writing and carry it away with them so that they continue to be good writers on their own. Internalizing conversation lets us work together, as Robert Frost says in "The Tuft of Flowers," whether we work together or apart.

In teaching students to talk with one another about their writing, one of the hardest things to do is to keep them from talking exclusively about the issue they are writing about and the opinions they have about it. Controversy is emotionally engaging and fun, but talking about issues does not by itself make students better writers. They also need to learn to talk about how they make writing judgments and arrive at writing decisions.

Take, for example, this made-up conversation between students about the very first step in writing: finding a topic. In this conversation, one student (we'll call him Bert) has to decide on a topic for an essay for his freshman composition course. The assignment is to explain to his classmates something that he learned in another course. He runs into his friend Ernestine. She's in the same class, sees the worried look on his face, and puts two and two together. Their conversation goes something like this:

> **Ernestine:** Hey, Bert, what're you going to write your comp essay about?
>
> **Bert:** Gee, Ernestine, I don't know.
>
> **Ernestine:** What courses are you taking besides comp?
>
> **Bert:** Music. Phys Ed. Psych. Physics.
>
> **Ernestine:** Which one do you like best?
>
> **Bert:** Physics. I'm doing great. I think I'm going to ace it.
>
> **Ernestine:** Why not write about that?
>
> **Bert:** No.
>
> **Ernestine:** Why not?
>
> **Bert:** No, Ernestine. No. Absolutely not. It's too hard. Nobody'd understand what I'm saying. Anyway, nobody cares about physics. They think it's boring. Everybody'd be bored.
>
> **Ernestine:** I wouldn't be. I liked physics in high school. I'm taking it next term. What're you doing in physics right now?
>
> **Bert:** Well, we just finished atomic structure and radiation.
>
> **Ernestine:** What about them?
>
> **Bert:** Well, uh . . . oh, Ernestine, no. I tell you I can't write about physics, and that's that.
>
> **Ernestine:** Aw, come on, Bert. What's radiation?
>
> **Bert:** It's energy. Different kinds of matter give off different kinds of energy.
>
> **Ernestine:** What kinds?
>
> **Bert:** Light. Light is radiation. There are different kinds.
>
> **Ernestine:** Bert, come on. What other kinds?
>
> **Bert:** Oh, X-rays, cosmic rays, particle radiation, that sort of thing.
>
> **Ernestine:** So, there you are. Write about them.
>
> **Bert:** Mm, . . . no. Too complicated. But you know what? I could write about what radiation does to you if you get too much of it.
>
> **Ernestine:** Do you have enough to say about that for a paper?
>
> **Bert:** Sure. The teacher lectured about it. Showed pictures too. Ugh. And you know, I remember seeing a TV show about it last spring. There's a section in the textbook about it, too. That may help.
>
> **Ernestine:** What could you say about it? What kind of position would you take?
>
> **Bert:** Well, maybe something like, Radiation changes cell structure. How about that?

Ernestine: What does changing cell structure do to you?

Bert: Mainly it gives you cancer and gives your children birth defects.

Ernestine: There you are, Bert. You've got a position—radiation changes cell structure—and two paragraphs to support it, one on radiation-induced cancer and one on radiation-induced birth defects. You're home free.

Bert: Gee, Ernestine, do you think so? Do you think people would be interested? Radiation sickness is really awful, Ernestine. Why, do you know what happens first if you get too much radiation? Your . . .

Ernestine: Wait. Wait. Stop, Bert. Don't tell me any more about it. Make the comp teacher sick, not me. Serve him right. But you know what?

Bert: What?

Ernestine: I'm not bored.

Bert: Gee, Ernestine, thanks.

Ernestine helps Bert a lot in this conversation, and Bert knows it. But she doesn't do anything that any undergraduate couldn't do, even without thinking much about it. She keeps the conversation from getting sidetracked by the issues that the topic raises. She helps Bert pull together experiences and sources that he had not connected before. As a result, in this conversation Bert begins constructing knowledge in writing as Latour and Woolgar's scientists do, by discovering "existing ideas" and some connections among them and by beginning to sort the strong connections from the weak.

Along the way Ernestine also helps Bert generate some enthusiasm for the topic by reaching for his feelings about it, plays dumb about it in order to elicit some details, helps Bert formulate a position on the basis of what he knows, helps him see a way to construct an argument by organizing what he knows, and encourages him. As it did for Mary (in Chapter 1), conversation makes Bert ready to write.

Teachers foster constructive conversations such as this one by creating classroom conditions in which such conversations can occur. The tools for creating those conditions are social reorganization and nonfoundational, constructive, tool-making tasks. The quality of student conversation and the quality of the judgments students arrive at depends on how well they negotiate among themselves to resolve their differences in judgment, how well they understand why such differences occur, and how well they evaluate and sort the information and experience that they have at their disposal.

Consensus-group tasks in writing courses differ with students' ability and experience as writers. Some of them involve familiar exercises such as collaboratively analyzing, diagramming, or combining sentences, revising sentences to improve their structure, simplifying complex or disorderly expression, reorganizing the sentences in disorganized or scrambled paragraphs, finding the thesis sentence or proposition in professionally written essays, inventing material to develop underdeveloped paragraphs, and so on.

Besides this consensus-group collaboration, writing courses also ask students to work in writing or editing groups. Some of the suggestions for reorganizing classes and designing tasks for consensus-group work sketched in Chapter 2 also apply to writing or editing groups. But writing and editing groups tend to be smaller than consensus groups—usually two or three students instead of five. And tasks designed for collaborative writing or editing tend to ask different kinds of questions.

One of the most reliable collaborative tasks used in teaching writing is the world's oldest means of publication and still the easiest, friendliest, and most economical one: reading aloud. Reading aloud in class turns displaced conversation (writing) back into direct, face-to-face conversation (talk). The resulting immediate response of a community of sympathetic peers helps writers develop responsibility for what they are saying and also helps them develop the courage to say it. It tends to diminish the obsessively private quality that makes writing so futilely self-involved for many writers. It gives writers a sense of a real live audience, a community of people who "speak the same language." It helps students begin to trust one another by turning an aggregate of solitary writers into a learning community and a workshop for working with words.

Reading one another's work and listening to one another's work read aloud gives students confidence in the value of their own words and ideas, because they learn that other writers are interested in what they have to say. Learning what their peers are interested in, furthermore, they get to know one another at a level of intellectual engagement, in many cases for the first time. And they become increasingly sensitive to triviality, excessive generality, and errors in usage and logic.

A second, more complex and intensive collaborative task used in teaching writing is peer review. In this case, students learn, first, to write a "descriptive outline" of another students' essay and, second, to write a peer review that tells the writer what in the essay is well done and how to improve the essay. Descriptive outlines ask students to "map"

a piece of writing—a paragraph, an essay, in some cases a whole book—
by identifying its parts and showing how they are related. They develop
writers' awareness as readers by developing their sense of form. Because
writers are always their own first readers, the better readers they are,
the better writers they are likely to become.

Tasks such as these and the others described in Chapter 2, along with
the routine procedures of collaborative learning, certainly seem harmless
enough in practice. But the collaboration they require and the nonfoundational understanding of knowledge they assume cut across the grain
of most college and university teaching today. In the next chapter we
begin to explore the depth of that cut, to see just how threatening it
may actually be.

Toward Reconstructing American Classrooms: Interdependent Students, Interdependent World

College and university teachers are likely to be successful in organizing collaborative learning to the degree that they understand the three kinds of negotiation that occur in the nonfoundational social construction of knowledge: negotiation among the members of a community of knowledgeable peers, negotiation at the boundaries among knowledge communities, and negotiation at the boundaries between knowledge communities and outsiders who want to join them.[1]

These three kinds of negotiation define both the practice of college and university teaching and the nature of college and university teaching as a profession. In Chapter 8 I will examine some of the professional implications of this distinguishing expertise. In the present chapter, after explaining the three kinds of negotiation in some detail, I will address some of their pedagogical and educational implications for colleges and universities and their teachers. In doing so, I will answer two questions: How does collaborative learning differ from foundational innovations in teaching? and, How does the thinking of college and university teachers about teaching have to change if change in college and university education is not to be superficial and ephemeral?

The first kind of negotiation that occurs in the nonfoundational social construction of knowledge is within a community of knowledgeable peers, among its members. Members of academic or professional knowledge communities such as law, medicine, and the academic disciplines negotiate with other members of the same community in order to establish and maintain the beliefs that constitute that community. Biochemists, for example (as we saw at the beginning of Chapter 3), review each other's work over the lab bench, and they read and respond to each other's published articles. This conversation within knowledge communities is what Thomas Kuhn calls *normal science* and, following Kuhn, what Richard Rorty calls *normal discourse*. As members of disciplinary and other kinds of knowledge communities, college and university teachers are fluent in the normal discourse of these communities.

The second kind of negotiation involved in constructing knowledge understood nonfoundationally occurs between different knowledge communities and is carried on at the boundaries where communities meet. Members of different academic and professional knowledge communities negotiate with one another in order to translate the language of one community into the language of another. They may do this so as to neutralize threats that one community seems to pose to the established beliefs of another, or they may do it to assimilate and normalize options that one knowledge community seems to offer to the other. Paleobotanists try to reconcile what they know with what the microbiologists are coming up with; New Critics defend themselves against what the deconstructionists have to say; physicists find themselves talking with historians, biologists with lawyers, ethnographers with literary critics. Kuhn and Rorty call this boundary negotiation *abnormal science* and *abnormal discourse,* respectively. Clifford Geertz calls it, somewhat less prejudicially if not necessarily more accurately, *nonstandard discourse.*

Nonstandard discourse is a demanding and uncertain kind of conversation. It is "nonstandard" because, in negotiation between two different knowledge communities, the language and ideas that one community accepts without resistance—for example, what they agree to count as a "real question" and an interesting answer to that question—is not likely to be accepted without resistance by another community. The standard that will prevail between two communities, if their boundary negotiation is successful, is a major part of what they have to negotiate. College and university teachers, as active members of their professional or academic communities, have to be able to engage in this nonstandard discourse of boundary negotiation between communities that they belong to and those that their colleagues belong to.

College and university teachers have to be especially adept at nonstandard, boundary discourse, because they have to engage in it professionally on two fronts. The third kind of negotiation involved in knowledge understood nonfoundationally occurs at community boundaries that may be even more difficult to negotiate than the boundaries that separate academic or professional communities. Teachers have to be able to translate at the community boundaries between the academic or professional knowledge communities that they belong to and uncountable numbers of nonacademic, nonprofessional communities that their students belong to. That is, they have to be able to translate the languages of academics and professionals into the languages of people who are not (yet) members of any academic or professional community, but who aspire to become members: from biologists to biology students, philosophers to philosophy students, literary critics to naive readers, and so on.

Mastering the linguistic improvisation involved in this third kind of nonstandard discourse—negotiation at the boundaries between knowledge communities and outsiders who want to join them—distinguishes a knowledge community's teachers from its ordinary members. More than anything else, this facility in negotiating what Mary Louise Pratt calls "contact zones . . . social spaces where cultures meet, clash, and grapple with each other, often in contexts of highly asymmetrical relations of power," defines the classroom authority of college and university teachers.[2] It also defines the cultural importance and cultural authority of college and university teachers outside the classroom and beyond the campus.

What makes boundary negotiation especially challenging is that people who are not yet members of the community of, say, chemists, philosophers, or literary critics are not simply members of no knowledge community at all. On the contrary, they are already stalwart, long-time, loyal members of an enormous array of other, mostly nonacademic, nonprofessional knowledge communities.

That is why negotiation between members of academic or professional communities and nonmembers is difficult. College and university students are decidedly not a *tabula rasa*. The language of caring, of counting to ten, of belligerence, or of baseball may be anybody's mother or father tongue, as the language of chemistry, say, can never be. So, although mere chemists have to be able to talk comprehensively as chemists with other chemists and, on occasion, perhaps, to a physicist, astronomer, biologist, or lawyer, college and university chemistry *teachers* have to be able to talk comprehensively as chemists also with all the Trekkies, romance-novel readers, canoers, computer hackers, fast-food restaurant assistant managers, and football players who aspire to become chemists or at least to learn something something about chemistry.

Of these three kinds of negotiation, the most important to college and university teachers *as* teachers is of course the third. Skill in negotiating between knowledge communities of which the teacher is a member and those who aspire to join them—students—requires understanding first of all that every college and university classroom—indeed, every college and university—is a community that, like all communities, has its own set of rules, mores, values, and goals, all of them accepted, more or less, by everyone in the community. They regulate everyone's deportment, relationships, and expectations. They are appropriate to the assumptions, shared by everyone in the community, about human nature, the human mind, and the nature and authority of knowledge. The depth and persistence of these conventions and assumptions result in one of the quiet, nagging truths of college and university education: we tend to forget much of the subject matter of the courses we have taken shortly after we complete them, but we do not easily forget the conventions that govern those courses and the values implicit in them.

The foundational conventions that govern traditional college and university classrooms assume (as we shall see in Chapter 12) that the authority of teachers lies in their function as curators of acknowledged touchstones of value and truth above and beyond themselves, such as treasured artifacts of art, literature, science, mathematics, and the universals of sound reasoning. The authority of college and university teachers from this point of view rests on the understanding that knowledge is a kind of substance contained in and given form by the vessel we call the mind. Teachers transfer knowledge from their own fuller vessels to the less full vessels of their students. Teachers impart knowledge that was imparted to them, as it was imparted to them.

The classroom social structure and conventions implicit in these foundational assumptions—what Pratt aptly calls "pupiling"—are familiar to everyone who has attended an American college or university.[3] They prevail with few exceptions today the world over, from the two Cambridges to Tokyo, from first grade to Ph.D. They are so familiar that we take them for granted. Like the curatorial role of college and university teachers, they have an ancient and honorable history, they remain educationally valuable under certain local circumstances today, and they probably will always remain so.

The social structure and conventions of foundational college and university education assume a one-to-one relationship between student and teacher. Students talk to the teacher, write to the teacher, and determine their fate in relation to the teacher, individually. This is true no matter how many students there may be in a class: three, thirty, or three hundred. There is no recognized, validly institutionalized, productive relationship among students. More accurately, traditional teaching assumes and maintains a negative competitive relationship among students. They are officially anonymous to one another, and isolated. Classroom learning is an almost entirely individual process. It is not just that most foundational teaching does not encourage students to collaborate. Most foundational teaching does not recognize collaboration as educationally valid. In fact, in traditional teaching collaboration is highly suspect. In some forms it is the worst possible academic sin: plagiarism.

The conventions of traditional teaching can be classified under two headings, the Lecture Conventions and the Recitation Conventions. Lecture Convention teachers tend to talk and perform; their students listen and watch. Recitation Convention teachers tend to listen and watch; their students talk and perform. Most college and university teachers combine these conventions in some proportion or other. For example, Lecture-Recitation teachers may choose students who talk and perform particularly well to talk and perform in place of the teacher. Then the teacher listens and watches along with the rest of the class.

The normal goal of Lecture Convention teaching is to provide answers, promote the authority of those answers, and enhance the authority of the lecturer providing them. Since answers imply questions, it would seem that the role that questions play in Lecture Convention teaching must be particularly interesting and varied. In most cases, however, it is not. Most lecturers answer the questions that they are prepared and willing to answer. They may or may not accept questions raised by students, or they may answer some and finesse others.

The most common Lecture Convention in which questions do play a major role is Socratic Dialogue. The conventions of this form of teaching derive from Plato's *Meno,* in which Socrates teaches a slave. In Socratic Dialogue, students do not ask the questions. Teachers ask them, and the role that questions play in teaching is tightly controlled. Teachers approve or disapprove the answers students offer in response to questions. They try to lead students to say what teachers might as well have said themselves, had they chosen to. The line of reasoning taken during the dialogue is the teacher's own, leading to a point that the teacher has decided on beforehand.

Recitation Convention teaching differs from Lecture Convention teaching by shifting to students the burden of filling class time. In outlining the requirements of the course, the teacher makes it clear that students will do most of the talking and performing, specifies what they will perform and talk about, and explains what kind of talk it should be. The teacher retains the privilege of interrupting recitations at will in order to evaluate what students say, correct it, or elaborate on it.

Forms of Recitation Convention adapted to special circumstances include the Tutorial Convention, the Seminar Convention, the Writing Course Convention, and the Teamwork Convention. In each of these, students present their work individually, in written or oral form. Then they discuss their work with the teacher or answer questions that the teacher asks them about it. In turn, the teacher evaluates, corrects, or elaborates upon the student's work.

The Seminar Convention is a cost-efficient version of the Tutorial

Convention. In tutorials, teachers meet students one at a time. In seminars, they meet them five to fifteen at a time. Tutorials and seminars both allow for considerable debate between students and the teacher and, in seminars under the teacher's direction and observation, among students. At issue is the quality of each student's live performance before the teacher in competition with other students. In a seminar a student sometimes replaces the teacher as the discussion moderator, but performance quality before the teacher is still the main criterion of judgment. Students who "take over the class" in this way become teacher surrogates. If they are wise and well adapted, they read a paper and field questions about their work in a way that is calculated to receive maximum approval from the teacher.

In the Writing Course Convention and its subgenre, the Creative Writing Course Convention, the teacher prompts students to comment on one another's essays, stories, poems, or plays. But in these classes, which are usually described publicly as being about writing, not about reading or criticism, teachers seldom instruct students in how to engage helpfully in the intellectually demanding, aesthetically sophisticated, and socially delicate process of commenting helpfully on the work of peers. As a result, students understand that their comments on one another's work are made not primarily for the benefit of fellow students. They are a performance before an audience of one, the teacher. In these comments students tend to become (as we noticed in Chapter 1) alternately sharks and teddy bears, providing cutting insult or effusive praise depending on their interpretation of "what the teacher wants."

The Teamwork Convention is most often found in engineering and the sciences, where it takes the form of research teams and in music, theater, and film in the form of ensembles and production units. It is the most nearly collaborative of all traditional forms of teaching. Assigned to a team, students work together on a project under the teacher's supervision. In some cases, all the members of the team are equally responsible for the quality of the work they do together. In other cases, the teacher evaluates a report written by each student on the team. At issue in most cases is what students accomplish together, the product of their cooperative effort. In educational teamwork at its best, the nature and quality of what students internalize and carry away from the experience is also at issue.

All four forms of the Recitation Convention allow teachers the prerogative of lecturing when they choose, a prerogative that many teachers frequently exercise. Science course laboratory work, for example, is a kind of recitation in which the student's response takes the form of actively manipulating material and instruments and then reporting that work in writing. But many labs are like the introductory undergraduate astronomy lab described by one of Sheila Tobias's informants, in which students saw no stars. The instructor spent every class hour working problems on the blackboard—in effect, lecturing. Some creative writing teachers fill large portions of class time reading their own work to their students. Some seminar teachers (the philosopher Edmund Husserl is reputed to have been a particularly egregious example) lecture incessantly, believing all the while that they are "leading discussion."

A student's responsibility, according to these traditional classroom conventions, is to "absorb" what the teacher, in one way or another, imparts. The teacher's responsibility is to impart knowledge to students and evaluate students' retention of it. Teachers evaluate students in the same way their own teachers evaluated them, and as the college or university in which they teach is likely to evaluate teachers, in terms of their "product."

Dissatisfaction with the conventions of foundational teaching is hardly new. It has grown throughout this century. John Dewey voiced it in the 1920s and 1930s. It reached a peak in the late 1960s and early 1970s, when leading college and university teachers made well-known and widely discussed attempts to change the nature of college and university teaching. Since that heyday of experimentation, widespread interest in innovation has waned, except for scattered recent attempts to repackage science education (discussed in Chapter 9); politically motivated efforts to change or enlarge the literary "canon"; efforts to "personalize" teaching in the manner of Roland Barthes; and a few largely speculative poststructuralist ventures (discussed in Chapter 11).[4]

Most of these recent attempts are likely to fail for the same reason that similar teaching innovations of the sixties failed, because their foundational assumptions about the nature and authority of knowledge remain unquestioned. The innovations of the sixties tended to be of two types, corresponding to the inner-outer polarity of the foundational understanding of knowledge. Both hoped to improve students' grasp of subject matter. One of the two alternatives was objectivist in approach, influenced by behaviorist notions of positive reinforcement, while the other was subjectivist, influenced by loosely thought-through notions borrowed from Rogerian group psychology.

One of the best known of the objectivist efforts to change the way college and university courses are traditionally taught was somewhat misleadingly called the personalized system of instruction, or PSI. In PSI, teachers determined procedures that students should follow and the results they should attain. Then they trained selected students to act as "proctors." Proctors reinforced both the procedures and the results achieved by those procedures. Thus, although PSI seemed to change the social relationship among students and between students and teachers by placing intermediaries between teachers and individual students, in fact it did not. It was a rigorously controlled "monitor" tutorial system of the sort described in Chapter 5. Proctors were, unequivocally for all involved, the teacher's agents—teachers writ small. Nor did PSI provide a vehicle for questioning the foundational assumptions that underlay it or in any way encourage such questions to be raised.

Taking the opposite tack from this objectivist approach, the motivating hope in subjectivist efforts to change college and university teaching was that students' emotional dependence on established authority could be overcome by giving them "complete freedom," defined as absence of direction from the teacher. These attempts at innovation equated freedom with individual enterprise. Their individualist emphasis reveals how deeply rooted these innovations were in traditional assumptions about the nature and authority of knowledge. The bottom line remained the individual student's "cognition." Lacking direction from the teacher and constructive relations with each other, a very few students—those who had already internalized the mores and practices favored by their teachers and who were comfortable in social isolation—showed themselves able to "handle" their "new-found freedom" by asserting their individuality. All the rest took one or another of the four alternatives that students typically have in traditional education: plodding acquiescence, cut-throat competition, self-destructive rebellion, or withdrawal.

The failure of these attempts to innovate without challenging the traditional understanding of knowledge tends to confirm John Dewey's observation that "the mere removal of external control" cannot guarantee "the production of self-control":

> It may be a loss rather than a gain to escape from the control of another person only to find one's conduct dictated by immediate whim and caprice; that is, at the mercy of impulses into whose formation intelligent judgment has not entered. A person whose conduct is controlled in this way has at most only the illusion of freedom. Actually he is directed by forces over which he has no command.[5]

Learning results, Dewey argues, when teachers exercise control indirectly through "work done as a social enterprise in which all individuals have an opportunity to contribute and to which all feel a responsibility." Productive community life of this sort, he insists, "does not organize itself in an enduring way spontaneously. It requires thought and planning ahead." Careful thought given to the social enterprise that controls the work is what the experimental teaching innovations of the sixties lacked. They rejected the tidy, reliable, well-understood, time-refined social conventions of traditional learning and the forms of schoolroom community life appropriate to the foundational understanding of knowledge. But they did not replace those conventions and forms with others appropriate to an alternative understanding of knowledge. Leaving the traditional understanding of knowledge implicitly in place and in many cases leaving students without guidance under stress, these honest efforts to innovate set themselves up to fail.[6]

Collaborative learning differs from these failed teaching innovations. It replaces the traditional social conventions of schoolroom community life with other conventions that students are, for the most part, already familiar with and can rely on for support under conditions of stress and that are appropriate to a clearly defined alternative understanding of knowledge. The social conventions of collaborative learning, which regulate deportment, relationships, and expectations, are of course not yet so time-refined as those of traditional teaching. Many college and university teachers are unfamiliar with them and with the understanding of knowledge appropriate to them. A good deal of conscious "thought and planning ahead" therefore still has to go into implementing them.

This thought and planning has to be directed toward organizing a classroom in which, as Dewey puts it, "all individuals have an opportunity to contribute something, and in which the activities in which all participate are the chief carrier of control."[7] In traditional classrooms, the teacher's intelligent judgment is exclusively in control. In collaborative learning, students, acting collaboratively, also exercise intelligent judgment, so their collaborative activities together with the teacher's become the chief carriers of control.

That is, the social structure and conventions of a collaborative classroom assume not a one-to-one relationship between student and teacher but, rather, a collaborative relationship among small groups of students and between the teacher and those groups functioning as classroom subunits. Students talk and write to the teacher and determine their fate in relation to the teacher. They do so, however, not as isolated individuals anonymous to one another, but organized in recognized, validly institutionalized, positive, productive relationships with other students.

Changing classroom social structure in this way changes not just how teachers exercise their authority but the very nature of the authority they exercise. It is therefore not the kind of change that teachers and students can merely acquiesce to. It has to be effected by thinking through and planning classroom social relationships in which authority is understood differently by teachers and students alike. It is classroom social relationships of this sort that collaborative learning establishes. In a collaborative learning classroom, no one's conduct is dictated by "impulses into whose formation intelligent judgment has not entered," and yet (as we saw in Chapters 2 and 3) a central issue is the locus of that intelligent judgment: the source of the prevailing authority of knowledge. By shifting the "activities" that are "the chief carrier of control" from those of a presiding individual to those of people working collaboratively, control is systematically reconstructed and relocated. It is located variously in student working groups of various sizes and complexity and in the knowledge communities that the teacher represents. The authority of the knowledge that each of these communities constructs varies according to the size and complexity of the community. That is, the authority of knowledge varies according to the intelligent judgment of the knowledge community that is at that moment in control in the classroom.

Collaborative learning therefore implies that teachers have to rethink what they have to do to get ready to teach and what they are doing when they are actually teaching. According to the traditional, foundational understanding of knowledge, teachers tend to think that the most important thing they have to do to prepare for teaching is to fill their own heads to overflowing with disciplinary knowledge and expertise so that they will have plenty in reserve with which to fill the heads of their students. Teachers stock up their own minds by reflecting reality as accurately as they can with their cognitive mental equipment, the mirror of nature we are all supposed to have built into our heads. Teachers read, do their research, and consult their notes. The mind's mirror collects images of the miscellaneous, unrelated elements that reality offers and presents those images to the other piece of mental equipment we are supposed to have in there, our inner eye. The teacher's inner eye discerns these images as coherently as it can, making sense of them by examining, interpreting, and synthesizing them according to some variety of mental structure, conceptual framework, or procedure of critical thinking and higher-order reasoning.

Once they have prepared themselves to teach, what teachers do when they actually set about teaching, understood foundationally, is reflect outward what their own inner eye has perceived, so that other people, their students, can reflect it in their mental mirrors and discern it with their inner eyes. Teachers reflect their knowledge outward by lecturing and leading students through their paces in recitation in ways outlined earlier in this chapter.

Throughout this process, the best teachers and the best students, we say, have insight. Theirs is "higher order" reasoning, because they have the clearest, most highly polished mental mirrors giving (when good teachers teach and when good students take tests) the most accurate, most all-encompassing reflection of reality, and they have the best trained, most sensitive, most discerning inner eyes to comprehend that reflection. In contrast, poor teachers, and students who learn slowly or inadequately are, as we say, "blind." Their mirrors don't reflect much reality, and the little bit they do reflect is inaccurate. Their inner eyes are insensitive and poorly trained. Theirs is "lower-order" reasoning. The reasoning of teachers must of course be of a "higher order," because their task is to "elevate" reasoning that we regard as being of a "lower order." Otherwise education would be a case, as we say, of "the blind leading the blind."

In contrast to this foundational view of what teachers do when they prepare and when they teach, the nonfoundational social constructionist understanding of knowledge implies that preparing to teach is not a process by which teachers stock up their own minds, and teaching is not a process by which they stock up others' in turn. Preparing to teach involves learning the languages of the relevant communities and creating social conditions in which students can become reacculturated into those communities by learning the languages that constitute them. That is, from this perspective, college and university teaching involves helping students converse with increasing facility in the language of the communities they want to join.

Thus, to teach mathematics, sociology, or classics is to create conditions in which students learn to converse as nearly as possible in the ways that, in their own communities, mathematicians converse with one another, sociologists converse with one another, and classicists converse with one another. To teach writing (as we saw in Chapter 3) is to create conditions in which students learn to converse with one another about writing as writers do, and it is also to create conditions in which students learn to write to each other as do the members of the community of literate people.

Setting out to teach this way leads teachers to ask themselves a set of questions that are quite different from the questions they ordinarily ask themselves. According to the foundational or cognitive understanding of knowledge, teachers ask themselves questions such as

- What's going on inside my students' heads?
- How can I get in there and change what's going on?
- What's the best way to impart to them what I know?

These questions arise when teachers believe that their job is to "reach" students and to empty into students' heads what teachers believe is filling their own. When teachers begin to think of their job instead as undertaking to reacculturate students into communities they are not yet members of, they tend to ask a wholly different set of questions. They no longer ask themselves subject-object questions about getting into other people's heads or teaching "how" vs. teaching "what." Instead, they ask themselves questions about what Thomas Kuhn calls "the special characteristics of the groups that create and use" the knowledge in question:

> How does one elect and how is one elected to membership in a particular community, scientific or not? What is the process and what are the stages of socialization to the group? What does the group collectively see as its goals; what deviations, individual or collective, will it tolerate; and how does it control the impermissible aberration?[8]

For college and university teachers, these questions have to be unpacked to reveal further questions about the social conditions in which students are most likely to gain fluency in the language of the disciplinary knowledge community that the teacher belongs to:

- What are those conditions and how can I best create them?
- How do the community languages my students already know reinforce or interfere with learning the language I am teaching?
- How can I help students renegotiate the terms of membership in the communities they already belong to?
- How can I make joining a new, unfamiliar community as unthreatening and fail-safe as possible?

In asking such questions as these, college and university teachers assume that learning is what Richard Rorty has called it. Learning, Rorty says, is not "a shift inside the person which now *suits* him to enter . . . new relationships" with "reality" and with other people. It is "a shift in a person's relations with others," period.[9] Teachers assume that their responsibility, as agents of educational reacculturation, is to help students make that shift. The best teachers, by this token, are those who mobilize students to work together in ways that make reacculturation possible. The best students are those who help effect constructive consensus by drawing both themselves and their peers into relevant conversation.

The most important tool that college and university teachers have at hand to help students reacculturate themselves into the knowledge communities they aspire to join is transition communities. Transition communities are small, new, temporary communities made up of people who want to make the same change. A teacher's role, besides helping students form transition communities, is (as we have seen in earlier chapters) to provide them with the tasks and occasions that will help them negotiate the transition they want to make.

Educational transition communities are sometimes misleadingly called support groups. This useful term was devised in the sixties by the women's liberation movement and the self-help mutual-aid movement to describe a basic reacculturative tool. Support groups are small autonomous or semiautonomous coalitions of people who recognize in each other similar needs and problems and learn to depend on one another to help fulfill those needs and solve those problems. Collaborative learning groups—for example, classroom consensus groups—are similar to support groups and in fact were first devised on the support-group model.[10]

Useful as it is, however, the term "support group" suggests that what is going on in the group is ancillary to something more important that those involved are doing somewhere else and which their work in the support group "supports." To call a "support group" a "transition community" has the advantage of suggesting that the most important thing going on—making a transition between established communities or constructing new communities yet to be established—is going on right there in that small local group, not somewhere else.

A close look at what goes on in transition communities suggests that what they really are is *translation* communities. They organize students into social relationships involving a "temporary fusion of interests" that allow them to relinquish dependence on their fluency in one community-constituting language (their "old" one) and acquire fluency in the language that constitutes the community of which they are now becoming members (their "new" one).[11] Enrolled in transition communities, students have a chance to learn and practice, relative to substantive issues, linguistic improvisation, that is, negotiation of the second kind listed at the beginning of this chapter. They carry on this nonstandard boundary discourse between the knowledge communities they belong to and one they do not belong to (the one in this case that they are trying to join), in order to reacculturate themselves to the standards—the language, mores, and goals—of that unfamiliar community.

The groups for learning medical judgment that Abercrombie reorganized students into were translation communities. In these groups, students translated the diverse languages they brought with them into the unfamiliar language of medical diagnosis that they were learning— the language of the new community that they aspired to join. The consensus groups that Harvard's New Pathways program plunges first year medical students into and Uri Treisman's math and science study groups are translation communities in the same sense.

Many of the students William Perry interviewed had organized translation, or transition, communities in their residence houses (as we shall see in Chapter 10), but Perry thought it beneath the dignity of an instructor at Harvard College to help organize them.[12] Like Abercrombie's and Treisman's students but outside the institution's curricular framework, Perry's undergraduates negotiated among themselves the diverse languages they brought with them from their homes, and they negotiated between these languages and the new languages provided by the liberal education they were undertaking.

Such subcultural transitional social units as these maintain the coherence of students' lives in transit. They give their lives—and their language—a measure of stability as they loosen or give up their loyalties to the communities they are already members of, give up the comforts and sense of identity pertaining to those communities, form loyalties to communities that are new to them, and experience the comforts and sense of identity pertaining to those communities.

A transition community is therefore an odd, unstable, ephemeral social entity. Instability is of course entirely appropriate to communities of fence-sitters gathered on the boundary or "contact zone" between (probably) quite incompatible communities, engaged in what Thomas Kuhn correctly describes as the "threatening process" of translation.[13] The language and paralinguistic symbol systems that constitute transition communities—conversation across community boundaries—is nonstandard discourse in a number of respects. As we shall see in the next section, some of its language, some of its conventions, and some of the beliefs, values, traditions, interests, and goals that its members maintain are those of the communities its members are leaving. Some are those of the community they hope to join. Still others are common only to the conversation of transition communities. Furthermore, this unstable mix is itself undergoing constant change.

As a result, membership in a transition community may often be, as reacculturation always is, stressful and uncertain. The conversation of transition-community members is dominated by talk about these stresses and uncertainties of reacculturation. Much of it is in-the-same-boat talk. Members talk about what it was like to be a member of the old community, what it may be like to be a member of the new, unfamiliar community, and what a pain in the neck it is to change: nostalgia, anxious anticipation, and complaint.

Transition community members also talk a lot about coping. They trade hints and tips, some accurate, many apocryphal, about how a person is expected to behave and talk as a member of the community they hope to join. As Abercrombie noticed, they refute and cancel out each other's presuppositions and biases. They practice using the unfamiliar community's constituting language—sometimes accurately and appropriately, sometimes not, under as many different conditions, some relevant and some not, and in many different settings, some relevant and some not—so as gradually to become fluent in it.

To say that through collaborative learning nonfoundational teaching teaches the "languages" that constitute established knowledge communities, such as the academic disciplines and the professions, does not mean, however, that what it teaches is fluency in the jargon and methodological consensus of those communities. That is precisely the purpose of foundational teaching and jigsaw-puzzle tasks (described in Chapter 2). Foundational teaching inculcates students with disciplinary jargon and well established methods. As my wife, Anthea, once put it while she was in law school (and in most law schools legal study is a foundational exercise if there ever was one), what she was doing there was learning how to quack.

In contrast, the purpose of collaborative learning is not primarily to teach students how to quack. Collaborative learning tasks are designed to generate conversation in which students learn to "speak differently" (in Rorty's phrase), to speak in ways unlike their former habits of speaking. So students almost inevitably pick up a good deal of disciplinary jargon along the way. But in collaborative learning the route to fluency in the language of a new community is paved with ad hoc intermediary languages that students devise themselves to serve their own purposes as they work through the assigned task. Like foundational teaching, nonfoundational teaching will almost certainly teach students to quack. But on the way they will also learn to gobble, honk, peep, and squawk.

Some of this ad hoc language sticks. It is this measure of residual nondisciplinary vocabulary, however small, that helps distinguish the results of nonfoundational teaching from the results of foundational teaching. It represents a precious resource: the grain of newly constructed knowledge that collaboratively educated students take away from the course with them.

The process of ad hoc translation that goes on in a transition group was illustrated in detail for me once during a class in which I had asked students organized collaboratively to subdivide a paragraph and describe how the parts are related, in order to write a "descriptive outline" of it. This is a nonfoundational constructive tool-making task appropriate to collaborative learning for two reasons. First, there is no "right answer," although there may be some clear options, the merits of which can be negotiated. Second, students undertake the task at first without a prescribed, disciplinary vocabulary to work with. They have to root around in their own collective experience and make use of whatever language they find there.

During this particular class, I (unintentionally) overheard a student explaining something to the other members of his consensus group about the paragraph I had asked them to outline. It contained, he said, a "transition between the whoosie-whatsis and the other thing." No one would call these terms elegant or professional. But for the time being, the expression served this student's purposes and the purposes of the group he was working with. It negotiated the boundary between languages that he and his fellow students knew and the one they were just beginning to learn, by cobbling together a variety of terms that every student in the group understood. To use a term of the Russian critic Bakhtin that has been fashionable recently among American literary academics, the expression was "heteroglossic." It drew on informal street-corner or beauty-parlor lingo ("whoosie-whatsis") and the plain, unvarnished speech of home, shop, and playground ("the other thing"), combining these with a new bit of classroom jargon ("transition").

Eventually, of course, these students replaced their rough-hewn, ad hoc linguistic tools with more efficient and appropriate terms as they explored further the nuances of the complex task they had been assigned. In fact, in any course taught collaboratively, adopting and culling linguistic tools to establish a transitional critical language is implicitly as much the point of the assigned task as the point that the task explicitly targets. In collaborative learning, college and university students learn to lift themselves by their own verbal bootstraps, making new language by borrowing from, renovating, and reconstructing the old. Their transitional terms emerge from the conversational history they share with one another and with their teacher, as they identify the task before them, formulate it, and do it.

The kind of translation at community boundaries that students do in collaborative learning is translation of an especially "thick" and complex kind. Students translate the languages that they bring to the task into a composite working vocabulary common to the particular small group they are working in. That's where, for example, my students working on descriptive outlines got the phrases "whoosie-whatsis" and "the other thing." While students are translating among each other's languages in this way, furthermore, they are also translating into their own new composite vocabulary the language in which the teacher posed the task, which is the language of the community they aspire to join. That's where my writing students picked up the word "transition."

To turn classrooms into arenas in which students can negotiate their way into new knowledge communities in this way, college and university teachers have to discover points of access or ports of entry to the relevant community that are appropriate to the varieties of nonmembers in their charge. They have to discover ways to help those nonmembers loosen their loyalty to some of the communities they are already members of — to "divorce" themselves from those communities, as Perry puts it — and marry instead into the knowledge community that the teacher represents.[14]

What teachers teach in this way is how to establish and maintain intellectually productive rapport and ways to renegotiate that rapport when the task is done. They help students learn to negotiate boundaries between the communities they belong to and communities their fellow students may belong to. They allow students latitude to define their individuality not as a stark and lonesome independence, isolated or alienated from others, but as a function of interdependence among peers.

For college and university teachers to adapt themselves to teaching of this sort, however, may require (as Chapter 1 suggests) a depth of change that is difficult if not impossible for individuals to accomplish on their own. It is a process of reacculturation best undertaken, and perhaps only undertaken with success, collaboratively. In this chapter we found William Perry's confused undergraduates undertaking it by working together to construct new speech, lifting themselves by their own verbal bootstraps with a transitional language constructed for the purpose. In Chapter 7 we will find engaged in the same process Thomas Kuhn's scientists facing a theory crisis and Bruno Latour's example of a mother and child negotiating the name of birds.

Collaborative learning is most likely to fulfill its promise when faculty members of whole institutions, or of coherent subdivisions within them, build transitional conversational units similarly committed to this painful, painstaking collaborative talking-through. The next chapter will explore the most promising way to begin this process of institutionalizing collaborative learning. It uses leverage gained through a form of collaborative learning that I have alluded to but not discussed so far: peer tutoring.

CHAPTER FIVE

Peer Tutoring and Institutional Change

Institutionalized peer tutoring began as an educational experiment during the early 1970s. Today it is an accepted part of American college and university education almost everywhere. Focused at first almost exclusively on writing, peer tutoring eventually found its way into general education or "core" programs and sometimes even into upper division courses. There is hardly a college or university now, from Berkeley to Brown, from Harvard to Hostos Community College, that could do without it.

The formula is simple and familiar. Working through academic departments or through some designated structure such as a "writing center" or "learning center," the institution selects undergraduates to work one-on-one with other undergraduates. Tutors meet students they tutor either individually or in small groups to talk through the academic problems that the tutees have brought to the session. The way they do it depends on the program's "philosophy" and how it is organized. In some programs, they may meet informally in a space set aside for them somewhere in the library, the student center, or a dorm, or they get together over coffee in the cafeteria. In others, they may meet formally in a classroom during class time set aside for the purpose by the teacher. Teachers may require detailed reports about what the tutor and tutee discuss and what the tutee accomplishes, or they may not. Tutors may work with tutees only when teachers send students to see them, or their meetings may be entirely voluntary, anonymous, and "drop-in."

The day-to-day, short-run educational effects of peer tutoring result from the fact that, regardless of the subject, the issues tend to come down in one way or another to reading (texts, documents, word-problems) and writing (papers, lab reports, exams). Peer tutors usually deal best with these issues, furthermore, when they assume that their tutees' academic problems result primarily from not being able to organize, synthesize, and apply what they know, or from not being able to negotiate the conventions of traditional classroom education.

That is, peer tutors work best when they do not regard students in the foundational way, as tablets waiting for imprint, but in a nonfoundational way, as members of a variety of knowledge communities, related and unrelated. What tutees need is help in translating the terms of the communities they are trying to enter—the academic and professional disciplines, people who read and write standard written English—into the terms of the communities they already belong to, and vice versa.

Peer tutoring based on this assumption can tip the scale from superficial and partial knowledge to a secure, mature, reliable, and possibly even creative understanding. As a process of intellectual and social engagement, it can involve students in one another's intellectual and social development. It can therefore help college and university teachers reach, indirectly, students who for a variety of reasons have not responded to direct instruction under traditional classroom conditions.

This important short-run, day-to-day effect of peer tutoring has been widely demonstrated. College and university teachers and administrators may be less aware of the potential long-run effect of peer tutoring. That potential was perceived and stated succinctly in a routine internal document promulgated by one American liberal arts college during the 1988–89 academic year. The genre and source of the document (an interim report generated in the office of the college president on progress implementing the college's "five year plan") attest to the fact that the views expressed in it are institutionally normalized: the report takes care not to say anything that is likely to raise hackles in any quarter of the campus.

One section of the report describes actions taken to enhance the college's well-established, well-supported, and successful writing center and peer-tutoring program. This section, like the report as a whole, pays appropriate attention to statistical and organizational detail. It notes, for example, that the college had recently added some fifty-three new peer tutors to its program. As a result, "2784 individual tutoring sessions were held" and "877 students attended group sessions." In this sober statistical context, the report makes the following striking assertion:

> Peer tutors have a potential to act as agents of institutional change, as revealed by . . . [the] faculty's acceptance [in one course] of the tutors' request for an all day faculty review (an experiment that proved to be an enormous success) and [in another course, the] professor's comment that a presentation to the department by the tutors resulted in changes in the way the course is taught.[1]

The tone of this passage and the facts of the case imply that, in this college and perhaps others, peer tutoring has already begun to have an impact well beyond its normal, expected, short-run, day-to-day educational effect on individual students. Furthermore, when this document says that peer tutors can be agents of institutional change, it is not referring to any old kind of change. It is referring to a particular and crucially important kind. When it talks about professors changing the structure of their courses and changing the way they teach a course as a result of suggestions made by peer tutors—that is, as a result of suggestions made by well-informed students—the document is talking about change that goes to the very root of the educational process. It is challenging traditional prerogatives and assumptions about the authority of teachers and the authority of knowledge. It is saying that peer tutors have the potential for helping to change the interests, goals, values, assumptions, and practices of teachers and students alike.

The passage also seems to imply that, in this case and perhaps in others, the institutional influence of peer tutoring may have two sources. One source is the peer tutors' own intelligence, persistence, political savvy, and understanding of educational issues. The other source is a full understanding on the part of faculty and administrators of the particular nature of the contribution that peer tutors can make to institutional change.

This chapter assumes that better understanding of that institutional influence can lead to a more widespread, systematic effort to tap the full potential of peer tutors. It answers the question, Why and in what way can peer tutors be effective, "as agents of institutional change"? The chapter argues, first, that the potential of peer tutors to serve as institutional change agents is a function of the degree of peership that tutors maintain between themselves and their tutees. Second, the chapter argues that peer tutors can contribute to institutional change for a particular purpose. That purpose is to foster in college and university undergraduates social maturity integrated with intellectual maturity—the capable intellectual interdependence described in the Introduction to this book.

Peer tutors can help colleges and universities work toward that goal by reaching beyond their immediate impact on students to bring about changes of four kinds: changes in relations among students, among teachers, and between students and teachers; changes in the prevailing understanding of the nature and authority of knowledge and the authority of teachers; changes in curriculum; and even (certainly in many cases the last domino to fall) changes in classroom practice.

The educational effects of peer tutoring, in the short and long run, depend on the degree to which tutors and their tutees are real peers. My dictionary (the *American Heritage*) defines *peer* as "a person who has equal standing with another, as in rank, class, or age." The editors emphasize this point, repeating it in no uncertain terms: "*Peer* refers to an equal, not a superior." In peer tutoring this equality means, first of all, that the students involved—peer tutor and tutee alike—believe that they both bring an important measure of ability, expertise, and information to the encounter and, second, that they believe that they are institutional status-equals: both are students, clearly and unequivocally.

In any college or university setting, of course, institutional constraints and native ability favor some students over others. Students are never absolutely equal in ability, knowledge, and expertise. Somebody always knows more or is quicker to grasp than somebody else. Furthermore, peer relations in an institution are never entirely autonomous and uncompromised. Most of what peer tutors and tutees talk about is sketched out, and in some cases stipulated, by the college or university curriculum and the tasks set by the teacher of the relevant course.

But what compromises the peership required for peer tutoring is neither institutional constraints nor native ability. Teachers and teacher surrogates compromise peership when they directly intervene in students' collaborative work and when they assign tasks that unavoidably imply or reinforce the authority structure of traditional classroom education. The resulting differences in degree of peership among students distinguish both educational practice and educational kind. They divide peer tutoring programs, which appear under many names and rubrics, into two categories, the monitor type and the collaborative type.

The difference between the two illustrates once again the distinction between foundational and nonfoundational teaching drawn throughout this book. In some cases, the term *peer tutoring* is used to denote direct, centralized, monitor-like tutoring that mobilizes undergraduates as institutional manpower for prevailing institutional ends. In other cases, the term is used as it is used in this chapter, to denote a kind of collaborative learning: indirect, polycentralized tutoring that mobilizes interdependence and peer influence for broadly educational ends. Most peer tutoring programs these days are a mixture of the two.

Monitor-type peer tutoring, sometimes called peer teaching or near-peer teaching, is similar to the PSI "proctor" system, described in Chapter 4. It differs considerably in history, practice, motives, and goals from peer tutoring that maximizes peership and collaboration. The limitations of monitoring are implicit in its origins, the nineteenth-century monitor system widely used in British "public" (what Americans call private or independent) schools. This system engaged older or more advanced students to undertake some of the more onerous chores of teaching, such as drill and review, and thus make life easier for overworked teachers. In the monitor system, teachers chose the "best" students, according to prevailing institutional and personal criteria, to act in their stead. Monitors then exercised authority derived from this appointment over much of the academic work and even over the personal lives of younger or less advanced students. Thus, both the source of the monitors' authority and the extent of their power compromised their peer status, often, as the history of the British public school system testifies, well beyond any significant educational effect.

The degree of peer status involved in collaborative peer tutoring and in monitoring is the crucial difference between them. Collaborative peer tutors are not surrogate teachers. Monitors are precisely that. A surrogate teacher is anyone who replaces the teacher in the social structure of institutional authority, whether inside the classroom or outside it. Monitors, or near-peer teachers, grade down from a species of junior faculty at the top (graduate teaching assistants, section men, lab assistants, graduate students employed as tutors, full-time or part-time) to undergraduate teaching assistants, who, because they are usually about the same age as the fellow students they work with, can seem very close indeed to being their status peers.

What distinguishes each of these categories from collaborative peer tutors is that they are set apart institutionally both by the teachers and administrators who rely on them and by the students who work with them. They are thought of, by faculty and students alike, as being especially well trained for what they do. It is sometimes said that they have been "professionalized." As a result, they are not regarded, and in many cases do not regard themselves, as sharing fully in the vicissitudes, burdens, and constraints of normal student life. In the case of undergraduate teaching assistants, furthermore, the distinction is established, maintained, and sometimes emblazoned by the traditional ways in which the institution "trains" them and organizes their relations with other undergraduates. They are select, superior students who for all intents and purposes serve as faculty surrogates under direct faculty supervision. Their peer status is so thoroughly compromised that they are educationally effective only in strictly traditional academic terms. As such, of course, they can be very effective indeed. Giving individual, personal attention, they fulfill the promise of traditional teaching, which (as we saw in Chapter 4) assumes a one-to-one relationship between the teacher and each individual student.

In contrast, collaborative peer tutors are not surrogate teachers, and they are taught to make that fact clear to their tutees. They see the institution from the same place their tutees see it, from the bottom up. That is, collaborative peer tutors work within the institutional constraints that their tutees experience.[2] This means, for example, that in most cases they do not mediate directly between tutees and their teachers. Peer tutors deal with classroom assignments as their tutees bring them in, beginning wherever it seems that the tutee bogged down—even if that means beginning at the very beginning. If they suspect that the assignment is miscopied or misunderstood, for example, they send the tutee back to the teacher for clarification, sometimes suggesting for the benefit of timid or frightened tutees how to ask questions that will get results.

Collaborative tutors may sometimes offer their own independent approach to the course's subject matter and method, but in contrast to monitors, their main purpose is to guide and support. When they instruct, it is to clarify that guidance and enhance that support. They engage in conversation with their tutees, helping them translate (as we saw in Chapter 4 and will see again in Chapter 7) at the boundaries between the knowledge or discourse communities they already belong to and the knowledge or discourse communities they aspire to join. The goal of this conversation between peer tutors and tutees is to help tutees internalize the conversation of the community they hope to join so that (as we saw the student we called Mary doing in Chapter 1) they can carry it on internally on their own.

This distinction between collaborative peer tutors and monitors is of course a matter of degree. No institutionalized collaborative learning, including collaborative peer tutoring, is autonomous. All of it is organized and directed by teachers or administrators, who are responsible for selecting and "training" peer tutors of whatever sort. Conversely, no monitor totally lacks autonomy. The educational effect of most monitors in helping students academically draws to some degree on their influence as their tutees' peers.

So, in saying that compromised peer status reduces the educational rewards that accrue from peer status, I am not saying that less learning necessarily occurs or that monitors are educationally of little value. Monitors give many students exactly the sort of help they want. But in saying that compromised peer status reduces the educational rewards that accrue from peer status, I am saying that the education provided is of a certain type. With less peership a different kind of learning occurs: more of the traditional, foundational kind, less of the nonfoundational kind that most people who are interested in collaborative learning, and thus most people interested in collaborative peer tutoring, are trying to bring about.

The degree of peership that tutors maintain with their tutees is governed largely by the way peer tutors themselves are taught to tutor. To some extent, of course, tutors teach one another to tutor, learning as they go along by watching one another and by exchanging tips and experiences. But most colleges and universities teach their peer tutors in some more systematic way, either in occasional meetings or, at best, in credit-bearing courses. The most effective tutoring courses are themselves collaborative. They help tutors learn to engage their tutees on substantive issues by fostering the tutors' own active membership in a coherent learning community.

When the subject to be tutored is careful reading and readable writing, for example, besides learning to write better while they coach others (other tutors in the tutoring class as well as their tutees), peer tutors can also undertake collaboratively a progressive set of analytical and evaluative tasks. These tasks can be on topics that emerge from their work as tutors, and they can focus on the form and substance of one another's writing: making distinctions, drawing inferences from data, adopting criteria, examining inferences according to those criteria, and formulating and explaining conclusions in useful ways.

A tutoring course that is itself collaborative can also help tutors consider the nature, risks, and potential of the nontraditional institutional role they play. The course can address institutional issues of a sort that college courses rarely address, such as the institutional status of students and teachers, and the relationship of peer tutors to one another, to college and university administrators, and to the general public, the latter often and most immediately represented by students' parents.

A course for tutors taught collaboratively can raise these issues in a particularly concrete way because of the ambiguities in a peer tutor's role relative to students and tutors on the one hand and, on the other, teachers and the institution. Discerning these ambiguities and discussing them in the tutoring course in a collaborative context can lead to discoveries about the educational implications of the limited role that peer tutors play relative to the fellow students whom they tutor—their peers. And it can lead to discoveries about students' role and their social and "political" place in a college or university.

In such a course, collaborative peer tutors can also learn some of the practical skills of dealing with people under stress. They can learn where students' most debilitating academic difficulties lie and how to deal with them, how to open conversations with reticent or fearful students, how to evade overdependent tutees, how to empower and encourage without raising expectations too high, and so on. In short, the course can help peer tutors bring to bear in an academic context the highest degree of social and institutional maturity they are capable of.

One of the most important goals of a tutoring course organized collaboratively is to prevent tutors from imitating their betters. Tutors have to learn how to guard against reverting to pedagogical type by becoming traditional, foundational teachers writ small. The temptation to revert is strong because, as one of the peer tutors I taught several years ago put it,

> Being in a position to look at and analyze another's work and not be judged yourself produces a tremendous feeling of power. This feeling is bad for me and the tutee because it puts us on two different levels, which makes it difficult to work together.[3]

Another tutor put the point even more revealingly. Through peer tutoring she became

> conscious that I have a tendency to want others to adopt my values . . . Power, I have found, is something I like having. For example, a classmate of mine came to the Writing Center to meet with his teacher. He saw me there in my role as a tutor. The next day in class he asked my advice about his English paper. I enjoyed his asking my advice. The fact that he values my opinion makes me happy. What makes me unhappy is realizing that I do to others what I've always hated others doing to me—just evaluating work, not helping to make it better.[4]

The tendency of many tutees to turn peer tutors into little traditional teachers by depending on tutors emotionally and academically reinforces this temptation to reestablish the traditional, foundational teaching relationship between peer tutors and their tutees. Collaboration in a tutoring course can help reduce the tendency for tutors to adopt the role of traditional teachers. It does so by restructuring relationships among the tutors themselves. Collaboration encourages students to accept authority for helping one another learn and to acknowledge the authority of other students—their peers—to help them learn themselves.

I began to understand both the potential of collaborative peer tutoring to act as an agent of institutional change and the sort of institutional change that it could foster when for several years in the early seventies I taught a tutoring course myself.[5] Some of the details of this experience are relevant here because they suggest two traits of peer tutors that can make them exceptionally effective as change agents within a college or university. First, they understand (to mix metaphors rather crudely) at both a gut and a grass roots level many issues that are central to the nature and quality—and hence the future—of American higher education today. Second, from that understanding derives a distinct self-confidence, an unusual, mutually confirmed authority. More than any other group of students on any college or university campus, peer tutors know what they are doing and know the value and significance of what they do.

Besides the hoped-for result of producing, semester after semester, groups of able, hard-working, effective peer tutors, the tutoring course I taught had a number of unexpected results. One of these was the peer tutors' striking insights into the difficulties experienced by students who asked them for help. The first surprise was the tutors' impression that they were not dealing primarily with failing students trying to stay in school. They were dealing with C students trying to get Bs, B students trying to get As, and A students trying to stay A students. Some of them were even dealing occasionally with graduate students. One, sworn to secrecy, had been approached by a member of the faculty for help on an article he was writing.

The records that the tutors were asked to keep of their work confirmed this impression. These records were anonymous. They included only the tutees' class, how well they were doing in school—in some cases their grade point average—and remarks about the particular problem that the tutor and tutee worked on. From the first day, even during the era of "open admissions" (for which I had originally designed the program), more than half of the students the tutors worked with were in the middle range of ability and accomplishment. Peer tutoring turned out not to be a service for new or nontraditional students, although it served them, too. It turned out to be a service largely for the sorts of students who had always gone to college and done well there.

The second discovery the tutors made had to do with the kind of problems these middle-range students asked for help on. Sympathetic faculty and administrators, myself among them, expected that most of the students who asked peer tutors for help needed work on "assimilating subject matter." We expected that in, say, writing, the students who asked for help had problems that could be solved by helping them learn grammar and "writing skills." But the peer tutors began to find that their students' difficulties seemed to have a deeper cause. One tutor, for example, stumbled on the close relationship of self and language, when he reported that "many students whose writing is weak" feel that weaknesses in writing expose "weaknesses in themselves." Similarly, in mathematics and related subjects, semester after semester tutors rediscovered "math anxiety," which Sheila Tobias has written so perceptively about.

That is, the tutors began to think that the academic problems of many students may not stem from lack of ability or instruction alone. Some students appeared to be intellectually paralyzed. Their preconceptions about themselves, about their education, and about the world beyond college seemed to limit their belief in their capacity to generate ideas out of experience, either in the library or in life. To account for such a state, some tutors felt that it was superficial merely to say that the students they dealt with had been poorly taught in high school or had watched too much TV. Their problems seemed to have an origin that was at once both broader and deeper, of an order that more sophisticated observers might call cultural and epistemological. Based on my own experience (reported in Chapter 1), that is certainly what I called it. Such students faced barriers to learning that were therefore intractable from the perspective of traditional college and university education.

If traditional classroom teaching had little effect on this educational paralysis, peer tutoring in many cases had considerable effect. Students who said that they did not know much at all about the subjects that they were supposed to be studying or that their teachers had asked them to write about, given the opportunity to talk with a sympathetic, knowledgeable peer, discovered knowledge they did not know they had. Many of them, the tutors found, could begin to identify and examine issues on these subjects, take positions on them, and explain them.

A gratifying confirmation of these observations about the nature and effectiveness of peer tutoring came from comments by an education reporter from the *New York Times* who asked one day to spend an hour alone with a half-dozen peer tutors. Their conversation seems to have rapidly become shop talk. He told me enthusiastically later that the sorts of things the tutors were doing with their tutees were exactly the sorts of things he had to do with many *Times* free-lance writers. He said he spent hours on the phone with them helping them pull their work together into some semblance of organization and coherence, getting them to deflate their style, wringing some understandable details out of their overgeneralizations, and bolstering their self-confidence. And to reach them, he had to learn to deal with them in much the same way as, he found, our peer tutors had learned to deal with their tutees.[6]

Related to the tutors' insights into the problems of their tutees was another unexpected result of the course: changes in the peer tutors' own academic work. Tutoring and its classroom counterpart, the organized, collaborative process of peer review, led in a single semester to dramatic improvement in the writing of some of the tutors, according to almost any measure: organization, style, perspicacity, balance, depth of understanding, tact. The tutors' willingness to read one another's writing and their ability to make constructive suggestions about it, instead of becoming (as we saw in Chapters 1 and 4) merely sharks and teddy bears, improved dramatically as well.

The literature on "cross age" tutoring in grade schools (older kids tutoring younger kids) has led me to expect some improvement in the tutors' academic work.[7] But nothing led me to expect that the thinking and writing of somewhat above-average undergraduates could "develop" so much so quickly through a process of peer interaction. Nor was I prepared for the degree to which the course tended to decrease the tenacity with which the tutors clung to familiar ideas and to increase their willingness to entertain new ideas. These developments were so rapid that it made me suspect that they were not "developments" at all. Rather, I began to suspect that the tutors had discovered, perhaps for the first time, an educational context into which they could adapt and bring to bear traits of maturity that they had already developed in other circumstances. Some of the tutors' comments when the class members debriefed one another during class discussion about their experiences as tutors, as peer reviewers of one another's writing, and as peer reviewees, confirmed this suspicion. For most of them, it was the first course they had ever had in which behaving in socially mature ways manifestly contributed to their success in the course.

A third unexpected result of the course was that it reduced the effect of one of the most serious and debilitating limitations of peer influence: the conservative tendency, potentially detrimental to academic development, that is seen in the anti-intellectual and anti-academic cast of many college and university social, athletic, and other extracurricular groups. As Newcomb and others have pointed out, although some extracurricular activities can help students learn social graces and can encourage change in personal values, they are also likely to increase students' tendency to conform to already established, comfortable, and even self-destructive patterns of behavior and thought. In the several "generations" of peer tutors that I dealt with, each class of which formed an exceptionally coherent group with its own distinct "personality" and style, this conformity never occurred.

The tutors themselves suggested why peer influence tends not to be a conservative force among peer tutors. Group solidarity is conservative, they said, because people in groups have power to reward and applaud one another for performing well within the conventions of the group and power to punish, humiliate, and exclude one another for infractions of the group's mores. These extreme responses tended not to occur among peer tutors, they suggested, for at least two reasons. First, most of them found that their growing loyalty to their class of peer tutors cut across their loyalties to other groups—ethnic communities, fraternities and sororities, teams, clubs. When I explained the process of reacculturation I had experienced myself (the tale told in Chapter 1) they were able to match my experience and even top it with added details and nuances. The increased awareness they garnered from these experiences tended, they felt, to "soften the edges" of their peer tutoring class group so that it was less exclusionary and cliquish than shared experience and expertise might ordinarily have led it to be.

The other reason they mentioned was, of course, that the peer tutoring group was constituted in large part for the purpose of reaching beyond the group to other students. The coherence of the group depended in part on its members acquiring expertise as translators at the boundaries between teachers and students. This is a trait that (as we have seen in Chapter 4) peer tutors share with college and university teachers and that for the latter (as we shall see in Chapter 8) has important professional implications. Some peer tutors are in fact more expert in this respect, or at least more aware of their expertise and of its significance, than some of the faculty members they deal with.

Group solidarity did not push the peer tutors I worked with into stereotypical responses for still another reason. The tutoring course taught them to subdivide the socially and intellectually tricky task of peer evaluation into elements so limited in scope as to seem unthreatening to group coherence. When I originally subdivided evaluation in this way, I did not do it for this purpose. I did it to make the peer tutors better readers of other students' writing and thereby make them more effective tutors. But learning some of the criteria that are appropriate to evaluation and how to apply them reasonably, temperately, and constructively turned out to have a happy by-product. The peer tutors acquired incrementally a new set of values based on a consensus negotiated with other members of their group of peer tutors. The result was increased willingness to evaluate one another's work reasonably, temperately, and constructively. It appeared that I had been teaching my peer tutors "academic judgment" much as M.L.J. Abercrombie had taught medical judgment to her diagnostics class (discussed in Chapters 1 and 10), and with much the same results.[8]

Another happy by-product was that many tutors understood, and in some cases for the first time, some basic aspects of thought and conceptualization. For example, they became aware of varieties of logical sequence and contradiction, both as tools for explanation and persuasion and as patterns of resistance in learning: for example, that lists can be used as an aid to synthesis and judgment and also as a barrier against them. Their own work improved because, as a result of identifying these problems in the work of their tutees and their fellow tutors, they began to identify and resolve them in their own thought and writing. As one put it, the academic problems he confronted as a peer tutor "seemed to be a mirror image of my own."

Most peer tutors did not formulate these issues in received philosophical or psychological terms but on the hoof, so to speak, and in the community languages they had at their disposal, like the "heteroglossic" working terms we saw students improvising in Chapter 4. One tutor offered a revealing example of the practical level at which peer tutors tend to become engaged with ideas. "I recall one student I tutored," he tells us,

> who avoided detail like the plague. He was writing a report on the book *Dibs, In Search of Self*, which is about a troubled boy who closed himself off from the world and about the method his teacher used to bring him back. In writing this paper, the student did nothing but generalize. He was worried that the detail of the book was too tedious and irrelevant to his paper. But together we delved into the book and extracted the necessary detail for solid support. From [working on this paper] both of us realized that it was those "tedious" details that made the book enjoyable. It was mainly the ability of the author to relate her thoughts to concrete detail that made her writing good.[9]

The apparent simplicity of the transitional language that this tutor uses in describing a "writing problem" should not obscure the fact that these two students, peer tutor and tutee, were grappling with sophisticated issues: the relationship of concrete and abstract, attitudes toward and evaluation of sources, and levels of reasoning.

They were also confronting another, still larger issue, frequently ignored, that underlies the difficulties many students have in attempting to learn the nature of the relationship between generalizations and supporting detail. The tutee's overgeneralized writing and his "worry" about "those 'tedious' details" reveal anxiety about the nature of writing itself, a desire to find a level of discourse that is appropriate to academic writing, and possibly confusion about the relationship between style and what he believes to be the importance of his own ideas. His anxiety betrays a feeling common among students that writers have to dress up what they want to say with big words and highfalutin phrases because ideas expressed at a high level of generalization are necessarily more important (less "tedious") than ideas expressed more concretely.

What the example shows, in short, is that peer tutors do not deal with ideas complete and in the abstract. They learn to deal with ideas in their fluid, incomplete state of change, ideas as they are developing through conversation and social exchange. And they confront the insecurity, personal interest, and proprietary attachment that all thinking people feel for their own ideas, especially when expressed in words on a page. In this way, peer tutors and tutees alike can become more intensely aware than most undergraduates ever become of the fragility and uncertainty—and the inherent excitement—of intellectual work.

My understanding of the potential of collaborative peer tutoring to act as an agent of institutional change and my understanding of the sort of institutional change it could foster increased when I found myself having to answer the questions my colleagues asked, both on my home campus and elsewhere, when I described peer tutoring and the tutoring course I was teaching. They asked questions like, "Do peer tutors need a certain amount of political savvy when they deal with the teachers of the students they tutor?" "Do you talk with your peer tutors about how teachers will grade the students they're working with?" and "What do you do about the faculty members who are opposed to peer tutoring?"

Questions such as these revealed an apprehension about peer tutoring that, naively, I had not anticipated. Every question had both a short and a long answer. Yes, I said, peer tutors do need some "political savvy"— that is, a measure of circumspection and tact—if they deal with the teachers of their tutees. Yes, I do talk with peer tutors about grading practices. And no, I do nothing about faculty members who were opposed to peer tutoring, since if they choose not to work with peer tutors or allow their students to consult them, they do not have to.

And yet every one of the questions my colleagues asked had a subtext that my short answers evaded. If college or university faculty members framed a question about tact as a "political" issue and anticipated opposition that, on the surface, seemed unlikely (Who could reasonably oppose a well-organized, faculty-governed academic support service that demonstrably made life easier all around?), they were already perceiving peer tutoring as a potential threat to entrenched academic values and practices. And if faculty members asked about the relationship between peer tutoring and grading, an issue that peer tutors should never be involved in, they were already perceiving peer tutoring as a challenge to teachers' traditional prerogatives and classroom authority.

The suspicion that peer tutoring had something to do with institutional "politics" and classroom authority became of more than passing interest (as well as of practical interest to the peer tutors themselves) when, over time, other aspects of peer tutoring that I have referred to in this chapter began to emerge. First, within a decade after peer tutoring was successfully instituted in a few American colleges and universities, it became an almost universal practice, institutionalized and depended upon at almost every kind of institution of higher education. Second, peer tutoring was everywhere serving not only students at risk—the "nontraditional" and the "underprepared." It was serving a broad spectrum of traditional, well-prepared college and university students. Third, this broad spectrum of students was bringing to peer tutors everywhere academic problems rooted in intellectual, emotional, and cultural issues that were unrecognized, unaccounted for, and largely unaddressed by traditional classroom education. Finally, peer tutors were addressing these academic problems, experienced everywhere by a broad range of students, with demonstrable success.

In short, it began to seem evident that peer tutoring was a form of collaborative learning that presented an alternative to traditional college and university education. It was being broadly institutionalized to the benefit of many students. And although it caused some slight tremors beneath the traditional academic landscape, massive opposition seemed unlikely. One case I happen to be familiar with illustrated the potentially persuasive force that peer tutors could exert even under the most adverse conditions. The story goes that a certain institutionally influential, newly elected English Department chair sent a highly reputable, well-published professor, a medievalist and Chaucerian, to get the goods on the college's new peer tutoring program. The chair's goal, not so subtly bruited about (it was a tacit plank in his election campaign platform), was to sink the program.

The chair knew that the Chaucerian in question had rigorously traditional views and no particular fondness for institutional innovation. What he didn't count on was that the Chaucerian was also a person of great scholarly integrity. He spent almost a semester slowly and methodically examining the program, including interviews with the peer tutors, one of whom turned out to be one of the best students in his Chaucer class. He attended a national convention of college and university teachers that under normal circumstances he would have considered beneath contempt. And in the end, he turned in a report, to the dismay of the department chair and to the relief of the peer tutors (not to speak of the program director), that convinced a dubious administration to support the program wholeheartedly.

My experience with peer tutors as a faculty member and, furthermore, as a teacher of the tutoring course, demonstrated that peer tutors can be sensitive to institutional issues to a degree—and to a depth—that many other members of the academic community, faculty and students alike, tend not to be. Even without thinking much about it, some peer tutors will learn collaboratively how to affect and change their academic environment. In this particular example, the factor in their academic environment that they set out to change was me.

Naturally enough, I began teaching the tutoring course with a set of confirmed views about how peer tutors should be "trained." To the tutors' advantage, I had an interest in the program. I was curious about

it, and I had become professionally invested in its success. I was therefore, it could be argued, vulnerable to their influence. For a while, things
went pretty much as I intended them to go. Toward the middle of the
term, however, the tutors suggested one day in class that the program
consider making some changes in the way the tutoring center was being
run. Some of these struck me, on reflection, as hmm, well, perhaps
worth trying.

But then those tutors had the audacity to suggest some changes in
the way I was teaching the course. An institutional program is one thing.
A professor's course is quite another. To these suggestions I found myself
less receptive. Whose course was it, anyway? I asked myself.

In fact, I blush to recall, one day I asked the class the very same
question. They laughed. Only gradually, as they worried me like a dog
with a bone, did they work me around to acknowledging that the answer
to the question might just be that the course was indeed not quite all
mine. Only gradually could I acknowledge that classroom authority, in
this course at any rate, might not be all mine, either. Whether I liked it
or not, by virtue of the fact that the peer tutors could all, if they liked,
take a walk, they contributed heavily to whatever authority I enjoyed
in that course. My classroom authority depended in part on their willingness to acknowledge it. And if the students in the course contributed
to my classroom authority, they might also have some claim to affect
the direction that the course was taking. They might even have some
useful expertise to contribute. In short, evidence that I could not gainsay
began to mount that "my" peer tutors were already acting as agents of
institutional change. And the evidence was firsthand. I was the bit of
the institution they were undertaking to change.

But this insight into the potential of peer tutors "to act as agents of
institutional change" raised more questions than it answered. For example, would my colleagues feel their influence in the same way and
the same degree? Probably not quite, although clearly that Chaucerian
had felt it. Hostile department chairs aside, the mere possibility struck
me as intriguing.

At the point of acknowledging this possibility it occurred to me for
the first time that a pool of suitably prepared (by which I mean, collaboratively prepared), thoughtful, articulate peer tutors might provide for-
ward-looking institutions a new resource that could be effective at every
level of decision making. The reason to consider drawing on this pool,
it seemed to me, would be that peer tutors have expertise that many
faculty and administrators lack. My peer tutors had shown me that they
had an intimate, hands-on understanding of the constructive and conversational nature of thought and knowledge. They had seen the social

95

construction of knowledge (of the sort we saw Mary experience in Chapter 1) repeated every day, and they repeatedly experienced it themselves. They had also witnessed and experienced themselves (with, for example, me) the many kinds of intricate and in some cases distressing relationships that occur between college and university students and their teachers.

The experience that administrators and faculty members have had with involving peer tutors in institutional decision making at every level confirms this impression. In many American colleges and universities since the sixties, undergraduates have contributed a good deal to institutional decision making, but with diminishing intensity and effectiveness. This decline is in part a result of the fact that the contribution is made in many cases by student representatives who are either elected members of student government or else faculty or administration appointees. Elected student representatives turn out, not surprisingly, to represent the limited interests of their constituencies, while faculty appointees turn out, also not surprisingly, to give voice to views that are little different from the views of those who choose them.

Student representation of this limited sort is of still less value if we regard colleges and universities not primarily as composites of quad, curriculum, and catalogue, but as composites of the people who, for the time being, walk the quad, teach the curriculum, and enforce the catalogue. The "institution," then, is precisely the interests and goals of these people, their values, what they know and how they know it, what they learn and how they learn it, what they teach and how they teach it, what they think of each other, how they treat each other, and the whole fabric of human relationships that exists invisibly within the walls of bricks and mortar.

Decision making in an educational institution understood in this way requires quite another sort of student representation: students seriously engaged in the same educational enterprise that the faculty and administration are engaged in, but with an informed, independent perspective. An institution's peer tutors comprise such a pool, if they have been suitably prepared, have plenty of expertise in tutoring, and meet a sufficiently broad range of student needs (possibly including, for example, peer counseling). College and university governance, from department curriculum to long-range institutional planning, could be profoundly affected by their influence. More to the point, students actively involved in collaboration, and neither afraid of it nor uncritically enamored of it as the solution to every problem that colleges and universities face, can help move whole institutions toward some of the changes explained in this book.

In these first five chapters I have discussed what I regard as the most important of these goals. They are changes in relations among students, among teachers, and between students and teachers; changes in our understanding of how we learn; changes in our understanding of what teachers do and of the nature of their authority; and changes in classroom practice. In the next chapter, I will discuss in that context a troublesome issue that is growing in importance and public visibility: how to fulfill the educational potential of electronic technology.

CHAPTER SIX

Mime and Supermime: Collaborative Learning and Instructional Technology

Collaborative learning implies changing what we think college and university teachers do when they teach. Changing what teachers do implies changing what they think knowledge is. The change this book recommends is from traditional teaching to collaborative learning. Traditional teaching makes foundational (or cognitive) assumptions about knowledge. Collaborative learning makes nonfoundational (or social constructionist) assumptions.

This last chapter of Part 1 illustrates, with the way we think about educational technology, in particular microcomputers and television, the relationship between teaching and our understanding of knowledge. In both cases, the visual intensity of the video screen and the obscurity of the electronic process that produces it reinforce the visual metaphor on which the foundational understanding of knowledge is based. Yet these foundational assumptions about knowledge and learning have caused most educational applications of television to fail, and they threaten the failure of most educational applications of microcomputers. This chapter says that understanding educational technology differently and applying it with different assumptions in mind may help us ensure its educational effectiveness and success. The chapter also looks forward to the discussion in Part 2 of broader changes in our understanding of college and university education.

We tend to think about educational technology in three related foundational ways. The first and most prevalent is objectivist. We think of television and microcomputers as sources of information derived from the external world. Those who favor this objectivist view tend to believe that to get the best results we should program television and microcomputers to help students discern reality more fully and accurately. We can do this, the argument goes, by using these electronic tools to provide access to masses of nuanced and intricately related information. Hence the importance of our ability to pack the Encyclopaedia Britannica, the Third International Dictionary, and perhaps the works of Shakespeare on a single fourteen-inch compact laser disk.

The second way we think in foundational terms about microcomputers and television is subjectivist. We regard them as aids to imagination and conceptualization. We encourage television producers and microcomputer programmers to devise whizbang shows and programs that we believe will help students synthesize information in increasingly sophisticated and complex ways. Among microcomputer subjectivists the most enthusiastic tend to believe in artificial intelligence. They take the position that a microcomputer is itself a "mind." To my knowledge, no one has quite yet thought of television as a "mind." But educational television enthusiasts do claim that television can "open minds" and "provoke thought."

The third foundational way we think of educational technology is elisionist. Elisionists tend to think that the most important educational goal is to effect a relationship between the two pieces of foundational knowledge apparatus that are supposed to operate in the human mind, the synthesizing inner eye and the reality-collecting and reality-reflecting mirror of nature. They regard microcomputer hardware and software as an electronic analog that helps students "make connections." Elisionists therefore tend to regard television as a "medium of communication." And they tend to think that access to a massive integrated data base is essential to the effective educational use of microcomputers.

Today the foundational understanding of knowledge underlying these views has been seriously challenged, and on that basis this book challenges traditional college and university teaching. As a part of that challenge, this chapter takes the position that the appropriate use of any educational technology requires giving up foundational assumptions and integrating technology with social relationships. Television and microcomputation can fulfill their educational promise only if we exploit their potential as mediators of intellectually constructive, educationally productive social relations: collaborative learning.

To understand how we might do that, we have to understand first the extent to which television and microcomputers are generically identical. They are both mimetic media. Television is a mime. A microcomputer is a supermime. Both generate, store, replicate, transform, and transmit electronic impulses in ways that human senses can "read," and in ways that seem to reproduce aspects of human mentality and of external reality. Both illustrate natural phenomena and mental exercises in animated diagrams, pictures, and sounds. Sometimes they even illustrate mental exercises that heretofore only a handful of people have ever comprehended and phenomena that are impossible for the eye otherwise to see, for the ear otherwise to hear, and for most minds otherwise to conceive.

The generic identity of television and microcomputers includes their capacity to open doors. Television extends access to college and university education by making the human "presence" in drama, film, demonstration, and lecture (including the evening news) available to everyone everywhere, bringing people together face-to-face without requiring them to leave their offices or homes and bringing current events—love, sport, ceremony, war, mayhem—into our living rooms. Similarly, microcomputers place the resources of great research libraries and laboratories within reach of everyone everywhere. Because they can illustrate a great range of natural phenomena and mental exercises, they also make it possible for teachers to teach to large numbers of students things that they could once teach to only a few, or could not teach at all.

Word processing is no exception to this extension of access. Ease of editorial revision makes refinement of verbal nuance possible for many who had never before had the leisure or patience to undertake them. In its most sophisticated form, so-called desktop publishing, word processing puts within the reach of almost everyone everywhere the ability to formulate the written word and cast it in eminently readable form, a process available until very recently only to those who could afford high-speed typists and talented graphic designers.

There are, of course, obvious differences between television and microcomputer programs, but they are differences of degree or scale, not of kind. Microcomputers exceed television as television exceeds telephone and radio. Radio, telephone, and television extend access to resources to large numbers of students well beyond large centers of study and learning. Microcomputers extend access to even greater resources. TV wows us. Microcomputers wow us more. Television can engage students deeply in their studies. Microcomputers can engage them more deeply still.

Even the most celebrated difference between television programs and microcomputer programs, instant interaction, is illusory. In the most striking and obvious form of interaction, between persons and machines, microcomputers win hands down. As machines, microcomputers can respond in microseconds with the all-but-infinite visual and auditory combinations that can be designed into "hyperprograms" and stored for instant access. Even word processing interacts with us at lightning speed. We push "help"; instantly, the program tells us what to do. We type s-a-u-s-e; instantly it says, Oh no, it's spelled *sauce*. In contrast, mechanical interaction with television is primitive. All we can do is turn it on, off, and from channel to channel.

But this interaction between person and machine is not the kind of interaction that counts. The interaction with television and microcomputers that counts occurs between two groups of people, those in front of the machine and those behind it: the people who use the machine and the people who produced the show or designed the program loaded into the machine.

Looked at this way, microcomputers are neither more genuinely interactive than TV nor so instantaneous as they seem. Rapid interaction with microcomputers is a technologically induced illusion. The machine's response, however infinitely diverse, is canned, just as taped television programs are canned. What the vast microcomputer memory stores is the disciplinary and cultural languages of the people who write the programs—the languages of the knowledge communities they belong to and the institutions they are part of or work for. Both TV producers and microcomputer programmers lock into the machine the language of their own communities of knowledgeable peers, and they oblige users to be fluent in that language or become so.

A trivial but revealing example is that old spelling demon of mine, *sauce*. In the single gesture of correcting my spelling, the word-processing program in my machine encapsulates and enforces a convention, fixed since roughly the mid-eighteenth century, that determines the orthographic representation of sibilant sounds in certain phonemic contexts in standard written English. More important, the program also encapsulates and enforces a deeply entrenched tradition based on that convention: that misspelled words in written texts reveal inadequacies the importance of which far exceeds the variation of a single letter in a single word. If you can't spell, the tradition goes, can you really have much between the ears?

Because television and computer programs lock in the assumptions, presuppositions, goals, biases, and limitations of those who program them, genuine interaction with both is deliberate and laborious. In many more cases than the industry would like to acknowledge, by the time commercially designed microcomputer and mainframe programs are debugged, packaged, and marketed, users' needs have outpaced them. It can take up to two years to produce a new computer program or even to correct or revise an old one. By that time, users' needs may well have changed again, sometimes drastically. The lag between the needs of microcomputer program users and the production and revision of programs addressing those needs can in fact make the rate of change in TV programming look prodigious. Our one demonstrably successful effort to put television to educational use, *Sesame Street,* for example, has changed in many ways during its twenty-year history through ongoing interaction between the show's producers and their audience. Interaction with commercial television through audience polls and ratings surveys occurs faster, because there's so much cash riding on it. But it may still be weeks or months after a show or advertisement first goes on the air that a negative audience rating finally results in the show's cancellation.

The first two steps toward using educational television and micro-computers effectively are relatively easy. We recognize that the most important educational relationships are social, and we therefore shift the focus of our attention from visual intensity and electronic instantaneity to a constructive interaction between users and producers or program-mers. The third step is the tough one. We have to recognize that the nature of the displaced relationship between students and producers or programmers is determined by a much more immediate one: the rela-tionship among the students using the machines.

This notion, that the impact of television depends on social relations among television viewers, does not come as news to producers of both commercial and educational television. They readily acknowledge that audience response to television, as one study puts it, is "clearly an *overt social process.*"[1] As long ago as 1978, research showed that "television viewing is an often-interrupted, frequently divided focus of attention." People do all sorts of things while they watch television. A significant portion of this "secondary activity" is "devoted to conversation and social interaction. . . . [This] conversation is not invariably distractive; about as often, it augments or complements television being viewed."[2]

People behave the same way when they watch educational television. A study some years ago by an Annenberg/Corporation for Public Broad-casting project, for example, neither mentions the socially mediative effect of television nor cites existing studies that demonstrate it. Yet the study offers plentiful evidence, apparently with no awareness of its implications, suggesting that as many as 30 percent of the students in the sample studied, even unprompted, turned telecourse programs into a mediated experience of collaborative learning by watching them "at home with family and/or friends."[3]

Classroom experience with microcomputers leads to much the same conclusion. Both when they watch television and when they work at microcomputers, except when the program's razzle-dazzle rivets them to the screen, students often talk to one another while the machine is on. They tend to cluster around work stations to help each other out, explain to each other how to fiddle the machine to get it to work, talk over the results they are getting, and debate the next move. In both cases, canned performance and conversation "augment and complement" each other.

This interaction between social relations and electronically mediated performance is reminiscent of the audience participation cult of *The Rocky Horror Picture Show*. This movie was popular in the seventies and is periodically revived. While it is shown, young people dress up as the characters who appear in the movie and perform ritually with each other. This social interaction among members of the audience becomes the most important event taking place in the hall. The incidents in that event happen not to the characters in the movie but among the "characters" who attend it. In fact, it is not accurate to say that people attend this movie. The movie attends them. The "audience" enacts the real drama, for which the moving picture is prop and staging. The professional performance is not the show. The professional performance creates conditions in which the real show occurs.

Microcomputer programs attend us in much the same way. Like television programs, they are props and staging, catalysts, provocations, and occasions for social interaction. Whether highly polished and "user friendly" or awkward and crude, the professionally programmed performance before us is subordinate to the social engagement that it induces among us. Of course, we cannot easily acknowledge that television and microcomputer programs are socially provocative parts of our lives in this way, because we find it hard to account for some of the facts of the case. In particular, we find it hard to account for the fact that we spend so many long hours watching television alone, seemingly isolated, solitary, and passive in front of that grand repository of imagery, the tube, and for the fact that we work so frequently alone in front of that grand repository of data, a microcomputer.

These facts are hard to account for because we think of what we are doing in foundational rather than nonfoundational terms. Understood nonfoundationally, a TV or microcomputer program is no more a repository than (as we noted in Chapter 1) a library is. It is a crowd of interrelated communities of producers, programmers, writers, designers, and technicians. Furthermore, we ourselves have internalized many of the vast, complex linguistic and paralinguistic symbol systems of word and gesture that constitute those communities, out of which television and microcomputer performances are constructed. Like Mary, whom we encountered in Chapter 1 carrying on an internalized conversation with her classmate at home, we carry with us to the TV or microcomputer our own membership in those communities.

We are able to engage in this internalized conversation, giving ourselves the wherewithal to watch and work alone, because the razzle-dazzle of television and microcomputer programs gives us such a persuasive illusion of "living presence." It convincingly apes not only nature and the human mind but also human communities. To watch young children absorbed in *Sesame Street* is to see that razzle-dazzle put to the use of reacculturating young human beings to the conventions of dozens of knowledge communities entirely new to them, from the alphabet to the shticks of vaudeville comedy. Television, as a colleague of mine put it years ago, is "an instructor and a friend."[4] So today are microcomputers. Ask any hacker. Ask any Nintendo-playing sick kid home from school. Ask the Nintendo-playing sick kid's mom.

In short, when we watch television or work on a microcomputer alone, our solitude is an illusion. Reading, studying, doing experimental work, watching *Dallas* or *Sesame Street*, crunching numbers, and word processing—all these are displaced social acts in which solitude is adventitious. Each of these performance events is permeated with internalized linguistic and paralinguistic symbol systems with which, as members of the knowledge communities they constitute, we construct our ideas, thoughts, feelings, and perceptions. We watch TV together (to allude to Frost's "Tuft of Flowers" once again), whether we watch it together or apart. We play Nintendo together, whether we play it together or apart. Isolated, solitary, and passive as we may seem before the tube and the keyboard, we are in fact always enmeshed in circle upon circle of invisible social relations, woven with the linguistic and paralinguistic symbol systems that constitute the knowledge communities of which we are members.

Any educational application of television and microcomputers that makes nonfoundational assumptions will strive to integrate these three social elements of knowledge and learning: socially constructed symbol systems, the displaced social relationship they effect between producers or programmers and their audience, and social relations among the people using the machine. In short, nonfoundational educational applications of electronic technology require using machines to prompt people to turn away from the machine and focus their attention instead on each other.

This requirement is the greatest barrier to changing the way we use television and microcomputers educationally. To traditional performers it is anathema to allow or, worse, to encourage people to turn away from the performance and focus their attention on anything else—least of all, perhaps, one another. The ancient and honorable goal of performers is to rivet the audience's attention on themselves. Not to compel an audience to focus its attention on the performance is to "lose your audience." Yet a calculated loss of audience in some sense is the goal of any program that marshals the social effects of television and microcomputation. Such a program must encourage people to turn their attention away from the tube and focus it instead on each other, carrying into the immediacy of social relations what they have experienced vicariously on the screen, either just then or at some time in the past.

It is becoming increasingly imperative that we design television and microcomputer programs for this purpose, because electronic media continue to increase their powers of social mediation. VCRs have freed television watching and the social engagement that television tends to bring about from the tyranny of channel programmers. VCRs and compact disks let us turn television not only on, off, up, down, and from channel to channel, but also forward when we get tired of the razzle-dazzle, and backward when we think we may have missed something while we were talking to each other. Compact disks free microcomputation and the social engagement it mediates from the tyranny of mainframe memory banks and telephone lines. This technology, and more to come, confirms and enhances the social impact of television and microcomputation, however much performers try to stamp it out with razzle-dazzle.

What measures, then, can producers and programmers take, with full awareness and the greatest possible competence, to fulfill the educational potential of television and microcomputers for constituting, mediating, and guiding the social conditions in which learning occurs?

Currently, most programs not only perpetuate but magnify the one-to-one social relations of traditional education that we discussed in Chapter 4. They replace relationships between a teacher and each individual student in a lecture hall or seminar room with one-to-one relations between teacher and each individual student across a campus or throughout an area of hundreds or thousands of square miles.

To transform these electronic programs and systems into tools that stimulate and mediate collaborative work and focused conversation among students, producers and programmers have to find ways to accomplish two ends. They have to engage people socially in transition (or translation) groups of the sort described in Chapters 2 and 4. And they have to guide the negotiations that go on among the members of transition communities that they have helped to establish. As we have seen, these negotiations are of two sorts: at the boundaries of communities that students are leaving and at the boundaries of communities that students are trying to join.

In this process, producers and programmers will find an important resource in the expertise of self-help mutual-aid group work. People form self-help mutual-aid groups autonomously on their own initiative when they feel they need help in order to understand their needs and satisfy them. But they may also form these groups semiautonomously at the prompting and with the encouragement and guidance of an institution such as a hospital, hospice, governmental program, college or university, or—potentially—a television or microcomputer program.[5]

To devise programs that help people at the computer keyboard or in front of a television screen to make contact not just with the authority that the program represents but with one another, producers and programmers will have to strive to "lose their audience" constructively. Software writers, dramatists, writers, directors, and performers will have to find ways to weaken the bond that glues people to the tube and intensify instead the excitement, interest, and understanding that people derive from conversation about what they are seeing or have seen on the tube. It may take some time for them to devise successful programs of this sort. They may even have to await research based on nonfoundational assumptions. As Chapter 10 implies, research of that sort does not seem to be just over the horizon at the moment. We may now be at about the stage in understanding the socially interactive aspects of television and microcomputers that people were at when they strapped wings to their arms in order to fly.

It is possible to say, however, that as a stopgap measure producers and programmers can get to work on at least three fronts: (1) designing learning tasks to be undertaken collaboratively and directed toward achieving consensus, (2) designing programs that help students learn the social conventions of working successfully in small, semiautonomous groups, and (3) designing programs that supply the information, assumptions, tasks, and evaluative criteria that guide collaborative work constructively and help people learn from each other.

At this stage only a primitive illustrative sketch is possible. Sequentially speaking, the purpose of the first segment in a collaborative learning television or microcomputer program would probably be to encourage people to draw themselves together on the basis of mutual interest into small working groups of three to seven, either in the same room or across a network. This first segment would not instruct but tempt, stimulating ice-breaking conversation among participants and ensuring that the impetus, origin, and sanction of each learning group came as much as possible from users, not from the authority of professionals.

Here, some of the methods and constraints of first-phase group work (discussed in Chapter 2) are relevant. In the first phase group members tend to confront the relevance of authority to their relationships with one another and to their work. For example, a program could propose "warm-up" games germane in some simple way to the topic but drawing on information contributed by students who have different backgrounds or interests or who are located in different places (weather, distances, names, relation to siblings—first, middle, only child, etc.—courses taken, career goals, and so on). This initial problem or task should be interesting or provocative but nonthreatening. It should be relatively easy for a group of students coping with the stress of working together for the first time to solve or accomplish. It should provide some experience in collaboration. And it should give the community its first success in arriving at productive consensus.

Following this introduction, program segments might ask students to solve a series of topic-related problems or do a series of topic-related tasks together, arriving at a consensus in each case that all or most of the members of the group can "live with." At intervals throughout the experience, and especially at the end, the program would take care to give collaborative groups a chance to debate dissenting views and to compare the consensus they have arrived at with the prevailing consensus of the relevant disciplinary community. It would also deal with the contradictions, false paths, and common errors that may occur in collaboration, perhaps even sending the groups back through the program again using the new information or point of view generated in this final phase.

For this purpose, the program could draw groups of participating students into a looping, interpretive process with any number of hypothetical combinations. It could provide means for feeding interaction among participants, as well as interaction between participants and the machine, back into the program. It would therefore allow the social relations among participants to modify the program as they go along. The program would "learn" as the ability of learning communities to govern themselves and as the ability of their members to learn from each other develop.

A program of this sort would not of course proceed entirely without whizbang and razzle-dazzle. The issue is the purpose to which they are put. Cartoons, animated diagrams, quiz-show and talk-show formats, and mixed forms such as the television adaptation of the children's microcomputer game program "Where in the World Is Carmen Sandiego?" suggest productive points of departure. There should be lots of laughs, maybe a few tears, lots of gut-gripping film clips, and plenty of appealing personalities, both hunks and hanks.

But throughout the experience, however clever and visually and auditorially stimulating the program may be, it would have to keep its eye on the ball. The ball is increasing people's effectiveness and efficiency in collaboration. Some of the primary tasks and models of performance and behavior—the elementary scaffolding of learning that we will discuss in Chapter 10, such as Bruner's "formats" and Latour's "black boxes"—may originate with the professional programmers who design the program. But control of the social process and control of many of the subsequent tasks has to remain in the hands of the community's members working together. And producers and programmers would have to be aware that it is at this point—in helping to devise subsequent tasks, including mutual evaluation—that participants may enter the second phase of group work, in which they tend to become more deeply concerned with issues of intimacy than with issues of authority (discussed in Chapter 2).

The growth in knowledge and ability that each participant could experience while working with a group through a series of collaborative learning television or microcomputer programs has five sources: (1) each person's existing skill and knowledge, brought out and guided by focused conversation, that is, the influence of the group and the design of the program; (2) the willingness of group members to submit their presuppositions and biases—their individual registration of experience—to the examination and influence of peers; (3) the experience of guiding, teaching, and influencing peers; (4) the confidence gained as each member of the community, with the support of other members, experiences and survives the risk-taking transitions involved in learning, and (5) the stress each group member experiences under the pressure of having to evaluate the work of other members of the group.[6]

Besides their use on campus in collaborative college and university classrooms, television and microcomputers can also be used collaboratively in "distance learning" programs at the ends of television, radio, telephone, and microcomputer feedback networks. The admirable goal of these projects is to provide people who cannot attend a college or university an opportunity to get a college and university education.

Most programs of this type are designed to harness the pervasiveness and persuasiveness of educational technology. Handicapped by foundational educational assumptions, however, they tend to ignore the social dimension of that technology. They encourage individuals to take their degrees working on their own by watching taped "classes," while maintaining their isolation from one another. To this standard formula, however, an eighteen-university consortium called Mind Extension University adds an ingenious and (to my knowledge) unique device. It asks students to take their exams in their local library, proctored by their local librarian. This innovation holds the germ of making "distance learning" more than a set of technologically updated correspondence courses. For reasons explained in the section on William Perry in Chapter 10, it turns "distance learning" into something like the experience of residential college and university education.

Involving local libraries and librarians as part of a "distance learning" program can fulfill this potential, though, only if the program revises the ubiquitous foundational understanding of what learning is and what libraries are. The reason that local libraries play an important role in the Mind Extension University program is that, as an MEU spokesman has put it, "Every community has one, and libraries have a quiet, studious atmosphere."[7] But this traditional notion of local libraries as a repository of knowledge offering an intimidatingly quiet, studious atmosphere is a foundational notion that librarians themselves have recently begun to challenge.

Joan M. Bechtel has argued the position, for example, that the most appropriate "new paradigm for librarianship" is "conversation."[8] The traditional views of a library as a "warehouse for storing books" and as "the heart of the college and university" or "the center of our intellectual life," Bechtel says, are equally archaic. Storing books, she points out, is only one of many services libraries provide these days. The heart of the intellectual life of a college and university is more likely to be, among other places, in "a group of friends who meet regularly for study and discussion."

Instead, Bechtel says, what libraries do is "collect people and ideas" and "facilitate conversation among people":

> the primary task . . . of the academic library is to introduce students to the world of scholarly dialogue that spans both space and time and to provide students with the knowledge and skills they need to tap into conversations on an infinite variety of topics and to participate in the . . . debate on those issues. . . . The preservation of crucial conversations, the first task of libraries, [serves] not only to preserve the record, but more importantly to ensure the continuation of significant conversations already in progress.[9]

In this description, even an academic research library sounds like a discreet version of what my local library becomes when school lets out, a place where the neighborhood kids talk about their work with each other, trade ideas, read interesting stuff to each other: a place to learn collaboratively. Bechtel's library, a library understood nonfoundationally, is a crowd of thousands of ageless voices tucked together in the stacks waiting to be heard and (literally) talked about and talked back to.

In some colleges and universities, librarians have already begun to put into effect, architecturally, this understanding of what libraries are. The newly renovated library at Lafayette College, for example, has small "conversation rooms" scattered throughout the building where students can get together for talk and study. It is a clear case of institutionalizing collaborative learning with bricks and mortar, and it is the direction that library design is taking in order to actively "facilitate conversation among people." Since libraries now maintain collections of microcomputers, along with videotapes and CDs, it seems a logical extension of Bechtel's principle to provide facilities in libraries for using them collaboratively along the lines developed in this chapter. (See the Appendix for more on architecture and interior design appropriate to collaborative learning.)

This nonfoundational notion of libraries and librarianship, together with television and microcomputer programs designed to foster both local and network collaboration at a distance, transforms "distance learning" into something as close to a "real" college and university education as it is likely to get. Students would not just sit in their local libraries taking exams in the studious quiet. They would meet in their local libraries to learn collaboratively in semiautonomous groups of interested neighbors, family members, and friends. Local libraries would become the heart of "distance" college or university education and the center of its intellectual life. At the far ends of the transmission network, local libraries would be the neighborhood locus of what, as we shall see in the next chapter, Michael Oakeshott calls the "conversation of mankind."

Part 2

Higher Education, Interdependence,
and the Authority of Knowledge

CHAPTER SEVEN

Education as Conversation

Collaborative learning makes the Kuhnian assumption that knowledge is a consensus: it is something people construct interdependently by talking together. Knowledge is in that sense, Kuhn says, "intrinsically the common property of a group or else nothing at all."[1] In an essay on the place of literature in education entitled "The Voice of Poetry in the Conversation of Mankind," Michael Oakeshott places this notion of knowledge as a community-owned social construct in an even broader context: our ability to participate in unending conversation is what distinguishes human beings from other animals. "As civilized human beings," Oakeshott says,

> We are the inheritors, neither of an inquiry about ourselves and the world, nor of an accumulating body of information, but of a conversation, begun in the primeval forests and extended and made more articulate in the course of centuries. It is a conversation which goes on both in public and within each of ourselves. . . . And it is this conversation which, in the end, gives place and character to every human activity and utterance.

On this premise, Oakeshott defines education as

> an initiation into the skill and partnership of this conversation in which we learn to recognize the voices, to distinguish the proper occasions of utterance, and in which we acquire the intellectual and moral habits appropriate to conversation.[2]

Oakeshott says here that education initiates us into conversation first, and by virtue of that conversation initiates us into thought. He reverses the common foundational understanding of the relationship between thought and conversation that has been eloquently stated in a recent defense of conversation as the mode of education at St. John's College: "Conversation is the public complement to that original dialogue of the soul with itself that is called thinking." The position taken in this statement is that we can talk with one another because we can think. Oakeshott's position and the position taken in this book is the contrary, that we can think because we can talk with one another.[3]

L. S. Vygotsky confirmed this view by showing that reflective thought is social conversation internalized. We first experience and learn what Oakeshott calls "the skill and partnership of conversation"—what I call here the craft of interdependence—in the arena of direct social exchange with other people. Only then, Vygotsky demonstrates, do we learn to displace that skill and partnership by dramatizing and playing out silently within ourselves the role of every participant in the conversation.

If we think because we can talk with one another, then it follows that we have learned the ways we think in the same way. As Stanley Fish has put it, all the thoughts we "can think and the mental operations [we] can perform have their source in some or other interpretive community."[4] The range, complexity and subtlety of our thought, its power, the practical and conceptual uses we can put it to, and the very issues we can address result from the degree to which we have been initiated into the craft of interdependence within the knowledge communities we belong to. Clifford Geertz would agree. "Human thought," he says, "is consummately social: social in its origins, social in its functions, social in its form, social in its applications."[5]

There are of course both benefits and liabilities to understanding thought as internalized conversation. One of the practical benefits is that logistics are no problem at all. We don't have to take the A train or United Airlines flight #221 to get together with ourselves for a chat. And in thought there are no differences among the participants in preparation, interest, native ability, or spoken vernacular. Every one of the internalized speakers we can dream up is just as loquaciously clever as we are.

Or just as laconically dull. This particular liability of thought understood as internalized conversation is illuminating from an educational point of view. If ethnocentrism, inexperience, personal anxiety, economic interest, and paradigmatic inflexibility (tunnel vision) constrain our conversation, they will constrain our thinking. If the talk within the knowledge communities we are members of is narrow, superficial, biased, or limited to cliches, our thinking is almost certain to be so, too. Many of the social forms and conventions of conversation, most of the grammatical, syntactical, and rhetorical structures of conversation, and the range, flexibility, impetus, and goals of conversation are the sources of the forms, conventions, structures, impetus, range, flexibility, issues, and goals of thought. Good talk begets good thought.

This functional relationship between conversation and thought informs Kuhn's notion that community life generates the conversation that constructs and maintains the community's knowledge and thought. And it also informs his notion that to understand a community's knowledge and thought, we have to understand the life of the community. Part 1 of this book has examined some pedagogical implications of this position. It says that if college and university students are to become members of sophisticated, complex, highly literate communities, they can best reach that goal by experiencing something like that community membership in class—through collaborative learning.

Part 2 places that educational goal, the practice it implies, and the nonfoundational understanding of knowledge that informs it into several broader educational and professional contexts. It talks about ways in which the academic profession is both similar to and different from other professions. It talks about how nonfoundational thought changes the way we think about scientific research and science pedagogy. And it suggests how collaborative learning and its understanding of knowledge as socially constructed can be integrated into diverse college and university curricular practices.

This first chapter of Part 2 introduces that broader discussion by placing college and university education, understood nonfoundationally, in the context of learning throughout life, understood nonfoundationally. By exploring some of the ways in which Kuhn's argument has been confirmed and elaborated, the chapter shows that from infancy to adulthood, education is an interdependent, socially constructive, conversational process.

Each of us initially accounts for the physical reality that shoves us around and the social circumstances we find ourselves in with beliefs cast as stories, fragmentary narratives that at first are ours alone ("Bobby pushed me, so I fell off the slide"). These beliefs become what we call knowledge when we "justify" them ("Ask the teacher. She saw him do it").

All of the many differences between the foundational and the nonfoundational understanding of knowledge boil down to differences in what the two mean by "justification." Foundationalists say we justify our beliefs by testing them against reality ("She saw him do it"). Nonfoundationalists say we justify our beliefs by testing them socially, against other people's beliefs ("Ask the teacher"). Richard Rorty succinctly states the nonfoundationalist position when he says that "we understand knowledge when we understand the social justification of belief."[6] From the very beginning of our lives we construct knowledge in conversation with other people. When we learn something new, we leave a community that justifies certain beliefs in certain ways with certain linguistic and paralinguistic systems, to join instead another community that justifies other beliefs in other ways with other systems. We leave one community of knowledgeable peers and join another.

The community we join may of course be only slightly different from the one we left. This is the case, for example, when we learn a new way to use semicolons or steal second base. Or it may involve reacculturation to entirely new values, habits, symbol systems, and expertise. This is the case when we first cross the street alone, pass the bar exam, or learn Chinese. Kurt Lewin offers the example of a group of watchmakers learning to become carpenters. To do that, Lewin says, they have to do more than just to use a hammer and saw. They have to learn to swear like carpenters, drink like carpenters, walk, eat, and tell jokes like carpenters. Learning involves shifting social allegiances because knowledge results from acknowledgment, the mutual agreement among knowledgeable peers that a belief expressed by a member of that community has been socially justified or is socially justifiable.[7]

At another level of analysis, any community we join may be only slightly different from the one we have left because, as sociologists have demonstrated, all communities are held together by the same sorts of "integration mechanisms." This similarity is especially evident among academic and professional knowledge communities in the western world. Intellectual indebtedness, shared expertise, technical knowledge, and traditions (Kuhn's "paradigms"), patterns of argument, patterns of approval and reward (citation referencing, publication, grant approval), levels of collaboration, trust, conflict, competition, and often even resources (university jobs, funding agencies) turn out to be largely the same in general outline, if not detail, from community to community.

In early infancy, and perhaps even before birth, we begin a lifelong process of reacculturation. Jerome Bruner has shown (as we shall see in Chapter 10) that even six-month-old infants engage in paralinguistic conversation with their mothers and other caretaking adults, and through these conversations infants construct and reconstruct knowledge from their earliest beliefs. Because their wellbeing depends on understanding their mother's language, both verbal and gestural, infants begin engaging in interpretive conversation with their mothers (and other caretaking adults) as soon as they can register and distinguish changes in physical attitude and gesture, tone of voice, and facial expression. And because a mother's wellbeing also depends in part on understanding and adapting to her infant's needs, infant and mother are to that extent knowledgeable peers. Together they compose a unique, minuscule, but culturally crucial knowledge community whose members are learning collaboratively.

Vygotsky describes a scene illustrating this process of community composition and collaboration that involves, as Bruner's experiment does, a six-month-old infant. The infant sees an attractive object—let's say, a shiny spoon—and extends his hand to grasp it. The spoon is out of reach. For a moment, Vygotsky says, the infant's "hands, stretched toward that object, remain poised in the air. His fingers make grasping movements."[8] The infant in this scene appears to be trying, at the most elemental level, to establish contact with a bit of physical reality. Shoved around by physical reality, he shoves back. He wants a response from the object or a relationship with it that corresponds to his reaching out for it. But the object does not cooperate in the effort to be known. Objects never do. For a moment, then, the infant reaches and nothing happens.

Then something does happen. The object still doesn't cooperate, but Mommy does. The infant's mother moves the object closer, so that the infant can feel it, look at it, put it into his mouth.

In this brief, mundane scene lies a key to understanding the non-foundational social constructionist understanding of knowledge and, not incidentally, collaborative learning. When infants reach for an object, they do not merely reach. They send a message. When Mommy or Daddy or some other caretaking person finally gets the message and responds, infants learn indelibly the importance of this seemingly irrelevant side effect. Our first effort to grasp an object, Vygotsky tells us, is the first step we take in learning to point. Pointing, Vygotsky argues, is

> an unsuccessful attempt to grasp something, a movement aimed at a certain object which designates forthcoming activity . . . When the mother comes to the child's aid and realizes his movement indicates something, the situation changes fundamentally. Pointing becomes a gesture for others. The child's unsuccessful attempt engenders a reaction not from the object he seeks but *from another person.*[9]

What Vygotsky's reading of this scene tells us is that knowing is not an unmediated, direct relationship between the subject and object. It is a disjunctive, mediated process involving the agency of other people. In learning to point we learn that acquiring knowledge has this underlying structure of social mediation. There is always another person—or several other people—directly or indirectly involved. The infant in Vygotsky's illustration eventually learns to know and master the shiny spoon by learning to know and master an adult's response to itself that it provoked by showing that it wanted to know the spoon. Infants begin to "understand [their grasping] movement as pointing," Vygotsky says, when they understand that their "object-oriented movement" has really become "a movement aimed at another person, a means of establishing relations."[10]

The experience is one of collaborative learning because when they finally get the message and respond, the mommies and daddies or other caretaking people involved have understood something about infants, especially this infant. They have learned a gestural word or phrase with which the infant is now able to converse. They have (perhaps) learned to watch out for some (possible) designated forthcoming activity on the infant's part heading their way. And—from the infant's point of view supremely important—they have learned to obey orders.

These moments in the lives of six-month-old infants contend seriously for the attention of college and university teachers, because the process implied can be traced from infancy through childhood to the learning of adults. Infant and mother learn what they need to know about each other by internalizing the language that constitutes their community, encapsulating the results of their ongoing conversations in conventions and routines—what Bruner calls "formats" and what Latour calls "black boxes." As infants grow and learn, becoming children and then adults, they incrementally replace membership in that first, small, closed knowledge community of mother and infant with membership in set after complex set of larger, more intricately constituted knowledge communities, each time laying down new sets of conventions and routines within which earlier ones are nested.

Once we acquire language, this lifelong learning process of reacculturation from knowledge community to knowledge community accelerates and becomes increasingly complex. In learning to name objects, young children are not engaging in a newly learned process but extending a process—pointing—that they mastered in early infancy. In childhood, just as in infancy, the nature of knowledge is such that "the path from object to [us] and from [us] to object passes through another person."[11]

Another scene that Vygotsky describes demonstrates how very complex and winding this path can become. The scene involves the actions of a four- or five-year-old child trying to take possession of a piece of candy by figuring out how to use some basic tools to advantage, in this case a stick and a stool. As the child works, she talks through her solution to the problem. But she does not talk in a state of fantasy involvement to the objects that concern her. She talks about them, and about herself, to *someone*. Sometimes she talks to another person at hand, in this case the researcher. Most of the time she talks to herself as if she were another person.

What is happening in this scene, according to Vygotsky, is that the child is using social speech instrumentally: that is, she is using speech to help get something done. Moreover, by the time she is four or five much of this child's "socialized speech (which has previously been used to address an adult) *is turned inward*. Instead of appealing to the adult, [she appeals] to [herself]."[12]

In Vygotsky's view, the process of development that has led the child to talk through her problem solving in this way is "the most significant moment in the course of intellectual development." That moment occurs when "speech and practical activity, two previously completely independent lines of development, converge." As soon as children incorporate speech and the use of signs into any action, Vygotsky says, "the action becomes transformed and organized along entirely new lines." Before mastering their own behavior, children begin to master their surroundings with the help of speech. From this moment on,

> speech and action are part of *one and the same complex psychological function,* directed toward the solution of the problem at hand. . . . The more complex the action demanded by the situation and the less direct its solution, the greater the importance played by speech in the operation as a whole.[13]

As a result of this engagement of speech in learning and thought, "every function in [our] cultural development appears twice: first, on the social level, and later, on the individual level; first, *between* people . . . , and then *inside*."[14] Instrumental speech therefore both helps us do everything we attempt to do and socializes everything we do. Conversation—direct, indirect, or internalized—makes even solitary tasks into collaborative ones. Once we begin to use speech instrumentally, we work together, whether we work together or apart.

Bruno Latour shows just how conversation and mastery of surroundings are related with an illustration that is similar to one of Thomas Kuhn's but goes well beyond it in its implications. Both stories are about parents teaching a child the difference between kinds of animals. In Kuhn's example, a father helps his son distinguish between ducks and geese. In Latour's example, a mother helps her daughter distinguish between birds and any other thing "that darts away very rapidly and disappears from view."[15]

The difference between Kuhn's scene and Latour's lies in the way in which language is involved in the process. Kuhn emphasizes ostension (pointing): the father says to his child, who has identified some birds incorrectly, "No, Johnny, that's a goose." But Latour knows what Vygotsky knows, that to point is already rudimentarily to acquire by naming in gesture. So he can show that the kind of conversation these parents and children are engaged in, reconciliation of contradictory assumptions, is a reacculturative linguistic process. That is, Latour construes the event as conversation in nonstandard, boundary discourse through which the child learns the community constituting language (the normal discourse) of English-speaking adults. The revealing details of Latour's story make it worth quoting at length:

> A mother is walking in the countryside with her daughter. The little girl calls "flifli" anything that darts away very rapidly and disappears from view. A pigeon is thus a "flifli" but so is a hare fleeing in panic, or even her ball when someone kicks it hard without her seeing it. Looking down in a pond the little girl notices a gudgeon that is swimming away and she says "flifli." "No" the mother says "that is not a 'flifli,' that is a fish; *there* is a 'flifli' over there," and she points to a sparrow taking off. Mother and daughter are at the intersection of two chains of associations; one that ties a ball, a hare, a pigeon, a gudgeon to the word "flifli"; the other one that . . . could indeed apply to several instances above—but not to the ball—and [the word] "bird" that would apply only to the pigeon and the sparrow. The mother, not being a relativist, does not hesitate to name "incorrect" her daughter's usage of the word "flifli." . . . "Flifli" recalls a set of instances that are not usually associated in the mother's language. The girl has to reshuffle the instances gathered so far under the word "flifli," under the new headings "bird," "fish," and "ball."

In this story, knowledge about what-is-associated-with-what cannot be separated from the conversation going on between the two people involved. There is not on the one hand "knowledge" and on the other "society." Instead, there are what Latour calls "trials of strength" in which knowledge, conversation, emotional involvement, and social relationships are inseparable. By exercising her native talent for linguistic improvisation, a young child translates and retranslates until she gets it "correct."

"Correct" of course means what is acceptable in the community that the child aspires to enter, her mother's community of standard-English speakers. As Latour points out, the child's mother is of course not a relativist locally, within the community of standard-English speakers. No one is a relativist locally. Locally we are all foundationalists. By definition, membership in a knowledge community means that everything we do is unhesitatingly correct or incorrect according to the criteria agreed to within that local community, the community we belong to and into which we acculturate our children. And acculturating her child is exactly what the mother in Latour's story is doing:

The child . . . does not know in advance how strongly her mother clings to the definition of "bird" and of "to flee." She tries to create a category that mixes everything that darts away, and she fails every time, confronted by her mother who breaks down this category. The little girl is learning what a part of her mother's world is made of: sparrows, balls, and gudgeons cannot all be "flifli"; this cannot be negotiated. The choice for the daughter is then to give up her category or to live in a world made of at least one element different from that of her mother. Holding to "flifli" does not lead to the same life as holding to "birds" and "to flee." The girl thus learns part of the language structure by trying out whatever her mother holds to. More exactly, what we call "structure" is the shape that is slowly traced by the girl's trials; this point is negotiable, this is not, this is tied to this other one, and so on. One sure element of this structure is that "flifli" has not got a chance of surviving if the girl is to live with English-speaking people.

As we mature, much of the kind of conversation engaging mother and daughter in Latour's story tends to go underground. We internalize it as thought. Along with it, as Vygotsky points out, goes much of the collaborative engagement and social relationship that conversation involves. As a result, even as adults working silently and alone, like the student, Mary, whose record of internal conversation we examined in Chapter 1, we are engaged in a process that is intrinsically collaborative, working together whether we work together or apart. When the children in Vygotsky's and Latour's illustrations are a year or two older, they will "say" much the same sort of things as they talk through their work, making the task collaborative in much the same way. What will be different is that they are not nearly so likely, except under stress, to say it aloud.

The fact that we tend to reexternalize thought under stress as direct or indirect conversation (talk and writing) demonstrates the continuing relationship of thought and conversation in adult learning, even when that relationship ceases to be readily apparent. It is stress that occasions our talking to ourselves ("C'mon, Anthea, you're going to be late," says my wife to herself as she heads out of the house for work). It is stress that occasions the rap sessions and endless dorm-room talk typical of late adolescence and early adulthood. As we shall see later (in Chapter 10), the undergraduates whom William Perry interviewed for *Forms of Intellectual and Ethical Development in the College Years* describe how their discussion of ideas, political presuppositions, and religious beliefs in dormitory bull sessions changed (or, in a few cases, hardened) opinions that they had brought with them to college. The testimony of Perry's informants shows that undergraduates feel a strong need to be accepted into the community that surrounds them when they arrive at college or university because they are aware that membership, by empowering them, tends to allay stress. "As soon as I become integrated into a new community and learn my way around and become able to control it," one student says, "I'm more willing to accept tentative answers, the double answers. . . . I'm less willing to accept them when I'm completely unintegrated [into the community], when I'm in a completely new atmosphere and have no connections."[16]

Thomas Kuhn's description of conceptual change in science also shows adults, working under stress at community boundaries, constructively reexternalizing conversation. Even in this case, which represents the most sophisticated, complex, and demanding kinds of thinking human beings ever undertake, "the path from object to [us] and from [us] to object" still "passes through another person." When the members of two factions of a scientific community experiencing a theory crisis try, working collaboratively, to reconcile incompatible assumptions on which their work is to proceed, Kuhn says, they cannot reconcile them through experimentation. The rules of experimentation are defined by those very assumptions. Nor can they resolve their differences at this level "simply by stipulating the definitions of troublesome terms" or by "[resorting] to a neutral language which both use in the same way." Any definition of terms that either scientist can accept as standard will be considered nonstandard by the other. That is, the two scientists can reconcile their incompatible assumptions only by boundary conversation, in terms that are nonstandard to both of them.

In that conversation, Kuhn explains, scientists must rely on techniques that are neither "straightforward, [nor] comfortable, [nor] part of the scientists' normal arsenal." They have to talk through their problem much as the child in Latour's illustration talks through with her mother her attempt to classify fast-moving objects. But in this case there is no "correct" answer because there is no established referent community the language and standards of which both scientists can accept. As a result, they have to start from scratch to build a new linguistic history common to both of them. They have to "recognize each other as members of different language communities" and then undertake translation as a substitute for fluency and as "a potent tool for persuasion and for conversation." They have recourse not only to language, but to language about language, talk about talk, engaging in a collaborative process in which they make language instrumental to the task of repairing language.[17]

There is of course a considerable difference in complexity between Bruner's and Vygotsky's six-month infants, Vygotsky's child getting the candy, Latour's and Kuhn's children naming birds, Perry's undergraduates rapping in the dorm, and Kuhn's scientists in a theory crisis. But it is a difference of degree, not of kind. The basic similarity among these examples is that none of them is a simple case of problem solving. In each case, the people involved are working within what Vygotsky calls their "zone of proximal development," trying to understand the world at the very frontier of their ability to understand it. To do that, they construct an ad hoc, transitional language that draws on whatever linguistic history they bring to the conversation and that eventually yields an agreed-upon language that constitutes a new community of knowledgeable peers. Then, sooner or later, they all internalize that conversation so that they can continue it alone. In each case, human beings travel the indirect path from the world to themselves and from themselves to the world through conversation with another person.

In all of these illustrations, two kinds of conversation are involved: normal discourse and nonstandard, boundary discourse. Both kinds of discourse occur in communities of knowledgeable peers, but the communities they occur in are constituted quite differently. Normal discourse occurs within established knowledge communities whose standards are unquestioned. Its goal is to maintain and confirm established knowledge. Nonstandard discourse occurs at the boundaries of established knowledge communities in ad hoc transition groups where the standards of no established community prevail. The goal of these transition groups is to effect reacculturation from one kind of normal discourse to another.

As I have argued elsewhere in this book (in Chapters 4 and 8) and as William Perry's informants show (Chapter 10), both normal and nonstandard discourse—conversations among members of both established communities and transition communities—are involved in college and university education. Of the two, nonstandard, boundary discourse is the more powerful and problematic. When Richard Rorty says that nonstandard discourse "is what happens when someone joins in the discourse who is ignorant" of the community's conventions "or who sets them aside," he describes precisely what happens in college and university teaching.[18] Students are outsiders. They enter their classes ignorant of the community-constituting language that the teacher speaks. In this "contact zone," to adopt Mary Louise Pratt's apt term for it, in which aspirations and expertise are "asymmetrical," they do not yet know what the members of that community "count as 'rational.' "[19] For example (as we shall see in Chapter 8), what Nobel physicist Richard Feynman wrote in a field he was not trained in, biology, turned out, he wryly reports to be laughable even to a friendly biologist. Similarly, to college and university teachers what students say and write can often seem to be "anything from nonsense to intellectual revolution."[20]

But what college and university teachers are not always aware of is that the converse is also true. To students, much of what teachers say is nonstandard discourse. Much of what college and university teachers say sounds to students, as Rorty puts it, either kookie or revolutionary. Either it sounds to them as if teachers don't really mean what they are saying or else, as one of Perry's informants puts it, it feels like "everything [is] *completely* changed."[21] Both teachers and students may be disposed to believe that this response is a measure of the students' dullness or the teacher's scintillating brilliance. It may sometimes, of course, be either or both. But it is more often attributable to vast differences in the languages that constitute the communities of which they are members.

The importance of collaborative learning is that it acknowledges these differences and creates conditions in which students can negotiate the boundaries between the knowledge communities they belong to and the one that the teacher belongs to. In the transition groups of collaborative learning, college and university teachers self-consciously generate non-standard discourse so that students can learn to engage in the normal discourse of the knowledge community they aspire to join. They generate this nonstandard discourse among students by assigning tasks that challenge the conventions of the communities that the students already belong to, contrasting those conventions implicitly with the conventions of the disciplinary communities to which the teachers belong.

College and university teachers pose the "trials of strength" negotiated by participants in boundary conversation in order to find "a certain amount of language that allows you to come to a conclusion, to reach agreement on something."[22] The child in Latour's illustration tests the strength of association of words in the language being learned in order to discover the strength of its various structural elements: which are acceptable and which are not. The same sort of testing is going on among Perry's undergraduates, between Kuhn's scientists, and in my student's ad hoc formulation, "the transition between the whoosie-whatsis and the other thing" (Chapter 4). Some elements of any such formulation will survive. Other elements will have to be replaced if the students involved are to become members of the community that the teacher represents.

This tendency of nonstandard discourse toward equilibrium, challenging and changing established normal discourse, results from its determination to become the new normal discourse itself. Nonstandard discourse aspires to establish its own values, goals, and standards as normal so that they too will "count as 'rational.' " Nonstandard discourse hopes eventually to become conversation in which everyone will agree on the "set of conventions about what counts as a relevant contribution, what counts as answering a question, what counts as having a good argument for that answer or a good criticism of it."[23] One of William Perry's students explains the source of this tendency toward equilibrium in this way:

> If you know that other people hold some of the same things valuable [that you hold valuable], it makes it much less of a strain, you don't have to question it intensely, whether this is all something you dreamed up to meet a special situation, [you] accept it as something you believe in, and other people believe in.[24]

In generating nonstandard discourse among students through collaborative learning, the most important skill that college and university teachers bring to bear, and can impart to their students, is skill in linguistic improvisation: translation. This skill is a professional requisite of college and university teachers because teachers and students belong to such different knowledge communities when they first encounter each other in a college or university classroom. In the next chapter we shall see that skill in translation across community boundaries sharply distinguishes college and university teaching from other professions.

CHAPTER EIGHT

Anatomy of a Profession: The Authority of College and University Teachers

What is the source of the authority that college and university teachers exercise? What gives them the right to teach? Called "professors," they normally believe (and the general public for the most part believes with them) that their authority as teachers derives from what they "profess." What they profess is the disciplinary knowledge and expertise that they gained in their postgraduate training (graduate school, medical school, law school) and that they maintain by "keeping up" through reading professional publications and attending professional conferences. Difference in disciplinary knowledge and expertise distinguishes one professor from another: a chemistry professor from a law professor, a professor of economics from a professor of music.

But this claim to a distinct disciplinary knowledge and expertise does not distinguish professors, or academic professionals, from other kinds of professionals, those whom we might call public professionals or professional practitioners. It does not distinguish law professors from lawyers, for example, or chemistry professors from chemists. Many public professionals command much the same knowledge and expertise that academic professionals command. The most apparent difference between them is the venue or domain in which they cultivate that knowledge and employ their expertise. Public professionals engage in research dedicated to advancing some civic or commercial end, applying their knowledge to the affairs to everyday life. Professors tend to engage in "pure" research and to disseminate knowledge. This difference is sometimes expressed in negative terms: whatever it is that professors do, it's merely academic.[1]

Recently, however, sociologists interested in the professions have begun to define professionals less in terms of what they know and can do, and more, as Magali Sarfatti Larson puts it, in terms of their "authoritative and authorizing" discourse. Professionals are people who use language that is "learned" or "knowledgeable."[2] At first glance this new way of defining professionals does not seem to distinguish academic professionals from public ones any better than the old way. Lawyers and law professors together are keepers of the language and lore of the law; chemists and chemistry teachers are keepers of the language and lore of chemistry.

But defining professionalism in terms of authoritative discourse turns out to be a useful tool. It allows us to acknowledge that even when academic and public professionals talk about the same things, they talk about them in different ways. They engage in different kinds of discourse. It allows us to say that college and university teachers commit themselves in particular to knowledge of and expertise in the distinctive, highly sophisticated kind of discourse I have described in earlier chapters: translation, or linguistic improvisation across community boundaries.

This chapter explores what this linguistic mastery implies about the authority of college and university teachers and about college and university teaching as a distinct kind of professional life. It argues that the nature of the professional life of college and university teachers depends on how they understand their authority as teachers. That understanding depends, in turn, on how they understand their preparation for teaching: what they think they know, how they think they know it, and what they think knowledge is.

The chapter necessarily involves, therefore, discussing the authority of colleges and universities and what justifies their existence. The stature and vitality of colleges and universities and the rationale for establishing them in the first place are products of the authority of those who teach there. Thus the authority, nature, and goals of colleges and universities also depend on what college and university teachers think they know, how they think they know it, and what they think knowledge is.

In every age, a teacher's right to teach derives directly or indirectly from the prevailing understanding of the authority of knowledge. We do not understand the authority of knowledge today as we have in the past. Therefore we do not understand the authority of teachers and the nature and goals of colleges and universities as we have in the past. Our understanding of knowledge has undergone a major change during the past half century. But we have yet to understand fully the effect of that change on the authority of college and university teachers.

This chapter traces briefly the history of the traditional understanding of the authority of teachers. It sketches the situation of college and university teachers today, at a time when the traditional understanding of knowledge is subject to serious question. And it explores the professionally distinctive, exacting, and problematical task that college and university teachers undertake: to negotiate boundaries among diverse knowledge communities. It assumes that many academics do this task well. But it also assumes that many may be less aware than they need to be of the complexities of the task, its internal contradictions, and its importance to the profession.

The history of our understanding of the authority of knowledge, and hence of the authority of teachers, can be divided roughly into two epochs: foundational and nonfoundational. The first is ancient. The second has barely begun. The epoch of foundational ways of understanding of nature and the authority of knowledge began in the mists of prehistory, well before the invention of colleges and universities, and is itself divisible into two long periods, pre-Cartesian and post-Cartesian.

In the pre-Cartesian world, people tended to believe that the authority of knowledge lodged in one place, the mind of God. Most teachers were priests—or priestly. They derived their authority from what they and their students regarded as their godliness, their nearness to the mind of God. The temple, the church, the synagogue, the mosque authorized college and university education, whenever and wherever it existed and such as it was. The most prominent exception seems to be the teachers of Athenian Greece, for whom knowledge was one of the civic virtues. But even then, the ancient Greeks' almost universal belief in the divine origin of civic laws and the status as absolutes of concepts such as "idea" and "soul structure" betrays the politico-priestly function of teachers for Plato and perhaps for Socrates as well.

Post-Cartesian assumptions emerge in roughly the seventeenth century. They remain explicitly potent today in the "cognitive sciences" and implicitly in the persuasion of most members of every other disciplinary community, professional and academic. In this post-Cartesian, or cognitive, foundational world, the authority of knowledge has one or more of three alternative habitations, each of them a secular version of the mind of God. Today we can believe that the authority of knowledge lodges in some touchstone of value and truth above and beyond ourselves, such as mathematics, creative genius, or the universals of sound reasoning. We can believe that it lodges in a person of genius: a Shakespeare, an Einstein, or a Freud. Or we can believe that it lodges in one or both of the two grounding entities of foundational thought: subjects and objects, mind and reality, creative inner selves and the universe of things.[3]

The authority of college and university teachers to teach in this post-Cartesian foundational world has its source in their nearness to the center of one of these three secular versions of the mind of God. In the first case, the touchstone theory, teachers derive their authority from identification with one or another of the acknowledged referents of value and truth from which we may believe the authority of knowledge derives. That is why we tend to regard mathematicians and scientists, for example, as having greater authority than, say, sociologists or literary critics. We believe that the "stuff" that mathematicians and scientists deal in is somehow more fundamental, more legitimate, sounder, and more "real" than what sociologists or literary critics deal in.

In the second case, the genius theory, teachers derive their authority from intimacy with the greatest minds. Most of us would readily acknowledge the superior authority of those who had the good fortune to study with, say, Freud, Faraday, or Faulkner. They would have touched the master, or—more to the point—the master would have touched them. They would therefore have greater authority than those who studied merely with disciples of Freud, Faraday, or Faulkner.

In the third case, the cognition theory, teachers derive their authority from being in direct touch with one or the other of the grounding entities of foundational thought: the essential object or the essential self. On the one hand, we tend to feel that teachers whose knowledge is confirmed by hands-on laboratory experimentation, say, have greater authority than those whose knowledge is based merely on a synthesis of research reports. Those who have studied the manuscripts of James Joyce's fiction have greater authority than those who have studied merely the edited texts and secondary sources. On the other hand, we tend to feel that poets, priests, psychoanalysts, and gurus—teachers whose knowledge is confirmed by access to some sort of direct pipeline to inner being—have greater authority than those who have merely studied inner selves at second hand through an acquaintance with liturgy, literature, or life.

Underlying the authority of college and university teachers from this foundational post-Cartesian point of view is the understanding that knowledge is a kind of substance contained in and given form by the vessel we call the mind. Teachers' mental vessels are full, or almost full. Students' mental vessels are less full. The purpose of teaching (as we noted in Chapter 4) is to transfer knowledge from the fuller vessels to the less full. The reason teachers need long summer vacations, it is commonly said, is to replenish their stock. The authority of teachers includes the responsibility to select from this stock which knowledge to impart and which not to impart.

The traditional, foundational criterion of selection among both students and teachers is what has been well established: intellectual precedent. This criterion is analogous to the traditional criterion of evaluation, memory: mental retention. Retention values human minds in which knowledge lasts a long time. Precedent values knowledge that lasts a long time in human minds. One kind of knowledge that traditional college and university education especially values because it is long-lasting is knowledge of the conventions of traditional education themselves. Teachers are responsible not only to impart knowledge that was imparted to them, but also to impart knowledge *as* it was imparted to them.

In contrast with this age-old foundational version of the authority of knowledge and thus of a college or university teacher's authority and right to teach, the nonfoundational version has only very recently achieved any kind of acceptance outside of esoteric philosophical conversations about extraordinary thinkers such as Nietzsche, Heidegger, Dewey, and the later Wittgenstein. The nonfoundational social constructionist understanding of knowledge denies that it lodges in any of the places I have mentioned: the mind of God, touchstones of truth and value, genius, or the grounds of thought, the human mind and reality. If it lodges anywhere, it is in the conversation that goes on among the members of a community of knowledgeable peers and in the "conversation of mankind" (discussed in Chapter 7).

That is, nonfoundational social construction understands knowledge, in Richard Rorty's terms, as socially justified belief. It assumes that each authoritative community, each community of interdependent knowledgeable peers, each academic and professional discipline, constructs knowledge in the distinctive, local language or paralinguistic symbolic system that constitutes the community. It assumes that what Karen Knorr-Cetina says of scientific knowledge is the case for all knowledge: that it is a "social occurrence" that emerges from "interaction and negotiation with others."[4]

Everybody in such a knowledge community "speaks the same language," the language that constitutes the community. Among academic and public professionals alike, a major element in this constituting language is what to outsiders seems like jargon, the disciplinary locutions and terms of art that add up to the normal discourse of the community. Speaking that language fluently defines membership in the community. Not speaking it fluently marks a nonmember. Mathematicians speak fluent mathematics. Nonmathematicians do not. Sociologists speak fluent sociologese. Nonsociologists do not. Classicists speak (or read) fluently not only one or more classical languages but also the prevailing idiom in which the literary criticism of classical literature or the history of ancient Greece and Rome is currently carried on. The rest of us do not.

Thomas Kuhn argued and Bruno Latour and others have confirmed (as I noted in Chapter 3 and will note again in Chapter 9) that this principle extends as well to scientific thought and scientific communities. Scientific knowledge does not change as our "conversation with nature" changes.[5] It changes as scientists revise the conversation among themselves and reorganize relations among themselves.[6] Generalizing Kuhn's view, Richard Rorty argues (as we saw in Chapter 7) that to understand any kind of knowledge we have to understand how people in communities of knowledgeable peers justify their beliefs among themselves socially: how knowledge is established and maintained in the normal discourse or community-constituting language of communities of knowledgeable peers. Stanley Fish calls these communities of normal discourse "interpretive communities."[7] They are the source of our thought and of the "meanings" we produce by using and manipulating symbolic structures, chiefly language.

In nonfoundational terms, therefore, the authority of college and university teachers derives from the fact that, by virtue of their exceptional fluency in the constituting language of the authoritative communities they belong to, they are the acknowledged representatives of those communities. We value mathematics teachers because they represent the community of mathematicians, sociology teachers because they represent the community of sociologists, classics teachers because they represent the community of classicists, and so on.

In every case, college and university teachers (say, for example, English professors) are the members of an authoritative community (in this case the community of careful readers and competent writers) whom the community charges with the responsibility of inducting new members. In accepting this responsibility, teachers set out to help students acquire fluency in the language of those communities, so that they become, if not necessarily new professionals, then people who are "mathematically minded," "sociologically minded," and so on. That is, students learn more than disciplinary jargon. They learn a particular kind of intense, flexible linguistic engagement with members of communities they already belong to and communities to which they do not yet belong.

The survival of the academic and professional disciplines depends on this process of reacculturation. Knowledge communities cannot get along without members who are committed to teaching, because without teachers communities die as soon as their current members die. Their knowledge ceases to exist. When there are no new mathematicians, physicians, lawyers, and classicists, pretty soon there is no mathematics, medicine, law, or classics.

The first difference between academic professionals and public professionals, then, is the obvious fact that public professionals practice their disciplinary craft and academic professionals teach it. In the past, the fact that knowledge communities have to initiate new members in order to perpetuate the community and its knowledge meant that practitioners of most professions took on apprentices. In most professions today, apprenticeship has long been obsolete. Those who make their living practicing their profession as a rule do not teach it, although some practitioners may contribute to the educational enterprise occasionally in some kind of adjunct or part-time capacity. Those who do teach the profession's craft do not as a rule practice it publicly except, again, in some kind of advisory or consultative capacity. They make their living teaching it as college and university faculty members.

The second difference between the academic and public professions is closely related to this division of responsibility. It is the difference in the source of their authority to practice as professionals, which results from the division. To initiate new members today, and to perpetuate the community and the knowledge that its members construct and maintain, knowledge communities have to find institutional homes for their members who teach. They must contrive to get those representatives employed, and keep them employed, by institutions of higher education. Because academic professionals have to be employed by academic institutions, their authority derives in part from the institutions that employ them.

This is not the case for most public professionals. True, like professors who teach at "top" schools, some doctors and lawyers acquire a high gloss by virtue of their affiliation with "top" hospitals or "top" law firms. But the professional authority of even these fortunate few, and certainly the authority of almost everyone else in the field, derives almost entirely from their membership in a single semiautonomous authoritative community, the professional community of physicians and lawyers. As a result, in most cases physicians and lawyers who find themselves unemployed have the option of opening up a private practice. Unemployed professors do not have that option. The authority of college and university teachers (including graduate or professional school teachers such as teaching physicians and law professors) has its source in their necessarily concurrent membership in two independent authoritative communities: an academic or professional discipline (chemistry, English, sociology, medicine, law) and the academic community of the college or university that employs them (USC, Asnuntuck Community College, Louisiana State, Johns Hopkins).

This divided loyalty does not result in a difference in *amount* of authority. It results in a difference in *kind* of authority, one that causes a good deal of unfortunate confusion. It affects what the educated general public, including college and university students, expect of professors, and also what professors expect of themselves. Most of us tend to place college and university teachers in the category of professionals we know best, that is, public professionals, especially the most common ones. For many of us, as Robert Welker has shown, the power, autonomy, public respect, and social status of teachers depend on the degree to which we think of them as being, for example, "like doctors."[7]

To understand the difference between the authority of academic and public professionals is to avoid this error and its consequences. Whenever we think that college and university teachers should do for us the sort of thing that public professionals do for us, we are bound to be disappointed. Likewise, whenever college and university teachers think they should be doing what public professionals do, and whenever they tell their institutions, their students, their students' parents, and the rest of the general public that that is what they should be doing or are doing, everyone—including college and university teachers themselves—is bound to feel short-changed.

The difference, in brief, is that whereas what academic professionals do for us is to reacculturate our children and ourselves, what public professionals do for us is to intercede between us and arcane but practical and obdurate realities: court cases and contracts, births and backaches. They fix things. They make things safer, healthier, more honest, less expensive or troublesome, more dependable or lucrative. When we confuse academic with public professionals, we tend to think that the purpose of college and university teaching is similarly to deal with arcane but practical and obdurate realities (medicine, law, classics, mathematics), and to fix things, make things safer, healthier, more honest, less expensive or troublesome, more dependable or lucrative. That is, we tend to think that the purpose of college and university teachers is to make us and our children smarter, better read, better informed, more competent, more polite, and more employable at high rates of pay. When college and university teachers confuse themselves with public professionals, they tend to expect these things from themselves and one another.

The authority of public professionals, furthermore, is almost exclusively a function of their practical relationship with the "center" of their disciplinary community, where the community's normal discourse is spoken in its purest form. Family doctors and company lawyers derive their authority from their "knowledge of medicine" or their "knowledge of law." That is, they derive it from their membership in the medical or legal community as certified by state boards of examiners and confirmed in everyday practice by the degree of their affiliation with the centers of their knowledge community. The "centers" of the legal community are major law schools and law firms, prosecutorial agencies, and the courts, especially the United States Supreme Court. The "centers" of the medical community are the major medical research laboratories, diagnostic clinics, and teaching hospitals.

Because the source of their authority is their practical relationship with a disciplinary center, the practice of public professionals is carried out mostly among professional community members, not between practitioners and clients. Of course, doctors and lawyers "see" clients occasionally, and to these clients they represent their professional community. But when my lawyer represents the legal community to me, she does not do so in order to turn me into another lawyer. She does so in order to win my case by dealing effectively with officers of the court. That is, my lawyer serves me by talking not primarily to me but to other lawyers. Similarly, I go to our family doctor (our personal representative of the medical profession), not so that he can help me become a doctor myself, but to have him cure my bug. He does that by calling explicitly or implicitly on experience and expertise he shares with his peers, with whom he is in more or less continual consultation.

Because the public professions are practiced mostly among professional community members, not between practitioners and clients, the language in which public professionals carry on their practice is in large measure the community-constituting language or normal discourse of their respective communities. Doctors and lawyers have recently begun to be persuaded to make their expertise more accessible to those who consult them, but such candor is not traditional. Until very recently, my doctor was likely to have confined his entire conversation with me to routine questions and a set of fairly curt instructions.

But because the source of their authority is quite different, the role that academic and public professionals play in society is in most respects quite different. Intradisciplinary practice is only a relatively small part of the activity of most academic professionals, because facilitating disciplinary practice is a minor part of the purpose of most institutions that employ them, even when those institutions are major research universities. The primary function of those institutions—even major research universities—is to teach. That is, their primary function is to reacculturate *their* "clients" into some degree of membership in the relevant knowledge communities. The primary professional relationship of the academic professionals who work in these institutions is not with other academic professionals but with students who aspire to join the knowledge communities that academic professionals represent.

Of course, relatively few of those who attend colleges and universities want their teachers to turn them into practicing academic professionals. But undergraduates do want their teachers to turn them into at least provisional members of the two authoritative communities that college and university teachers represent. They want to learn to talk, think, and behave to some degree as, for example, mathematicians or sociologists do: they want to become mathematically or sociologically or classically "minded." And they want to learn to talk, think, and behave to some degree as the people do who, ultimately, employ college and university teachers by establishing and maintaining the colleges and universities in which they teach: they want to become members of the "liberally educated" general public.

"Liberally educated" has become a somewhat dubious label for that linguistic flexibility the teaching of which quite appropriately preoccupies most college and university teachers. Yet most academics seem not yet fully aware of the underlying nature of this preoccupation or its source. Its nature is the identification and negotiation of community boundaries.[8] Its source can be traced in large measure to the occupational complexity I have been describing: college and university teachers represent disciplines that do not employ them, while housed in colleges or universities whose goals are not disciplinary but that do employ them, promote them, and give them tenure. This little-understood aspect of college and university teaching is crucial to understanding the reacculturative nature of college and university education.

In their activities within both of the authoritative communities they belong to—discipline and school—most college and university teachers engage in the normal discourse that is currently acceptable at the community's center. They talk fluent school-shop as readily as they talk fluent discipline-shop. The normal discourse of their disciplinary communities is determined by community members who are doing the scholarship and research that the community acknowledges to be the best new work in the field, by what everybody seems to be talking about this year at the conventions and conferences run by the discipline's professional organizations, and by the editorial judgment of community members who control the principal journals in the field. The normal discourse of a college or university community is determined by the institution's current successes, stresses, and needs. The principal players in the faculty and administration tend to talk mostly about maintaining their school's values and standards, improving the literacy of American youth, promoting the coherence and rigor of liberal education, and so on. Their agenda, in short, is to maintain the quality and integrity of their own college and university and to maintain college and university teaching in general as a satisfying way of life.

What makes the game worth the candle is that while college and university teachers are representing the centers of both of these two authoritative communities—discipline and school—they are also negotiating intensely and extensively at the boundaries of both communities. Much of the interest, complexity, and excitement of college and university teaching derives from the tension between these two kinds of normal discourse and these two kinds of boundary discourse, and it derives as well from the challenge of trying to reconcile or maintain equilibrium between them. It can be a rough, rugby-like sport, seldom played by public professionals. Either you love it or you don't.

Those who would reconcile or maintain the equilibrium between community boundary talk and center talk need to distinguish between the *boundaries* of authoritative communities and their *margins*. To be at the margin of a community is to be of limited or "marginal" importance to it. It is to be working on projects or to be cultivating interests that have minimal current significance for the majority of community members. In mathematics, "problem solvers"—those who spend their time puzzling out classic mathematical conundrums unrelated to larger mathematical themes or issues—are usually regarded as marginal. In literary studies, local antiquarians—those who cultivate the "-ana" or personal effects and mundane artifacts associated with an author (Joyce's laundry tickets, Melville's cane) tend to be marginal. Most historians consider most genealogists marginal. To be marginal means to be tenuously related to what is going on at the center and therefore to be wholly subordinate to that center while being almost totally neglected by those working there.[9]

In contrast, a community's boundaries are directly and vitally related to what is going on at the center. At the boundaries of a community, community members engage in the community's most heated controversies, do what most community members regard as its intellectually most exciting work, and confront those outside the community who most seriously challenge its constituting consensus, values, or mores.

At community boundaries, therefore, the coherence of a community is most in danger of becoming destabilized and threatened by nonstandard discourse. Nonstandard discourse occurs (as we saw in Chapter 7) when members of two communities who do not accept each other's standards try to talk to each other. At community boundaries, those outside the community—that is, members of other communities—seek to open doors into the community's discourse, find out what's going on inside, object to it, change it, or make it their own. This kind of challenge forces communities to expand, depriving established community members of their exclusive proprietary possession of the knowledge that the community has constructed. Nonstandard or boundary discourse therefore potentially threatens the standards of both of the communities involved in the negotiation, the challengers and the challenged.

As a result of this potential threat at the boundaries of a knowledge community, one of several things may happen. Boundary conversation may lead to a standoff; neither community gives way. Or the challenged community's ranks may expand to include the challengers as new members. Or the challengers may sweep the field, in which case the old community disappears as its members die off, as in Max Planck's example of what happened to Ptolemaic astronomy: the Ptolemaists did not convert to Copernicanism; they died, and the Copernicans took over.[10]

The terms that challengers and members are most likely to negotiate at the community's boundaries are terms that are well established in the language used at the community's center. But the relative importance to a community of its boundaries and its center is suggested by the fact that the center is not "located" by negotiations going on there but by negotiations going on at the boundaries. If the terms that a community negotiates with outsiders significantly and irreversibly change so that the community's boundaries move or change, the center is compelled to move. If the work being done at the center does not change when the boundaries change, it will quickly become merely a marginal by-whorl or eddy beside the mainstream of the profession. Weaken the community's boundaries or dismantle them altogether and the center disappears along with the rest of the community.

In contrast, when the center of a community moves (that is, when the language used there changes), the community's boundaries may or may not change. If the center moves but the boundaries do not—that is, if the normal discourse used at the center changes but the terms negotiated at the boundaries do not change—then the change at the center is illusory or superficial, and evanescent. This means that work at the boundaries of every discipline as currently established is never marginal, whereas work at the center is always in danger of being marginalized whenever the center shifts in response to change at the boundaries.

In the case of most knowledge communities, this process of boundary maintenance, negotiation, and change is normally hidden, or at best very hard to discern. The general public caught a glimpse of it going on several years ago, however, when the term *superconductivity* began to appear in newspapers everywhere and on the evening news.

Superconductivity is the ability of some materials at temperatures close to absolute zero to conduct electricity with little or no resistance at all. In the very recent past, physicists had about given up trying to find substances that would conduct electricity without resistance at higher temperatures. Before 1986, research on the ability of materials to conduct electricity at higher temperatures had become a marginally funded enterprise. Few articles were published on the subject. It was not the kind of promising work that bright young physicists went into if they wanted to work at the center of the field or if they wanted to obtain tenure in a college or university physics department.

All that changed suddenly in fall, 1986, when J. George Bednorz and K. Alex Mueller announced that they had gotten a bit of ceramic of a complicated copper oxide to conduct electricity with practically no resistance at the temperature of liquid nitrogen, easily achieved with existing technology. They were able to confirm their success with simple, dramatic, visual demonstrations, such as floating a magnet in midair. Other scientists easily replicated their results.

Suddenly, practical superconductivity seemed possible. It moved from the professional margin of physics to the center of professional life. Since no one had the slightest idea why a ceramic should conduct electricity at any temperature, much less in arctic "warmth," a good deal of theoretical physics—physics at the outermost boundaries of the field—was suddenly up for grabs. Research projects that made assumptions that excluded the possibility of high-temperature superconductivity, previously "central," were left beached on the margins of the profession.

Assaults on disciplinary boundaries do not always dismember a discipline in this way, of course. The general public has been privy recently to the failure of such an assault. Shortly after the superconductivity announcement, two chemists announced that they had achieved so-called cold fusion: nuclear fusion at room temperature and pressure, something that physicists had been doing only under conditions of high temperature and intense pressure, at great public expense. Once again physics was being attacked at its very core. Nothing in existing theories of nuclear behavior could explain these results.

Unfortunately, B. Stanley Pons and Martin Fleischmann could not provide a simple, dramatic demonstration of their discovery. Worse still, their results could be replicated only fitfully and by only a few of the physicists who tried. After several months of tense conferencing here and abroad, the physics community rejected the idea as riddled with errors. Physicists closed ranks, repulsing assault at the boundaries of their community. The center remained intact. High-temperature, high-pressure, high-cost fission experiments went confidently on. Experimentation on "fission in a bottle" retreated to the unfunded margins of the profession, where a few diehards continue to tinker away at it.

The play between boundary negotiation and center maintenance that academic professionals undertake as teachers every day for their bread and butter is hardly ever as dramatic and well publicized as these episodes in high science. But it can be just as complex and challenging. College and university students are not full-fledged members of either of the authoritative communities that their teachers belong to: discipline or school. Their teachers therefore act ad hoc, from class to class and from day to day, and as academic and often personal mentors, advisors, and counselors, to open those communities to outsiders. Teachers thereby expose both of them—the communities and the outsiders—to incoherence, chaos, and change. Because constructing, maintaining, and monitoring boundary conversation is their primary responsibility, their professional goal is to leave their college or university, their discipline, and their students not quite the way they found them. Whereas the goal of public professionals is to construct, repair, normalize, preserve, and answer questions, the goal of academic professionals is to deconstruct, analyze, unsettle, evaluate, ask questions, and initiate change.

Change is the goal of academic professionals even when they act in their most conservative and placid capacity as curators of the intellectual traditions. For example (as we shall see in Chapter 9), most science teaching today has become heavily curatorial. Just as a high goal of most museum curators is to make sure that the great objects of creative art are exposed to the eyes of the public, a high goal of most college and university science teachers is to make sure that their students can recognize and reproduce great scientific truths, often in the form of solutions to routine problem sets. Similarly, a high goal of most English teachers is to make sure that their students have read the great literature in that language. Such tasks as these are necessary to maintain cultural coherence. But as paradoxical as it may sound, college and university teachers succeed in maintaining cultural coherence only if they manage to change their students. In the long run, they may also change their disciplines, by changing how their disciplinary colleagues understand the issues and artifacts with which they are concerned.

In order to change students, understood nonfoundationally, the expertise of successful college and university teachers has to include an understanding of community life, because change in knowledge, understood nonfoundationally, is change in community life. College and university teachers should know, for example, something about traits that all academic and disciplinary communities share and do not share, not only among themselves but also with the communities that their students already belong to: their families, religious and ethnic groups, clubs, gangs, and cliques. They need this knowledge in order to engage and guide students' negotiations (described in Chapter 4) as they reacculturate themselves from the set of knowledge communities they belong to into the set of communities they hope to join.

Knowing what makes student and disciplinary communities tick and how to keep them ticking is necessary to successful college and university teaching, and that, of course, is just another way of describing the difference between academic professionals and public professionals. Knowledge of community structure, the way language constitutes communities of knowledgeable peers, is not expertise that, on the whole, doctors and lawyers, affiliated mainly with the centers of their disciplines, need to have. But interceding between members of different semiautonomous authoritative communities by translating the language of one community into another—for example, translating the language of professional communities into the languages that the rest of us understand—is the task that college and university teachers in every field undertake all the time. Their expertise includes awareness of the potential glitches, difficulties, threats, and misunderstandings that are inherent in any effort to translate. It includes awareness of terms and expressions that seem similar across community boundaries, but are not; terms that are not translatable, or only barely so; and terms that seem to be grossly different, but whose denotations are in effect all but identical.

College and university teachers most fully exercise their unique, complex authority when they help students learn how to navigate the white water of nonstandard boundary discourse. That is, they exercise it when they lead students to understand (with regard of course to the communities at hand, their particular college, their particular discipline) how language constitutes communities of knowledgeable peers. They exercise it when they lead students to understand how knowledge communities function as social units, how communities are organized, what holds them together, how they are related to each other, and how they are alike and different.

When I say that "liberal education" is an exercise that reacculturates students into the knowledge communities that their teachers represent, then, I do not mean that the role of college and university teachers is to initiate students into varieties of academic and professional jargon. I mean, precisely, that their role is to initiate students into the linguistic awareness, engagement, and flexibility illustrated in Chapter 4. My point in this book is, of course, that collaborative learning is the most effective way to do that.

All of us experience the risky, stressful process of translation ourselves whenever we learn anything at all: in a classroom, on the job, poring over a book, at work at a laboratory bench. Everyone who tries to learn a new "subject"—mathematics, sociology, history, whatever—and everyone who undertakes research that has any pretence at all to originality is confronted with new language—language that is, to that person, nonstandard discourse. For that reason, as most college and university teachers recognize, the first few hours in a college or university course in some unfamiliar field, and perhaps many hours after that, can be among the most disconcerting experiences anyone ever has.

As I noted in Chapter 7, the Nobel physicist Richard Feynman has left us an amusing record of that disconcerting experience in his story about taking a graduate course in cell physiology, a field far outside his own. He "wrote up" "informally" some of the research he did in connection with the course and sent it to a biologist friend. His friend "laughed when he read it" because "it wasn't in the standard form that biologists use," and Feynman had "spent a lot of time explaining things that all the biologists knew." Furthermore, and perhaps worse from Feynman's point of view, when his friend rewrote the paper, Feynman himself could no longer understand it.[11]

To guide students as they navigate nonstandard discourses as Feynman did requires recognizing it as nonstandard discourse and acknowledging both its difficulty and its value. Guidance then entails helping students to tolerate the risks and stresses that everyone experiences who tries to engage in it. Finally, to help students to domesticate nonstandard discourse, teachers must translate it into the normal language that constitutes an authoritative knowledge community. In the next chapter we will examine the contribution that this process can make, specifically, to college and university science education.

CHAPTER NINE

Science in the Postmodern World

Scientists construct knowledge interdependently through a conversational process that includes displaced or indirect conversation: writing. Latour and Woolgar demonstrate that (as I have explained in Chapter 3), "the construction of scientific facts" is "a process of generating *texts* whose fate (status, value, utility, facticity) depends on their subsequent interpretation" by other scientists. Karen Knorr-Cetina's research confirms this conclusion. Knowledge is what is said—or perhaps what can be said—in some language, by members of some community, to other members of that community. The editors and peer reviewers of a scientific journal represent such a community. When they interpret a research report as acceptable for publication, they turn what the article says into knowledge.[1]

This nonfoundational understanding of scientific knowledge as a social construct tends eventually to the conclusion that the sciences do not discover necessary, universal truths. The British historian and philosopher of science Nicholas Jardine resists that tendency. Jardine agrees that scientific inquiry is interpretive, constructive, and diverse. But he also argues that traditions of scientific inquiry are distinguished by long-established, local, everyday details of research practice which he describes as

> methodological continuities of long duration associated with the use of particular types of instrument and with particular routines of observation and description . . . for example, [the] remarkable continuities over several centuries in the traditions of practices and competences associated with microscopes, telescopes, and surveying instruments . . . and routine methods of naming, ordering and describing living beings.[2]

These practical continuities, however diversely and locally maintained, Jardine argues, add up to a tradition of pragmatic thought that does yield knowledge independent of local limitations. Jardine, in short, would accept Quine's notion (as Rorty paraphrases it) that "a necessary truth" is merely "a statement such that nobody has given us any interesting alternatives which would lead us to question it."[3] But he would accept it with the proviso that the goal of scientific inquiry is to try to reduce the odds to zero, with regard to some statements, that anyone will give us any such interesting alternatives. Central to the pragmatic tradition of the sciences, Jardine argues, is the belief that some statements calibrated against precedents and standards can be interpreted as approaching asymptotically the status of "global or absolute reality."[4]

This chapter assumes that scientists are the bearers of this interpretive tradition of pragmatic thought and that it is a tradition central to Western culture. The professional expertise of scientists is the interpretive ability, in collaboration with other scientists, to construct, manipulate, and calibrate models and symbol systems. The chapter also assumes, however, that most of the time in most college and university science courses, scientists do not present themselves as bearers of an intellectual tradition. They present themselves as something like museum curators, whose job is to accumulate, maintain, and display curious and useful facts about the natural world.

These two roles, scientists as curators of scientific knowledge and scientists as bearers of a culturally central pragmatic intellectual tradition, are not inherently contradictory. Clearly there is a relationship between the knowledge that science accumulates and the intellectual tradition that contributes to its accumulation. Nevertheless, it would seem that acquainting students with science as science is actually done, in order to help them become members of the pragmatic intellectual community that science teachers represent, should be among the first priorities of college and university science education. To acquaint students with the wonders of nature, however attractively and accessibly, should at best be a somewhat distant second on the list of educational priorities.

This tension between the way scientists do science and the way they tend to teach science has resulted in the most pressing problem that college and university science education faces today. In a widely read report on the topic, Sheila Tobias has stated the problem concisely: in the past twenty-five years "the proportion of college freshmen planning to *major* in science and mathematics fell by half."[5] Tobias proposes to solve that problem by fine-tuning science pedagogy and changing "classroom culture." In this chapter I draw on evidence that Tobias presents, but I dissent from her foundational assumptions. As a result, I disagree with the solution she proposes. In my view, it does not get to the heart of the problem.

The heart of the problem is what students learn about science from the way they learn science. Based on the nonfoundational understanding of scientific inquiry sketched by Callon, Jardine, Knorr-Cetina, Latour, and others, I argue here that college and university science students should learn science as a pragmatic intellectual tradition and that they will do so if they learn to construct, interpret, manipulate, and calibrate scientific models and symbol systems collaboratively.

To teach science in this way would not be to display what scientists believe they know about the natural world and the changes it undergoes. Instead, it would be to teach the interpretive, constructive, collaborative process by which scientists build models of the natural world. Chemistry teachers, for example, would of course continue to explain what electrolytes are and how they dissociate. But their primary task would be to create conditions in which students learn how and why chemists construct the model they call "electrolytes," how they construct and manipulate symbol systems that express changes in that model, and how they calibrate such chemical models and symbol systems as "actual reality."

Science education of this sort would benefit science students by involving them in study that offers intriguing risks of uncertainty and ambiguity and an opportunity to grapple with comfortable, long-held beliefs. And it would benefit science teachers by helping them come to terms with the troubling difference between the way they conduct their professional lives as scientists and the way they try, as college and university science teachers, to induct new members into that professional life: between the way they do science and the way they teach it. Thus to teach science as interpretive, constructive, and collaborative would require adapting to the needs of science courses the procedures of collaborative learning.

Among the most recent and most thoughtful suggestions for increasing the number of American young people entering science as a career is to make science classrooms more "attractive and accessible."[6] There is a lot to be said for this suggestion: it seems to make sense, and it would undoubtedly make life a lot more agreeable for a lot of American undergraduates. On this principle, therefore, Sheila Tobias recommends Dudley Herschbach's revisions in Harvard's Chemistry 10. By "setting a different mood," in the class, chatting amiably with students on occasion, releasing them from enslavement to "the curve," and allowing them a second chance on difficult topics, Herschbach doubled enrollment and improved test performance.[7]

As a solution to the problem of declining enrollment in college and university science courses, however, a rhetorical and administrative change of this type does not affect what students learn about science from the way they learn science, because it does not resolve tension between the way scientists do science and the way they teach science. It does not come to terms with the most damaging objections students make to their introductory college and university science courses: that they are intellectually barren. Tobias's informants, for example, complain that their courses made science "into a craft, like cooking . . . where if someone follows the recipe, he or she will do well."[8]

What encourages science teachers to continue to present science as a craft or as a curatorial enterprise is the traditional individualistic, foundational understanding of science. Tobias and her colleague John S. Rigden have made these traditional assumptions explicit. Science, based in their view "on empirical evidence, not on authority," is a "systematic method of conversing with nature."[9] Science teachers, by this light, have to testify to the certainties and truths that scientists have adduced in that lonely conversation with nature by means of that systematic evidentiary method.

Fortunately for the future of science education, the traditional assumptions that underlie the way the sciences are normally taught have been under siege for at least a quarter century by a set of vigorous alternative assumptions. According to this alternative, science is not a methodical evidentiary process but one of interpretive construction. Latour and Woolgar show, for example, how interpretive construction plays out in the everyday working lives of scientists. They demonstrate that scientists do carry on a conversation, but not with nature. The conversation scientists carry on is with one another. Scientific knowledge, then, is what the members of some scientific community say, or perhaps what they can say—directly and indirectly, in speech and, even more important, in writing—to other members of that community.

The tectonic shift in our understanding of science represented by this socially constructive understanding of science is one that college and university science teachers can no longer ignore. Reading Tobias's evidence with nonfoundational assumptions in mind suggests quite a different solution to the problems of science education. It suggests that college and university science students should be learning collaboratively how scientists confront the uncertainties and ambiguities of science by collaboratively constructing, interpreting, manipulating, and calibrating scientific models and symbol systems. In short, college and university science students should be learning how to "talk science" *with* one another and "write science" *to* one another.

There is of course no guarantee that teaching science as a pragmatic, interpretive intellectual tradition—that is, as a collaborative, interpretive, constructive encounter with scientific uncertainty—would increase the number of American young people taking science courses. But it would almost certainly bring about a change in the kind of college and university student who persists in a science major. Such a change is likely because the current crisis is due not just to a decline in the number of students who go beyond the introductory science courses to major in a science but to the *kind* of students who go on. Many students who continue in science today are attracted to science by the same thing that attracted students twenty-five years ago: the tendency of science teaching to satisfy their "need to be gripped, grasped, and compelled" by Nature (capital N) and its tendency to appeal to their hope of discovering in science a tidy world full of certainties, "a world without loose ends."[10]

Fewer intellectually talented students today feel that need and harbor that hope. As a result, the vision of science presented by science teaching as compellingly certain and coherent now disenchants many students. That is why they are more likely to be tempted away from science, as Tobias's informants had been, by the humanities and social sciences, where they find the quality that they fail to find in their science courses: the intellectual rewards and excitement of trying to cope with uncertainty, ambiguity, and a world full of loose ends.[11]

Most science teachers are familiar with the portion of the student population that these intellectually talented and adventurous students leave behind when they go. Science courses tend to be saturated with students of the sort that one articulate informant described as "clean cut and serious . . . intellectual warriors" who seemed "bored," "scared," and "dull," were not "particularly interested in making friends or seeing each other outside of class," seemed to "lose patience" with "silly 'why' questions," and were satisfied with (or perhaps dependent upon) educational experiences that ask "only for a simple exhibition of skills required."[12]

Looking at the decline in undergraduates opting to study science in terms of kind rather than just number changes our understanding of the problem considerably. It does not suggest only that students avoid science because they are unprepared for its rigors. It suggests that, whereas in the past twenty-five years the needs and hopes of intellectually talented college and university students have changed, the needs and hopes that science teachers feel called upon to satisfy have not. If so, then the solution to the problem of declining enrollment is not to adjust pedagogy so as to make introductory science courses more user-friendly. The solution is to design introductory college and university science courses that will hold the interest of intellectually more adventurous students and suggest to less adventurous ones, early on, that for them some career goal other than science might be more realistic.

What kind of introductory college and university science course is likely to do that? Does "intellectually more adventurous" necessarily mean "tougher" and "more rigorous"? Not necessarily. But it almost certainly means more collaborative, more conceptually intriguing, and a lot less tidy.

A complaint that appears in the notes of several of Tobias's informants hints what such a course might be like. Several record a spontaneous tendency to challenge traditional scientific certitudes. One of them comes to the conclusion that "the law of conservation of energy . . . [is] so 'artificial' as to be 'bogus' " because of all the "qualifiers" that "you have to include . . . to make the balance come out right." Another records his suspicion that some of the conventions involved in the calculations he is asked to do in studying Newtonian mechanics, quantities such as "normal force" or "the force perpendicular to the contact surface," are "not really understood" but are "made up . . . just to make the calculations work out." Still another, taking chemistry, arrives at a similar conclusion about the lattice energy curve representing attractive forces among ions.[13]

What troubles these students is not the difficult concepts they have to bend their minds around. What troubles them is the issue of belief in scientific knowledge. They are resisting the scientific orthodoxy presented to them in introductory science courses, the belief that "facts are facts and . . . [that] there is, in the final analysis, only one right answer."[14] Each one is asking the question, To what extent are those scientific facts believable? Does scientific knowledge correspond exactly to the physical processes to which it seems to refer? If so, how? If not, then how does scientific knowledge "work," and what function does it perform? How much confidence should we really be placing in the scientific knowledge that we generally accept?

An introductory science course taught as a pragmatic intellectual tradition would take this issue of belief in scientific knowledge seriously. For example, instead of suggesting, as Tobias does, that in questioning conventionally stipulated definitions, the student of Newtonian mechanics was only "playing with language," the course would begin by recognizing that the student really was on to something. He had caught physicists themselves playing with language, and in doing so he had discovered that the issue of belief in science is a troubling one even at high levels of scientific sophistication.

When pressed, of course, the scientists who taught these students told them that many of the conventions of science are "really just . . . a way of freezing a system at a moment of time, a descriptive tool," and that "nothing works across the board."[15] No scientist would deny that scientific knowledge involves a great deal of uncertainty and language-play at every level. The point, however, is that for these students the uncertainties of science are not marginal issues. They are central issues.

For this reason, the uncertainties of science and the interpretive and constructive nature of science should be found at the center of introductory college and university science courses, not at their margins. There are at least four reasons for placing them there. First, the concerns about the uncertainties of science that Tobias's informants expressed are widely shared. Second, we are better prepared today than in the past to discuss the uncertainties of science cogently. Third, the issue of belief in scientific knowledge is relevant to postmodern notions of liberal education. And fourth, the belief issue is relevant also to a significant, coherent change in pedagogical practice that is already under way in colleges and universities throughout the country.

The issue of belief in scientific knowledge is already on many students' minds waiting to be addressed when they enter a college or university science classroom. As Karen Knorr-Cetina puts it, science is "no longer taken for granted as a social resource," even by the general public. The "crisis of legitimacy" in science, widely discussed in both academic journals and in the popular press for more than a decade, concerns everyone, lay people, beginners, and scientific experts alike.[16]

The crisis of legitimacy of the sciences is confirmed and fostered, furthermore, by a change in the relationship between scientific communities and other academic and professional knowledge communities. During the past twenty years or so, science has become less of a universal model of thought by becoming less of a source of explanatory metaphors in other disciplines.

For some three centuries—roughly speaking from Newton to Einstein—the empirical, "positivist" language, assumptions, and methods of the sciences were revered as the most powerful intellectual processes ever devised. "Unscientific" disciplines—the humanities and, especially, the social sciences—aspired to increase their rigor and influence by making themselves over in the image of what they supposed to be "scientific."

In the humanities and social sciences during the past quarter century or so, however, what Clifford Geertz calls a "refiguration of thought" has occurred. The "nonscientific" disciplines have turned increasingly away from science for intellectual models and metaphors and turned increasingly instead to one another. Social scientists these days, he points out, "are chattering about actors, scenes, plots, performances, and personae, [while] humanists are mumbling about motives, authority, persuasion, exchange, and hierarchy."[17]

As a result of this tendency of "many social scientists no longer [to] imitate the sciences" and to draw analogies "from the crafts and technology," the sciences have lost some of their intellectual cachet. Tobias is certainly right that science is "too little 'spoken' in the nation's households" today. But equally to the point, science is "spoken" less today in the conference halls and publications of scholars in every field.[18]

To ignore the issue of belief in scientific knowledge, therefore, is only to suppress it. And to suppress it is to divide potential science students into the two categories they tend to be divided into today: students who willingly submit to being mystified by unreasoned belief in scientific certainty, and students who opt out into other fields which they find "more interesting," fields that tend to demystify knowledge by addressing rather than suppressing the issue of belief in our understanding of knowledge.

The second reason for teaching science as a pragmatic, interpretive intellectual tradition is that today the uncertainties of science, along with the uncertainties of every other field of knowledge, are easier to deal with systematically than ever before. In fact, we now have a well-honed set of tools for dealing with them. To use them to create conditions in which students could learn how scientists accommodate inexactitudes, uncertainties, conventions, arbitrariness, and language-play would be to teach science as a pragmatic intellectual tradition.

It is of course primarily for scientists to say how this should be done. But it is clear that at the center of the issue of belief in scientific knowledge will be found a set of questions about the relationship between language and what it "refers" to. Does language "name things" and therefore correspond in some inherent way to ideas, objects, and actions? Or is the relationship between language and things purely conventional? And if it is purely conventional, then what can it possibly mean to "know" something?

In science, this question of "reference," hence the issue of belief in scientific knowledge, becomes the question, What does it mean to "explain" a physical phenomenon? In many cases this question comes down to the application of mathematics, which, as most scientists readily acknowledge, is from the very start adventitious and artificial. As the teacher of one of Tobias's informants puts it, what matters in the sciences is finding a mathematical concept that "works."[19]

Even relatively unsophisticated introductory science students sense the artificiality of applied mathematics. Several informants raise the issue explicitly. One of them says, for example, that "what her professor and her recitation instructor thought they were doing to *explain* the difficult material (describing physical phenomena in terms of the laws of physics [expressed in mathematical formulas]) didn't *feel* like an explanation" to her. Another states the underlying principle outright: "formulas are used to describe strange, unknowable quantities, or [express] relations that are necessary merely for consistency."[20]

What these students intuit is that mathematics is a construct—a systematic contrivance of signs. The criteria for the integrity and authority of these signs are internal coherence, elegance, and depth. Mathematics is a language, a kind of writing, a form of discourse. The application of such a highly artificial system to the physical world results in a kind of fiction—stories that mathematicians tell. In science, mathematics is a wonderfully consistent, and therefore wonderfully convenient and useful, analogy or metaphor.

Certainly a mathematical statement may turn out to correspond consistently to a physical process that it is applied to, but there is nothing about mathematical language that makes such a correspondence necessary. For scientific innovators, that is, scientists who are the first to apply some mathematical system to some seemingly regular physical process, a mathematical statement is a means of justification. As the first to discover that some mathematical system or other "works," scientific innovators use the right mathematical statement to justify, before a particular community of scientists, a set of beliefs that they have arrived at in order to gain that community's agreement and acceptance. Once the community agrees that the application "works," the mathematical statement becomes entrenched in the language of the community. No longer is it regarded as an analogy or metaphor. Acceptance by the community, by virtue of the statement's predictive power or methodological efficiency, transforms it for all intents and purposes of that community (although perhaps only for the time being) into an analog of the physical process in question and an explanation of it.

Tools for analyzing the referentiality of language have been developed and sharpened in discussion among literary critics for some twenty years. One way students could approach the interpretive, constructive way in which scientists achieve and maintain a practical relationship between mathematics and the physical world would be by exploring the scientific implications of this discussion.

The discussion has two parts. The first part hinges on the linguist Ferdinand de Saussure's case that language does not refer to things in the world or to the "ideas" that we maintain for them in our minds. Instead, Saussure said, language functions by reference to other language, the conversation going on within the relevant discourse community. Use of a term depends on conventions agreed upon among those who are fluent in the language being spoken. It is a process that even amateur scientists and lay mathematicians will recognize going on currently and throughout the history of math and science.

The second part of the referentiality-of-language discussion is about what this assumption of Saussurean linguistics must mean to our sense of "knowing" something. This issue emerges in the philosophy of Ludwig Wittgenstein, for whom what we call "knowledge" is one or another "language game." True statements for Wittgenstein are moves in the particular game being played; changes in knowledge are changes in the rules of that game; and "a necessary truth," in Richard Rorty's paraphrase, is "a statement such that nobody has given us any interesting alternatives which would lead us to question it."

In pursuing this discussion, literary critics ask, If fictions such as the great novels, plays, and other cultural artifacts that we treasure do not "refer" to "life" or even to our "idea" of life, then just how do they "work," and what functions do they perform for us? Applied to science and mathematics, the questions would presumably be similar: If fictions such as models of electrolytes, $E = mc^2$, and other scientific artifacts we treasure do not "refer" to "nature," or even to our "idea" of nature, then just how do they "work," and what functions do they perform for us? To my knowledge new analytical tools such as these have not yet been applied broadly and systematically in teaching the sciences. But they are now there for the asking.

The third reason for teaching science as a pragmatic, interpretive intellectual tradition is that it would return the sciences to their legitimate place in the curriculum of "the liberal arts and sciences."

There are of course as many definitions of a liberal education as there are curriculum committees trying to define it. But most of these definitions have in common three goals: (1) to introduce students to the depth and complexity of human thought by becoming familiar with some of the principal beliefs that we human beings hold about ourselves, about each other, and about the physical world; (2) introduce students to some of the ways human beings arrived at those beliefs; and (3) introduce them to some of the ways in which those who hold those beliefs justify them to themselves and to others.

The beliefs of science are, or should be, among the beliefs that students become familiar with through a liberal education. Some sixty-five years ago, Alfred North Whitehead officiated with high hopes at the marriage between the liberal arts and sciences with the publication of his Lowell Lectures, *Science in the Modern World*. For some thirty years the encouragement and counsel of that widely read volume kept the marriage intact. Today, however, science courses and the liberal arts curriculum have been divorced for decades, largely by common consent. As a result, students frequently complain with good reason, as one of Tobias's informants puts it, that undergraduate science courses "train" students, they do not "educate" them.[21]

In the 1990s, *Science in the Modern World* is a historical document. To many of us, its foundational scientific and philosophical assumptions seem antediluvian. Yet Whitehead's motive remains valid. To Whitehead, those who do not understand the cultural importance of the sciences are, in his word, provincial. To teach the sciences as an interpretive enterprise would help reduce this provinciality. Approaching science as a pragmatic interpretive tradition would contribute to liberal education by showing that, along with literature, philosophy, religion, music, history, and the arts, scientific knowledge comprises a set of beliefs. It would show how these beliefs are justified, how they become established, how they have been challenged in the past, and how they are being challenged today both from within disciplinary communities and from without.

The fourth reason for teaching science as a pragmatic, interpretive intellectual tradition is that in focusing on the uncertainties of science it would make possible the organized, open-ended conversation that is necessary for genuine collaboration among students and hence for the cultivation of the craft of interdependence. Tobias offers an example of one kind of collaboration, a student's experience in a chemistry "tutor room":

> I would go in, sit down at one of the three tables with some other people I didn't know [the student says], and pretty soon we would all be discussing the material and working the problems together. Whenever we were stumped, we could bring one of the tutors over to the table to help us out. It was a very good system. Here we had a solid block of

time . . . to interact with other students, work problems, discuss and actively learn the material we were covering in the lecture.[22]

The microconversation that occurs among students working together in small groups like this one helps them improve their grades by giving them an opportunity, as another student puts it, to "practice 'talking physics' " and of course to practice writing physics as well.[23] This is the principle underlying Uri Treisman's program organizing university science and math students into mutually reacculturating, self-help study communities at Berkeley and Texas, and it is also the principle underlying M.L.J. Abercrombie's research in teaching medical students.

Yet simply adding "small groups" to science classes, without integrating collaboration systematically into the course by changing the nature of the tasks that students undertake together, will not achieve the fluency in the language of the relevant scientific community that an interpretive approach to science can achieve. The problems that this chemistry student and her fellow students were solving together were closed-ended, result-focused jigsaw-puzzle tasks of the sort discussed in Chapter 2, the kind of tasks usually found in problem sets. In the context of an interpretive course, in which the goal is to confront the uncertainties of science as well as its certainties, problems of an open-ended, interpretive, tool-making kind, such as those described and exemplified in Chapter 2, would make peer-group work more rewarding still.

Under these conditions, that is, in collaborative learning, student conversation would go beyond helpful cooperation and teamwork to active construction of knowledge, although of course of limited scale and authority. The microconversation that goes on in peer-group work tends to model the conversations in which scientists construct knowledge, whether those conversations are direct (person to person), displaced into publication or interaction with computer programs, or internalized as thought. The same principle could be applied to lab work, which today has been subordinated to the authority of the lecture hall. Instead of assuming students' fluency in the relevant scientific language, lab work would assume that the lab is where that fluency is to be acquired. Lab work would also approximate the practice of science as Bruno Latour and Steve Woolgar demonstrate it in *Laboratory Life*: conversation—spoken and written—among scientists making sense out of what they observe by negotiating their differences.[24]

If foundational assumptions have affected college and university science teaching in ways I have described in this chapter, they have also affected research practices and results. This is especially the case in research in fields such as education, the social sciences, and philosophy of science. In the next chapter I will examine several examples of work in which that effect is evident.

CHAPTER TEN

The Procrustean Bed of Cognitive Thought

The belief that knowledge is socially constructed and learning socially interdependent has only recently entered the public discussion of college and university education. In the past, that discussion made cognitive assumptions exclusively, and almost all thought and research about knowledge and learning were pursued in cognitive terms. We have rarely questioned these foundational terms and assumptions, despite the fact that almost a century ago the overdetermined, hierarchical myth of cognition they draw upon began to reveal itself as unsuited to understanding knowledge as a property of human interdependence.

Five classic cases—represented in the work of M.L.J. Abercrombie, William Perry, Jerome Bruner, Bruno Latour, and Nicholas Jardine—illustrate the procrustean constraints that cognitive assumptions impose on thought and research. In the first, by the investigator's own admission, cognitive terminology fails to explain a central anomaly. In the second, developmental thought, foundational in its premise, precludes understanding the message being sent by some of the study's most perspicacious subjects. In the third, cognitive assumptions and language prevent a synthesis that would increase the significance of the work. And finally, suggesting the depth and intractability of the problem, in two cases cognitive assumptions implicit in the language used to talk about knowledge undermine the carefully crafted writing of two leading proponents of the social constructionist understanding of knowledge.

Through these case studies, this chapter offers a critique of the long-standing debate about learning and education as it has been carried on in familiar, well-established cognitive terms during roughly the past forty years.

The first case is M.L.J. Abercrombie's 1959 study, *The Anatomy of Judgment*. Jane Abercrombie was a highly respected biologist at University College, London. When the faculty of the university's medical unit,

155

University Hospital, asked her to review the way they were teaching medical students the key element in successful medical practice, diagnosis, the conclusion Abercrombie drew was that students who learned diagnosis collaboratively became better diagnosticians than individual students working alone.

> They tended [she wrote] to discriminate better between facts and conclusions, to draw fewer false conclusions, to consider more than one solution to a problem, and to be less adversely influenced in their approach to a problem by their experience of a preceding one.[1]

This was a significant result, and the research that led to it was exemplary. Yet by her own account, Abercrombie's ability to explain the evidence that led to her remarkable conclusion was limited. When she tried to explain why medical students learn diagnostics better in groups than they do working alone, she had at hand only the language commonly used in her day to discuss knowledge and learning, the foundational language of cognition. That language, she perceived, could make no sense of the results that her study led to.

The problem Abercrombie faced was that she had to make a cognitive assumption, that knowledge is an entity formalized by the individual mind and verified against reality, fit her noncognitive evidence that the process of learning judgment is not an individual phenomenon but a social one. Learning judgment, she saw, occurs on an axis drawn not between individuals and things but among persons. Yet Abercrombie's explanation sticks doggedly, as it must, to cognitive terms. Her conception of learning is organized on an inner-outer, subjective-objective axis. She talks about "the relation between the inside and outside worlds" and the successful creation of accurate mental forms or "schemata."[2]

To her credit, however, Abercrombie saw, and acknowledged, that an explanation couched in those terms just would not wash. Her abortive attempt to make a square peg fit a round hole led her to assert that there is something wrong with the cognitive assumptions she was using. Cognitive assumptions disregard what she calls "the biological fact" that the human being "is a social animal." Her honest appraisal of the facts led her to face squarely the question that has always haunted those cognitive assumptions: "how [do] human relationships influence the receipt of information even about apparently non-personal events"?[3]

Abercrombie failed to answer this question. But in trying to answer it, she made the prescient observation that people learn judgment best in groups; she drew the sensible inference that we do so by talking each other out of our unshared biases and presuppositions; and she made in passing a pregnant suggestion: that the social process of learning judgment that she observed is a function of language and "interpretation."

With these insights, Abercrombie stood at the verge of social constructionist thought. She came tantalizingly close to understanding her medical students not as so many cognitive mental devices in which myste-
rious "insights" occur, but as knowledgeable peers learning a new
community language, the linguistic and paralinguistic interpretive language of medical diagnosis.

A second example of the way cognitive thought has limited our understanding of the nature of knowledge and learning is the research
reported in William Perry's influential book, *Forms of Intellectual and Ethical
Development in the College Years*. This book, extending Piaget's developmental studies of young children to the intellectual development of
young adults, has made an indelible impression on the thinking of many
college teachers and administrators and on our understanding of higher
education generally.

The book's importance begins with Perry's documentation of a fact:
in the past fifty (now seventy-five) years, since roughly 1920, our understanding of knowledge and learning has changed radically. We once
assumed, Perry reminds us, that "knowledge consisted of facts in a single
frame of reference." Now we assume that "knowledge [is] contextual
and relative." This change, Perry speculates, is only the most recent
phase in a tendency toward assimilating cultural diversity that needs,
for its fulfillment, "a new social mind" and "a new realization of community."[4]

In observing that educational change is somehow a function of social
change, Perry implies that the most important educational issues today
hinge on a social understanding of knowledge, not a cognitive one. Our
most important educational concerns today, as Abercrombie discovered,
are about relations among persons, not relations between persons and
things. Learning as we must understand it today, Perry implies, does
not involve people's assimilation of knowledge. It involves people's
assimilation into communities of knowledgeable peers. College and university education, accordingly, is a process of leaving one set of knowledge communities and joining another.

Perry accepts this principle in theory but resists it in practice. He
denies that to create communities of knowledgeable peers among students is a legitimate part of rationally and consciously organized college
and university education. He prefers to rely on "spontaneity." He believes that to try to foster knowledge communities among undergraduate
students by using "particular procedures or rituals" would be to exercise
an unprofessional lack of restraint or would turn out to be a clumsy and

perhaps crass gesture that would despoil a delicate fruit: touch student knowledge communities, as Lady Bracknell says of ignorance, and the bloom is gone.[5]

Perry's politely dismissive tone suggests that he did not fully recognize the implications of his study. The cognitive language of the book's title tells us why. Perry's "forms" of intellectual and ethical development are the mental structures, cognitive frameworks, and procedures of higher-order reasoning sought by cognitive research. Drawn by the all-but-irresistible gravitational pull of these cognitive assumptions, Perry veers at crucial moments sharply from the most logical and most valuable conclusion of his argument.

This shift is evident in his summary of what happens to students in the course of a successful undergraduate education. "In our records," he tells us,

> the students appear to bring with them the expectation of identification with the college community. [But they] . . . simply transpose to the college the same sense they have developed in the community from which they come. The pressure for change therefore emerges from them as anomalies of experience from within the boundaries of this community. If they do not react so violently as to reperceive the entire [college] community as "other," divorcing themselves from it, they must assimilate the anomalous experience in ways that will force adaptations in the structure of their assumptions, opening the closed system to the progression of changes traced in this report.[6]

A close reading of this passage reveals a telling break in coherence. Through the opening clause of the last sentence, ending with the phrase "divorcing themselves from" the college community, Perry speaks of knowledge and values as a function of students' relations with other people: first their relations with the communities they come from and then their relations with the college community they enter. The thrust of the passage up to this point is clear. At first, freshmen enthusiastically commit themselves to joining the new college community. Soon they realize that membership in this new community presents them with a choice. They must renegotiate their membership in the community they have left behind. Or else they must reject membership in the new community that the college invites them to join. Perry conveys the seriousness of this choice between communities with a social metaphor. Students have to "divorce" themselves from one community in the act of marrying into another.

What is striking about the passage, however, is that just as Perry makes this crucial inference, he evades the resolution demanded by the logic of the social metaphor. In the final clause of the paragraph, he stops talking about knowledge and values as if they were a function of the students' relations with other people. He reverts instead to talking about knowledge and values as if they were a function of mental forms. Suddenly, learning stops being a readjustment of the relations with people that is involved in contracting membership in new communities of knowledgeable peers. It becomes instead a readjustment of the structural elements of students' inner lives effected by assimilating experience.

Logical incoherence of this sort pervades the book. Many passages draw inferences from data that lead to understanding undergraduate development as a collaborative process. Perry's allusions to the work of Thomas Kuhn suggest that he is drawn to understanding knowledge as a social entity and learning as a social process. Yet when the chips are down, the book treats undergraduate development in cognitive terms as involving "forms of thought" and "meaningful interpretation" by an inner "seer" or "increasingly complex experience."

Perry masks his ambivalence about the nonfoundational social constructionist implications of his argument by trivializing the social element in students' learning. He reduces it to the need to keep friends. He suggests that the impetus to change may "seem" to come from the students' peers but will really come from within individual students themselves. And he regards students' "new sense of community among peers" as a sort of tacked-on "comfort" that "can provide the required strength" and "environmental sustenance" for inner growth. The new undergraduate communities that students join, furthermore, serve only to "balance" the "loneliness" that they experience as the price of their "new inner strength." According to Perry, the stark, lonely, hard-won, courageous individualism of that "new inner strength" is the true prize of a college or university education, or at least of one gained at Harvard College.[7]

What saves Perry's book from this ambivalence about the social implications of its argument is that many of the more mature informants among the group of undergraduates he studied are not at all ambivalent in their perception of learning as a social process. Many of them see their undergraduate education quite explicitly as a transfer of loyalty from one knowledge community—the one they came from—to another knowledge community, the college community of student peers.

One student's testimony about this process is so compelling that it merits quotation at length. This student commuted to college for three years. During that time his education was wholly a classroom affair. As a result, his college education suffered in the way that, as Arthur Chickering has shown, the education of commuters almost always suffers.

This student never felt the life-changing impact typically felt by most resident undergraduates. He never had a "sophomore year."

In his senior year, however, this student moved into a residence hall on campus. He recalls the effect of that move in the following way. "The first surprise," he tells us,

> was that after three years here, I could still step into something so completely different; different types of people with different interests. . . . When I was transposed into this from living at home, I was confronted with a great many more attitudes about ways of doing things than I had seriously considered before. . . . One thing I've tried to do, which was a response to living in, was to think out much more carefully just where I wanted to stand—not that this was always possible. You couldn't say, "I stand here" and then live like that, because part of it was in a way, doing a little bit of everything, and then trying to come back to what you thought you should be doing . . . back to what I was serious about.[8]

What seems immediately clear from this report is that the student's new community of peers is not the "comfort" and provider of "strength" and "sustenance" that Perry would like to suppose. On the contrary, the undergraduate community challenges the student's complacency. What another informant calls simply "talking to roommates and other people in the dorm" does for this student what three years of classroom exposure to Harvard faculty failed to do. It forces him to make decisions and choices and at the same time blurs the distinctions on which those decisions and choices must be made. Other students that Perry interviewed tell us in more detail what this marrying into the student residence community involves. It challenges them to define their individuality not as starkly and lonesomely independent but as *inter*dependent members of their new undergraduate community of knowledgeable peers.[9]

As Perry would surely have noticed, if he had not been confined, as Abercrombie was, by the assumptions of cognitive thought, his students' testimony had an untutored but consistently Kuhnian, social constructionist force. Trying to reconcile incompatible religious and social views, they behaved like scientists trying to reconcile incompatible theories. Neither group can resolve its differences "simply by stipulating the definitions of troublesome terms" or by "resort to a neutral language which both use in the same way." Both groups engage in a collaborative process in which they "recognize each other as members of different language communities and then become translators," debating their heretofore unquestioned assumptions until, as one of Perry's informants says, they find "language that allows [them] . . . to reach agreement on something."[10]

The real importance of Perry's book, then, is not the mythic mental "forms" he infers but the evidence of the social construction of knowledge that his students so generously provided him. Their conversation at community boundaries illustrates the process of nonstandard discourse. To paraphrase Rorty, they engage in the kind of conversation that occurs when people do not yet agree on the conventions that will guide their conversation and actions; do not yet agree about how to evaluate what anyone says; and do not yet agree about what counts as a relevant contribution, a satisfactory answer to a question, a good argument or a good criticism of it. Their purpose is to reacculturate themselves through the process we saw going on in several examples in Chapter 1. Their purpose, that is, is to outgrow the limitations of their current knowledge: to exceed the "norms of the day" of the communities they currently belong to.[11]

The third example of the way cognitive thought has limited the potential of research into the nature of knowledge and learning is the work of Jerome Bruner. In an intellectual autobiography, *In Search of Mind*, Bruner has readably summarized his long, illustrious career.[12] There, he describes one of the experiments that established his preeminence, the one in which, with a simple but ingenious device, he showed how, even at the tender age of six months, we human beings can control our environment systematically. He did this by supplying some six-month-old infants with pacifiers wired so that by sucking on them the infants would produce effects that they could see. By sucking they could focus at will a blurred picture that was propped up before them, and blur a focused one.

This experiment demonstrates what Bruner calls "enactive" knowledge, which he describes in the language of inner-outer, subject-object foundational cognitive thought. Infants can learn how to affect their surroundings (by sucking to focus or blur a picture), he says, because their minds are equipped even in infancy with a "hypothesis generator" that gives them the ability to "form either higher-order action routines or more generalized 'cognitive maps' of their world."[13]

But Bruner's cognitive account, like Perry's, masks an ambiguity in his experimental results and limits the implications that can be drawn from them. The picture that Bruner's infants were focusing and blurring was a mother-surrogate, and the pacifier they sucked on to focus or blur it was a breast-surrogate. Bruner's experiment therefore reproduced a portion of the conversation that is carried on through touch and glance between mother and child, the conversation that D. W. Winnicott describes in, for example, his charming brief essay instructing parents on "The Baby as a Person."

To understand Bruner's scene, therefore, does not require the foundational machinery of "hypothesis generators," mental models, and "cognitive maps." It is a scene of negotiation carried on in a paralinguistic symbol system. It models the way in which infants and mothers construct the knowledge that they share in a conversation of touch, vocal tones, and facial expression. And that negotiation, however linguistically inarticulate, is as complex and rewarding as the one we saw (in Chapter 7) Latour's child engaged in, learning from her mother to distinguish a bird from a ball and a fish.

Just as Latour's little girl learns "part of [her mother's] language structure," by distinguishing and classifying words according to their relations with other words, the infant learns part of its mother's paralinguistic vocabulary and grammar by distinguishing and classifying gestures, vocal tones, and physical attitudes. And just as the girl's survival among English-speaking people depends on her making those distinctions correctly, the infant's emotional and physical survival depends on its understanding correctly its mother's gestural language.[14]

To construe Bruner's scene as a conversation, therefore, is to enlarge its implications. It confirms Vygotsky's observation of six-month-old infants establishing contact with reality through a mediated process involving the agency of other people. More striking still, construed in this way, Bruner's data revise Vygotsky's conclusions about the importance of the four- or five-year-old child's instrumental use of language, which Vygotsky calls "the most significant moment in the course of intellectual development."[15] Bruner's experiment tells us that that process does not wait for speech. It begins much earlier in life, as soon as infants can feel changes in physical attitude, hear tones, and see gestures and facial expressions—perhaps even (as more recent research suggests) before birth.

Unlike Winnicott's, however, Bruner's data are sparse. He records only a fraction of the infants' part in conversation with their mother-surrogates. He does not record, for example, whatever was also going on with his infants' fingers, elbows, knees, and toes. Winnicott records this negotiation in detail: infants look and gesture in diverse ways; caretaking adults reciprocate. Not only do infants often "follow an adult's gaze as if to find out what she might be looking at," caretaking adults also follow the infant's gaze to find out what the infant is looking at. Then they respond accordingly, often by putting whatever-it-is within the infant's reach, or else by putting it safely out of the way.[16]

But even with Bruner's sparse data, his results can be accounted for in a more rewarding way than in cognitive terms as "skilled activity." Understood nonfoundationally, the matrix of the infants' thought is neither self nor world, but rather the small knowledge community, mother-and-infant, to which the infant belongs. More specifically, the matrix of the infant's thought is the community-constituting linguistic and paralinguistic symbol system in which the members of that small community construct and justify their beliefs.

The experimental scene does suggest, as Bruner might say, some kind of "intention directed behavior" on the part of both infant and mother. But the intention that directs their behavior is not, as Bruner has to assume it is, an effort by a foundational self to affect a foundational object. In this conversational drama, intention too is socially constructed. What Bruner was observing, then, can be described to greater effect as, in Erving Goffman's sense, selves in the making: the primary acculturation of an infant that occurs by way of negotiation with another socially constructed self—in real life, a self still under construction as it negotiates with this particular infant: the mother's self.

In short, as with Abercrombie and Perry, a nonfoundational social constructionist account of Bruner's evidence has greater explanatory power than a foundational, cognitive account. Interestingly, Bruner himself implicitly permits a nonfoundational account when he concedes that "*some* concepts [can] exist only by virtue of language."[17] To have generalized this principle one more step (to the position that all knowledge exists only by virtue of linguistic and paralinguistic symbol systems) would have strengthened Bruner's useful notion of "formatting." A "format," he says,

> is a little microcosm, a task, in which mother and child share an intention to get something done with words. . . . Formats are little pieces of the culture—but crucial little pieces, for they are the first chunky bits of culture from which the child will generalize. Sufficiently circumscribed to permit an easy assessment of what one's partner is up to, they allow for correction of misinterpretation, and for negotiation of intention of meaning. They are indeed a means of entering the language and the culture simultaneously.[18]

So far, this paragraph could easily be mistaken for a nonfoundational, social constructionist account. Infant and mother learn by interpreting each other's behavior, each negotiating an understanding of what the other "is up to," both correcting "misinterpretations" and both encapsulating the result in a convention or routine that Bruner calls a "format." At a crucial point in the passage, however, cognitive assumptions lead

Bruner, as they did Perry, to misconstrue the process. As we grow older, he says, these formats

> become increasingly dependent upon skill in language and, in time, can be *constituted* when needed by language, without the stage setting required earlier. One does not need the mother-created, scaffolding format of the early years. One *creates* them, imposes them by learning the linguistic conventions for doing so—converting by convention whatever situation one encounters into an occasion for indicating, requesting, warning, congratulating, whatever.[19]

In this second half of the passage, it is increasingly evident that Bruner does not regard as social the constructive process that he describes. He sees it as individual, foundational, and cognitive. The individual mind "creates" the "scaffolding" needed for learning without the "stage setting" of conversation with others. Thus Bruner's foundational assumptions lead him to oversimplify the process of internalizing linguistic and paralinguistic conventions by taking the part for the whole. The nonfoundational understanding of the process would be that infants internalize the entire primary social relationship between infant and mother, constituted in looks, touch, and gesture. As the infant grows up, it does not replace mother. It subsumes membership in the closed community of infant and mother, burying it more and more deeply within larger, more comprehensive, and ultimately more rewarding communities. From the very beginning, *knowing* is a complex of such memberships in infinitely nested, overlapping linguistic communities. *Learning* is a process of reacculturation from one community to another.

Indeed, Bruner's cognitive account of this scene of primal conversation, because it assumes that mothers (and other caretaking adults) remain "constant throughout" while infants change and grow, suggests the possible metaphorical origins of cognitive thought itself.[20] The binary subjective and objective terms of cognitive thought appear to be characters in a mythical drama that replicates the primary negotiation between infant and mother. This negotiation appears, much displaced, in the cognitivist image of heroic epistemological confrontation between self and other, subject and object. It is the drama that Freud seems to have in mind in *The Future of an Illusion* when he says that even "our conviction that we can learn something about external reality through the use of observation and reasoning in scientific work" may involve the sort of "erotic illusion" that fulfills "the oldest, strongest, and most urgent wishes of mankind."[21]

What the cognitive myth suppresses is the uncomfortable reality that mothers (and other caretaking adults) are constant and unchanging only in childhood wishes. No emotionally coherent parent remains constant, least of all those in close relationship with infants and young children. Infants of course change more than caretaking adults. But as attentive parents know from experience, the power of infants to reconstruct the behavior and feelings of adults is formidable.

Read in nonfoundational terms, therefore, Bruner's data help account for both cultural coherence and cultural change. The values of a mother's ethnic community and the values of her community with an infant rarely exactly coincide. In some cases they differ considerably. Kuhn and Rorty both tell us that changes in knowledge are due to the disruptive presence of "outsiders"—nonmembers of the community—and to the nonstandard discourse or boundary conversation that they inflict on knowledge-community members. Read nonfoundationally, Bruner's experiment suggests that this culturally disruptive influence begins potentially with the birth of every child.

In discussing these three examples of research into the nature of knowledge and learning—Abercrombie's account of her research in working with medical students, Perry's account of results working with college undergraduates, and Bruner's account of his work with infants—I have reinterpreted them. This reinterpretation is itself part of a boundary conversation between two authoritative communities. It is an attempt to translate the language of one community of knowledgeable peers (the community constituted in the foundational language of cognition) into the language of another community of knowledgeable peers (the community constituted in the language of nonfoundational social construction).

Inevitably, something gets lost in translation. The work of all three, Abercrombie, Perry, and Bruner, was conceived in cognitive terms on cognitive assumptions to make a cognitive point. In translating each one, I have lost some of the detail and much of the symmetry of both the original research plan and the resulting account. I have undertaken the translation, however, because in each case important data will not "fit" cognitive assumptions, resulting in anomalies that the researcher has despaired of, rejected, or disregarded. In each case, the translation leaves some of the less important data unaccounted for but yields greater explanatory power than the original.

That a translation from foundational to nonfoundational terms should be necessary to gain this explanatory power is of course no discredit to Abercrombie, Perry, and Bruner. The powerful effect of foundational cognitive language on our thinking about knowledge and learning can be evident even in the work of writers who seem to have converted more or less wholeheartedly to nonfoundational assumptions and vocabulary. Even the most rigorous of social constructionist writers can find their language defeating their assiduous efforts to avoid, or at least to bracket, the ubiquitous traditional vocabulary of cognition with which we normally talk about knowledge and education. The language of this book, too, is certain to fall occasionally into the same trap.

The undertow of foundational locutions, running so deep in the language that they affect normal grammar and syntax, can disrupt even the most self-consciously nonfoundational argument. Sometimes that undertow only trips writers up for a moment. Perhaps in haste or as a result of losing concentration (even Homer nods), they forget that when we native Foundational speakers speak and write Nonfoundational we are all speaking and writing a foreign tongue. They forget (as we can all too easily do) the depth of the influence that foundational thought has on us and how far into our accustomed vocabulary any translation must therefore reach.

In the case of a momentary lapse, however, most writers easily regain their nonfoundational equilibrium. Their argument seldom suffers from more than a passing distraction. Even Bruno Latour, one of the most sophisticated of those currently studying the implications of nonfoundational social constructionist thought for understanding science, does not entirely escape this sort of momentary lapse. For example, in the second edition of Latour and Woolgar's influential book *Laboratory Life: The Social Construction of Scientific Facts*, the authors omit the word *social* from the subtitle and explain at length in a postscript why they did so. Their reasoning is that, in the phrase *social construction*, the word *social* has been, historically, "primarily a term of antagonism, one part of a binary opposition." The other part of this binary opposition is "technical content" or "scientific content."[22]

The term *social construction*, they argue, is therefore a revisionist cognitive term. Once we accept that all interactions are "social," the term "social" merely replaces "individual" or "inner" with something fuzzier but more currently acceptable to cognitivists. Once we leave cognitive thought behind, "the social study of science has rendered 'social' devoid of any meaning." As a result, Latour and Woolgar courageously but incautiously assert, "we . . . simply ditch the term."[23]

Acceptable as this reasoning may be as a species of wishful thinking—based on wishes I share—I would argue that the word *social* has to remain in the phrase *social construction* as a pointed reminder, at least for the current generation. Latour and Woolgar themselves demonstrate, in the course of arguing that we should cavalierly ditch it, what can happen when we do. At the beginning of the Afterword, in which they explain their decision to abandon the term *social*, this paragraph appears:

> There is a traditional tendency to chase and hound the "real" meaning of texts. Years after the initial publication of a volume, defenders and critics alike continue to argue over "what was actually intended" by its authors. As a welcome relief from this spectacle, literary theory has increasingly disavowed this kind of textual criticism. The current trend is to permit texts a life of their own. The "real" meaning of a text is recognized as an illusory or, at least, infinitely renegotiable concept. As a result, "what the text says," "what really happened" and "what the authors intended" are now very much up to the reader. It is the reader who writes the text.[24]

In this passage, determined as they are to emphasize the social "construction of scientific facts," Latour and Woolgar nevertheless reveal their own trace of not yet wholly reconstructed foundational premises. The individualist, relativist, reader-response argument, that "what the text says" is "now very much up to the reader . . . [because] the reader . . . writes the text," contradicts the thesis of *Laboratory Life*. There, as in the relevant work of Stanley Fish (discussed in Chapter 11), it is not *the* reader but *readers*—interpretive communities of knowledgeable readers—who, through negotiation to consensus, construct fictive "readings," fictive understandings of "what the text says," "what really happened," and "what the authors intended." Of course in writing "the reader" Latour and Woolgar have merely slipped. Of course they meant "readers." But their slip nevertheless suggests, as I have said, the strength of the undertow of cognitive assumptions.

Even in *Science in Action*, in which at considerable length Latour unpacks his notion of the "constructed" nature of scientific knowledge, there are signs that, in spite of himself, he remains, perhaps ever so slightly, ambivalent. In one passage (which I have quoted at length in Chapter 7) Latour describes a child learning to call those small feathered creatures that fly "birds." But he comments on this passage, equivocally, that the child is "confronted by a choice about which group to belong to or which world to live in." The alternatives Latour provides here suggest that he has not yet quite made up his mind himself about which linguistic group to belong to, foundational or nonfoundational. The phrase "which world to live in" is inappropriate to Latour's nonfoundational argument. Applied to a child learning what birds are, it implies that knowledge involves foundational contact between her synthesizing mind and an external entity, a "world." The phrase "which group to belong to" is an appropriately nonfoundational, social constructionist expression implying that knowledge involves reacculturation into a community constructed way of dealing with what Richard Rorty calls the physical reality that shoves us around.[25]

Among philosophers, historians, and sociologists of science, however, Latour is certainly not alone in the difficulty he has in extricating himself linguistically from "the social-cognitive dichotomy" that is, as Knorr-Cetina puts it, "useless" and "obsolete." In her case this difficulty appears in passing in clauses such as "conceptual interaction emerges from . . . different universes of knowledge or belief" and "(scientific) data . . . refer to some reality they represent." It appears also in her tendency to refer to the "generation" of scientific knowledge as if that word were an unproblematic synonym of the "construction" of scientific knowledge.[26]

Nicholas Jardine exemplifies writers in whose work the damage is somewhat more serious. The foundational undertow not only occasionally trips him up, it threatens in some passages to sweep his nonfoundational argument away into a maelstrom of unreadable convolutions, confusions, and infelicities. This seems to happen when he takes unnecessary linguistic risks not at the periphery of his argument but at the very center of it.

The most striking of these risks is to use a conspicuously foundational term in a resolutely nonfoundational context. Letting the camel's nose under the tent flap in this way opens him to greater danger than he is aware of, with the result that he gets hit from behind. The implications of the foundational term—that is, the presuppositions and beliefs of the foundational community from whose vocabulary he has borrowed the word—begin to assert their prerogatives. The word insists on reverting to type as the name of an entity that has an existence of its own and that obeys laws of its own, rather than remaining what Jardine wants it to be, the name of a certain agreement among the members of some community or other. Soon the temptation to use the word in a foundational way overwhelms his vigilance. What began as a lucid argument in nonfoundational terms turns into a muddled argument in contradictory terms.

In *Scenes of Inquiry* Jardine takes this risk because he wants to support the position, intuitively unexceptionable in western culture, that, in spite of the tradition of pragmatic reasoning on which the sciences are based, through "calibration against precedents and standards" scientists do in some cases arrive at what he calls "global or absolute reality." In offering alternative terms here, Jardine does suggest, as Latour's alternative terms do, a not yet fully resolved ambivalence about which linguistic group to belong to, foundational ("absolute") or nonfoundational ("global"). Still, Jardine is making an important point in a nonfoundational social constructionist argument both about science and about the history, philosophy, and sociology of science, and it is entirely possible to make the point without smuggling foundational assumptions back in. Scientists may be said in some cases to arrive at "truth" for all intents and purposes (as I suggest in Chapter 9), by virtue of their commitment to approaching asymptotically—"as a limit," as mathematicians say—a "reality" assented to "globally."[27]

But confusion on this point leads Jardine twice to use a foundational term in a nonfoundational context. His thesis is the nonfoundational notion that philosophers, historians, and sociologists of science should shift their attention "from scientific doctrines to the questions posed in the sciences," in particular a scientific community's selection of questions that its members agree to call "real questions."[28] But for these "real questions" and negotiations about them, Jardine chooses (from the ocular, foundational metaphor of the mirror of nature) the phrase *scenes of inquiry.* Jardine's argument survives this choice, although his repeated reference to "scenes" in place of "real questions" is likely to cause some readers to puzzle and reread. He might have made his task a bit easier by adopting some other term with literary cachet, such as "episodes" of inquiry, that would not run this risk.

In the second instance, however, Jardine nearly destroys his argument in a key chapter (Chapter 4, "Explaining Scenes") by adopting an even more conspicuously foundational term, "cognitive frame." In foundational thought, "cognitive frame" refers to a universal mental entity with which (to grossly oversimplify) the *res cognitans* or inner eye (characterized in one way or another) gives form and meaning to the mind's view of the *res extensa*, a reflection of the real world in the mirror of nature (characterized in one way or another). What Jardine means by the term, however, is admirably nonfoundational: a "cognitive frame" is "the totality of the beliefs and commitments of a community" that affect the community's decisions about which questions they will acknowledge as "real questions."[29]

The tension between this stipulated meaning of the phrase "cognitive frame" and its conventional meaning in the epistemological tradition ripples through the chapter in which Jardine uses it. The term has two deleterious effects. First, Jardine tends to generalize about "cognitive frames" in ways that suggest that he thinks of them, even if only momentarily, as universal entities: personified actors on a stage doing things, a stage on which other personified entities also do things. For example, we find him saying not that *communities adopt* "cognitive frames" that "attach major importance to considerations of" something or other, but that *"cognitive frames" themselves* attach major importance to considerations of something or other. And he also tells us that certain assertions "play the role of foundations in a cognitive frame."

The second unfortunate effect of using the term is stylistic paralysis. Bear in mind that I am talking here about a writer of philosophical prose (a genre not universally known for vigor and lucidity) who is capable of knock-your-socks-off paragraphs like this one:

> Perhaps most insidious of all the bases for dismissal of sociologists' and historians' findings . . . is faith in the destiny of science, the belief that whatever the local aberrations of scientists the juggernaut of science is fated to go on revealing truths about nature. This superstition is oddly tenacious. It seems that we have tacitly invested in the fate of science much that was once openly invested in sacred and spiritual histories of mankind with their promises of redemption and millennium.[30]

With his confidence as a writer evidently undermined by the contradictions implicit in the term "cognitive frame," however, throughout the first half of his Chapter 4 Jardine's normally fluent prose cramps and falters. The result is one distressingly obscure, convoluted sentence after another. Jardine just can't seem to spit it out, anxious, perhaps, that he has inadvertently lured his disciplinary colleagues to look most predatorially right here for a chance to string him up by his analyticophilosophical thumbs.

Take for example this tone-setting sentence at the very beginning of the chapter, a sentence that has the rudimentary, uncomplicated task of preparing readers for the next step in Jardine's argument by reviewing the argument up to now: "Reality of questions in a community has been explicated in terms of evidential considerations to those questions."[31] Rewritten in something like the readable style of most of the book, the sentence comes out: "I have already explained why communities call some questions 'real questions.' They believe that there exist, or could exist, evidential considerations relevant to answering them."

For the next seven pages Jardine discusses with consistent stylistic ineptitude the presuppositions that comprise his notion of "cognitive frames." Throughout, the argument is turgid and unnecessarily difficult to understand. Then, for the most part and none too soon for the grateful reader, with cognitive frames behind him, Jardine's writer's cramp disappears and his style becomes once again lucid and vigorous.

The reinterpretation of Abercrombie, Perry, Bruner, Latour, and Jardine that I have undertaken in this chapter suggests that fruitful discussion of college and university education must begin with liberating ourselves from the language and assumptions of cognition. As Latour and Woolgar put it quite pointedly, we are all still "fundamentally hampered by the legacies of a philosophical tradition."[32]

The examples explored in this chapter also imply that liberating ourselves from this tradition will not be easy. All of us have been educated for twelve to twenty-odd years in the foundational language of cognition and according to its assumptions. With few exceptions, education on cognitive principles and in cognitive terms is the only kind of education we know and the only way we know to talk about knowledge and learning.

As a result of this cognitive bias, when we see students learning judgment in groups better and faster than individually, as Abercrombie did; when students, such as Perry's informants, tell us that they learned more, faster, and better in the dorm talking with their peers than in their professors' classes; and when we see infants learning in collaboration with mothers or mother-surrogates to do things we never imagined they could do—when any one of these things happens, we have difficulty accounting for what we see, much less understanding it. We tend to treat it as an anomaly or as ancillary to the central educational issues, which, as we all know much too well, must be cognitive issues.

Abercrombie's medical students, Perry's undergraduates, and Bruner's infants all continue to speak to us in nonstandard discourse when they tell us about the social nature of knowledge and learning. Each invites us to engage in a challenging and somewhat threatening boundary conversation. Only recently and tenuously have foundational assumptions about knowledge and learning begun to lose force. Only recently have we begun to develop the means to replace traditional, foundational cognitive epistemology with another understanding of knowledge equally powerful and more appropriate to present and future needs of American college and university education. In the next chapter we will examine some recent efforts to do just that.

CHAPTER ELEVEN

A Plurality of Forces, Desires, and
Not Wholly Commensurable Visions

The debate about knowledge and learning, and by extension about college and university education, is a long-standing one. Traditionally it has been carried on in cognitive terms. During the past quarter century, however, cognitive assumptions have increasingly shown themselves to be of dubious value. A small, highly respected community of college and university teachers has tried in the past two decades or so, therefore, to put new assumptions into play. These assumptions are the less familiar nonfoundational ones sometimes called "postmodern" or "poststructuralist." This chapter, like the last one, is a critique of the debate about knowledge, learning, and the nature of college and university education. But whereas Chapter 10 is about how this debate has been carried on in cognitive terms, this chapter is about how it is now being carried on in nonfoundational terms.

The debate has recently changed direction abruptly, in part because many people now tend to agree that the world is undergoing profound change and that college and university education based on traditional, cognitive assumptions (sometimes in this context called "structuralist") no longer prepares students adequately to live in it. Because the most threatening issues in the world today are multicultural, our ability to communicate instantaneously and threaten massively one another's lives has made effective interdependence a necessity everywhere.

This issue comes to a head for most college and university teachers when they have to confront highly visible, unavoidable, and, to many, disturbing changes in the class, gender, race, and ethnic background of the American undergraduate population. For some, that confrontation occurs (as it did for me in the experience described in Chapter 1) when their college or university changes its admissions policies. For others it happens when all-male or all-female colleges go coed; when regional populations begin to include large numbers of new migrant or immigrant groups; when a foundation or the government offers funds to study or provide academic services for (that is, to acknowledge actively the existence of) diverse groups already in their student population; when courts enforce civil rights laws banning "separate but equal" facilities; when interest groups such as women, gays, the elderly, the physically handicapped, or the poor assert their rights; and even, on campuses still predominantly homogeneous, when professional pressure to diversify faculty and student populations, or public interest in doing so, finally hits home.

Stated in nonfoundational terms, the central educational question raised by these changes is, How can college and university teachers help students renegotiate their relations with the communities they come from while at the same time helping students reacculturate themselves into the communities they hope to join? This issue is just as important for students entering the larger community of diverse peoples from prosperous middle-class suburbs or from ethnically homogeneous, urban, working-class neighborhoods as it was for (say) a child of Mexican immigrants, such as Richard Rodriguez, or a child of black middle-class parents in the segregated South, such as Supreme Court Justice Thurgood Marshall, entering a community of highly educated, prosperous, white middle-class professionals. The issue is important because it is what Philip Roth calls "the quintessential American cultural task," which is "to negotiate . . . between the demands of the past . . . and the demands of the future."[1]

To date, college and university teachers tend to answer this question about renegotiation and reacculturation exclusively in curricular terms. What they need to do, they assume, is make sure that every student will become familiar with some of the texts and artifacts prized by peoples not embraced by the Western cultural tradition. This is not an unreasonable response, but it is a foundational one. It assumes a basic tenet of liberal humanism: empathy. Empathy is the process by which liberal humanists traditionally believe we understand other cultures. We imagine ourselves "into" the people we encounter or "into" characters we read about, and thus "see the world as they see it." It is a prime instance of what I have called in Chapter 6 the elisionist element in cognitive thought.

Most college- and university-educated people can recall, for example, being asked in humanities or literature courses to try to put themselves in Achilles's place or to empathize first with Ishmael and then Ahab. Lionel Trilling tells us that instructions of this sort assume that the "fictive persons" rendered in the texts we read can be experienced as if they had actual existence, as if their "values" were available to assessment, as if their destinies bore upon one's own, and as if their styles of behavior and feeling must inevitably have a consequence in one's own behavior and feeling.[2]

Assumptions of this nature lead humanities and literature departments to debate "the canon"—the list of books they believe undergraduates should read and discuss—and lead college and university administrations to establish women's studies and ethnic studies programs. The goal is to provide access to treasured texts and artifacts outside the Western cultural mainstream. It is an admirable goal, and many faculties and administrations strive with admirable honesty and integrity to reach it. Curricular decisions such as these are an important part of determining the direction of a college or university education. That is why, behaving typically as a college teacher, in Chapter 12 of this book I offer my own (presumably nonfoundational) curricular answer to the question about how colleges and universities can appropriately renegotiate and reacculturate their students.

But for many reasons, some explained in Chapters 4, 7, and 8 and some explained here, traditional assumptions about the nature of knowledge no longer give college and university teachers the direction they need as they fulfill their curricular responsibilities. Worse, to address the question through curriculum development alone seriously misconstrues the nature of the issue and underestimates its complexity.

Rodriguez himself, along with many others, has amply testified that the process that the question refers to—renegotiating membership in communities we come from while reacculturating ourselves into communities we hope to join—is a kind of covalent negotiation. It is not "assimilation." As Philip Roth maintains, that "is much too weak a word" to describe the process accurately because it has "too many connotations of deference and passive submission." Roth calls the negotiation instead "a two-way engagement . . . an interchange . . . an amalgamation of values and traits that [constitutes] nothing less than the invention of a new American type, the citizen with multiple allegiances."[3] Janus-like, the principals look anxiously in two directions at once. Their left hand always knows, distressingly, what their right hand is doing; whatever either hand does influences what the other hand does and can do. That is why the negotiation requires a high degree of linguistic flexibility and an ability to work interdependently across community boundaries on complex, intellectually and emotionally demanding issues.

Today that negotiation is occurring in classrooms throughout America—primary and secondary school classrooms as well as college and university ones. But college and university teachers are just now beginning to understand how the basic premises of the kind of education they are responsible for, college and university education, must change in order to answer the questions raised by negotiation and reacculturation.

The most pervasive effect that the increasing cultural diversity of college and university students has had so far is a tendency to redraw traditional academic and professional disciplinary boundaries. During the 1970s and 1980s, many ambitious college and university teachers began to challenge, modify, and in some cases even abandon the methodology and subject matter of the traditional academic and professional disciplines they were trained in. Besides the ethnic studies movement, typifying these changes were the deconstructionist and feminist movements in literary criticism, the nonfoundational understanding of knowledge in its various manifestations represented by Thomas Kuhn and his followers, a refiguration of thought from largely Western images to more diverse ones, and a general tendency to demote Western culture from a position of unquestioned preeminence.

Having challenged traditional disciplinary assumptions, however, college and university teachers engaged in this postmodern or poststructuralist discourse ran headlong into another, related challenge. Their colleagues and the educated general public began to ask: What would constitute poststructuralist college or university teaching or poststructuralist college and university education? How can communities of college and university teachers who maintain poststructuralist assumptions induct new members—their students—into those communities? In terms of conceptual as well as class, race, gender, and ethnic commitments, how can college and university teachers help students cope with the anguish generated by the kind of negotiation-out-of and reacculturation-into reported, for example, in Rodriguez's widely read book?

Thomas Kuhn led the way toward poststructuralist, or nonfoundational social constructionist, thought, but then fudged questions like these. Kuhn argued that scientific knowledge is not the objective truth we thought it was. It was constructed by communities of knowledgeable peers. Even so, he then claimed, nothing in the education of scientists needed to be changed. Partly as a result of this educational position of Kuhn's, scientists more or less turned their backs on the issue, with the results taken up in Chapter 8. Similarly, while arguing that knowledge in no field of study leads to universal truth as Western culture always presumed it did, most college and university teachers have continued to teach in ways that imply that nothing needs to be changed in college classrooms but curriculum: the books students read, the pictures they look at, the music they listen to, and the questions teachers ask about them.

Nevertheless, a few eminent scholars, most of them in the humanities, have addressed the issue of education appropriate to college and university students in the late twentieth century. The results of this effort are limited, however, by the fact that those involved in it are not all equally aware of the implications for college and university teaching of adopting nonfoundational assumptions. Most of them evade some or all of the social implications in the terms they adopt. The element that most overlook or, when they are aware of it, address only obliquely, is the key element in the nonfoundational understanding of the authority of knowledge: interdependence among peers.

The first and most thorough of these poststructural commentaries on college and university education is Stanley Fish's book, *Is There a Text in This Class? The Authority of Interpretive Communities.* This book records the intellectual and professional odyssey, beginning in 1970, that transformed Fish's views from foundational to nonfoundational. The central issue addressed in Fish's book is the central issue addressed in this one, the authority of knowledge: as Fish puts it, "what gives us the right to be . . . right." Fish argues that the authority of knowledge is "situated": "The thoughts [we] can think and the mental operations [we] can perform," he maintains, "have their source in some or other interpretive community." As a result, we ourselves are "as much a product of that community (acting as an extension [*i.e.,* as a member] of it) as the meanings it enables [us] to produce."[4]

Fish's book has its origin in his practice, both as a literary critic and as a college and university teacher. As a critic, Fish explores in rigorously nonfoundational terms the notion that we "construct" any text we read, reading there what the interpretive community we belong to constrains us to read. Just as, in Kuhn's view, to learn science is to join a community of scientists of a certain persuasion and, in Rorty's view, to learn anything at all is to join a community of those who socially justify their beliefs in a certain way, Fish says that we learn to read by joining the community of those who "interpret" in one way rather than another. To be a member of such a community is to be "situated" in "a structure of assumptions, of practices understood to be relevant in relation to purposes and goals that are already in place," but that are "not abstract and independent but social."[5]

In promulgating these nonfoundational literary critical views, Fish sketches a teaching method that is in many respects consistent with them. In some parts of his sketch of nonfoundational teaching Fish slips into foundational terminology, just as (in Chapter 10) we have seen

Jardine, Knorr-Cetina, and Latour doing. But most of these slips can with little loss be translated into nonfoundational terms consistent with Fish's literary critical views. For example, Fish says that his goal as a teacher is to "[break] down the barriers between students and the knowledge they must acquire."[6] This sentence construes knowledge as an objective entity, students as subjective entities, and teaching as an elisionist effort of overcoming barriers to communication between them. In more rigorously nonfoundational terms, Fish's goal would be described as helping students negotiate boundaries between the interpretive communities that they are already members of—for the most part their home communities incorporating the class, racial, ethnic, and gender presuppositions constructed by those home communities—and the community they aspire to join by taking Fish's course.

His procedure for reaching this goal is to identify "knowledge with something that [his students] are already doing, and then [ask] them to become self-conscious about what they do in the hope that they can learn to do it better." Or, Fish says, putting it somewhat differently, teachers have to "back up to some point at which there [is] a shared agreement as to what [is] reasonable to say so that a new and wider basis for agreement [can] be fashioned."[7] He assumes, of course, what he could assume with considerable impunity where he was teaching at the time (Johns Hopkins), that there would always be some such shared agreement ready to hand in any group of students that he would be likely to teach. Had he been teaching at, for example, the City University of New York during open admissions or a similar institution, he might have found a point of reasonable shared agreement harder to come by.

Again, stated in nonfoundational terms, Fish's procedure is this: having identified knowledge as constructed by the interpretive communities that students are already members of, he helps students make a transition to membership in another community, one in which self-conscious practice is part of the knowledge it constructs. What college and university teachers do in general, by this token, is begin by helping students discover the socially constructed "repertoire" of the "situation"-constituted communities they already belong to. Then they help students "expand" that repertoire by renegotiating their membership in the communities they come from, while at the same time they help students negotiate their way into another "situation"-constituted community, the community they hope to join. The process Fish describes is therefore similar to the one we saw Perry's undergraduate informants describe in Chapter 10. Teaching does not effect "a rupture but a modification of the interests and concerns [as well as assumptions and practices] that are already in place."[8]

This "modification" involves, first, engaging students in interpretation according to the rules and conventions of the interpretive communities they already belong to, with the goal of helping them understand that they already know a good deal; second, helping them describe that familiar interpretive practice in a transitional language (of the sort described in Chapter 4), derived in part from the constituting language of the communities they are already members of; and third, helping them apply the same procedure again, but this time using the language of the interpretive community that the teacher represents, the community they aspire to join that Fish alludes to with the phrase "do it better." This new language, then, provides students with what Fish calls a greater "awareness" than they have had before of the "probable (and hidden) complexity . . . [of] the workings of language."[9] Becoming aware of the hidden complexity of language is Fish's phrase for acquiring the capacity for the kind of intense, flexible linguistic engagement I explore elsewhere in this book under the rubric of translation.

In short, for Fish, college and university teaching is reacculturative. The central issue is helping students to establish their membership in familiar communities on new terms and helping them become fluent in the language of the communities that their teachers represent. Fish acknowledges that it is up to college and university teachers to determine what students must learn so that they will be able to conform to "the standards and accepted practices that [are] in force" in their teachers' classrooms.[10] Teachers make that determination because they are the sole representatives in their classrooms of relevant, larger, more authoritative knowledge communities—their own disciplinary communities and those even more populous communities of "the liberally educated," of writers of standard written English, and so on. At the same time, teachers have to acknowledge, as Fish does, that those standards and practices, understood nonfoundationally, do not have inherent or universal value. They are of value only insofar as they constitute the communities that students join by virtue of learning them. They are the languages of the interpretive communities, cultures, or "situations" that they seek admission to by undertaking a college or university education.

As strong and well worked out as Fish's nonfoundational position is, however, he is ambivalent about the college and university teacher's obligation to foster reacculturation into these communities. He demonstrates this ambivalence in several ways. For example, he is clearly talking about reacculturation out of a community constituted by a language that allows only relatively unself-conscious conversation, and reacculturation into a community constituted by a language that allows conversation of relatively greater self-consciousness. But he masks this reacculturative process by saying merely that students learn to do the same thing "better." Or, again, in one mood he readily acknowledges the authority that teachers exercise in order to fulfill their disciplinary and institutional obligation to foster reacculturation, that is, authority derived (as explained in Chapter 8) from their dual membership in their college or university community and in their disciplinary one. Students learn what they know, he says, "because they are told by their teachers." Yet in another mood, Fish denies that complex authority when he describes "the teacher's classroom authority" as an "accidental fact."[11]

Fish's ambivalence also appears in his limited recognition of the complexity of reacculturation. He makes the correct and pregnant observation that "stability in the makeup of interpretive communities . . . is always temporary. . . . Interpretive communities grow larger and decline, and individuals move from one to another." No one is "trapped forever in the categories of understanding at one's disposal (or the categories at whose disposal one is)."[12] Yet Fish does not relate this social fluidity and the instability of knowledge communities to what happens when students change "situations" with the help of a teacher or their peers. That is, he does not relate it to changing social relations among students and between teachers and students.

Perhaps most tellingly, Fish demonstrates his ambivalence to the reacculturative implications of the nonfoundational understanding of knowledge by reserving his most rigorous use of social constructionist terms and most rigorous nonfoundational analysis for discussing literary critical practice. He is thorough, consistent, and clear about the relevance of interpretive communities to literary critical reading. But he describes his teaching method in mixed terms—foundational and nonfoundational. He therefore leaves the nonfoundational implications of his classroom practice blurred, confused, and inadequately explored. For example, besides speaking, as I have pointed out, about "barriers between students and . . . knowledge" as if knowledge and student selves were foundational entities, he also talks about increased awareness of the complexities of language while at the same time talking about students acquiring "a mind . . . more sensitized." And he talks about what it means to "acquire" knowledge as if knowledge were a species of property exchangeable among individuals acting on their own instead of being, as Kuhn puts it, "the common property of a group or else nothing at all."[13]

Despite these unreconciled and unexplored elements in Fish's book, his nonfoundational treatment of educational issues is a good deal more coherent and thoroughly developed than most other attempts to explain the role that poststructuralist thought can play in college and university education. Some contributions to this discussion are affected only marginally by a nonfoundational social constructionist understanding of the nature and authority of knowledge. Others are more deeply affected by it through a commitment to postmodern literary critical notions such as deconstruction, feminist theory, psychoanalysis, or some combination of these. Most appear in two collections of essays, *The Pedagogical Imperative*, edited by Barbara Johnson, and *Theory in the Classroom*, edited by Cary Nelson. More recent, more coherent, and in general somewhat better informed are Mary Louise Pratt's call for "the pedagogical arts of the contact zone" and Gerald Graff's rediscovery that reading is a species of conversation.[14]

Authors in the Johnson and Nelson volumes are frequently pushed off balance by foundational assumptions embedded in the language we normally use to talk about knowledge and education, just as we have seen that Fish (in this chapter) and Latour and Jardine (in Chapter 10) can occasionally be. Foundational assumptions and foundational language, unanalyzed and unbracketed, appear most often in these essays as those traditional heroes of the foundational melodrama in its educational manifestation, form and content.[15] For example, the essays describe teaching as involving "methods of reading or interpretation" applied to "historical and philological facts" (DeMan); as "a process" or "procedures" giving "access to information" (Felman); as a "revolutionary consciousness" that reveals the contingency of politics and economics (Ryan); as "principles and evaluative criteria" interpreting "a restricted set of objects" (Schroeder); or as "an interpretive strategy" applied to a "subject matter" called "popular culture" (Grossberg).

Some essays in these books also pay obeisance unawares to the universal forms and other absolutes believed foundationally to lie behind or beneath knowledge and learning. One of these is Truth, as in " 'the true nature of things' " that, platonically, "one does not know" (Johnson). Another is the Inner Self, as in the notion that teaching should involve "an intersubjective rhetoric" (Wells) or an effort to effect "penetration of interiority" (Gallop).[16]

These lapses into foundational language in talking about college and university teaching have a common source. The teachers whose work appears in these volumes have a thorough grasp of the fields of study in which many of them have built significant academic reputations. But to the issues of authority of knowledge and learning implicit in teaching and scholarly research, most of them, like Fish, do not apply the same degree of rigor or self-awareness. The result in most cases is a nonfoundational understanding of college and university teaching that is inconsistent and insufficiently examined. Many of these writers sense the problem and describe it in the disciplinary language they have at hand. But most of them offer little more than idealized, highly generalized, fragmented, or severely abbreviated solutions, further compromised by foundational terms.

The essays are nevertheless important for what might be called their proto-nonfoundational educational thought: ideas that manage almost to escape the influence of latent foundationalism and thereby advance our understanding of the relationship between the authority of knowledge and the authority of teachers. Constance Penley introduces students to "nonauthoritative knowledge . . . resulting from a collective endeavor" and explains how "the social system rationalizes ['natural'] qualities into structures of inequality." Richard Terdiman encourages teachers to make the "transparency" of "social interests, structures, positions" visibly opaque and thereby identify and understand them as a "system governing meaning." Vincent Leitch asks teachers to analyze "the constituting powers of *language*." And S. P. Mohanty describes his effort to lead students "to question the self-evidence of meanings" so as to "disrupt" the "flawless discourses of knowledge," the teacher's as well as their own.[17]

Many of these implications of a nonfoundational understanding of college and university education are synthesized by Shoshana Felman. Felman's psychoanalytical terms illuminate the integral relationship between the authority of knowledge and the authority of teachers by demonstrating the relationship between (socially constructed) institutional authority and (also socially constructed) emotion. That is, Felman explores the relationship between, on the one hand, political and social interests constructed and manifested in language and, on the other, deeply rooted personal needs similarly constructed and similarly manifested in language.

The problem with traditional college and university teaching in Felman's view, following Freud and Lacan, is that like many "discursive human relations" it is informed with an illusion of mastery, self-sufficiency, and self-possession — Barbara Johnson's "One-ness of individual mastery." Because most teachers and students alike remain ignorant of the source of this illusion, and of its overwhelming force, they conspire to make their ignorance an "integral part of the very *structure* of knowledge." In these terms, then, the source of the authority of teachers is students' willingness — indeed their desire — to bestow authority upon their teachers, and their teachers' willingness—indeed their desire—to have students bestow upon them that authority. In this matter as in many others dealt with in this book, only those who are faultless can cast the first stone with impunity. Still, it may be worth pointing out that dependence on this illusion of mastery, self-sufficiency, and self-possession is a probable cause of the tendency among the writers I discuss in this chapter to evade some of the social implications of adopting nonfoundational assumptions when talking about college and university teaching.[18]

Felman's position is that in order to change their understanding of the structure of knowledge, college and university teachers have to undercut these forces that entrench hierarchical authority. To do that, she says, they have to begin to regard what they do, not as "the transmission of ready-made knowledge" but "the creation of a new *condition* of knowledge." This new condition has to restrain the conspiracy of students and teachers to bestow and welcome authority. One way college and university teachers can contribute to creating this new condition is by using their "knowledge of the functioning of language, of symbolic structures, of the signifier, knowledge at once derived from—and directed towards—interpretation." Here once again, becoming aware of the hidden complexity of language and developing linguistic flexibility is central, not only to teaching the humanities and social sciences but also, as we have seen in Chapter 9, to teaching the sciences as well.[19]

In turning teaching and learning into interpretive acts, Felman argues, teachers would no longer understand them as exchanges between something that goes on inside teachers' heads and something that goes on inside students' heads. Instead, they would understand them as the sociolinguistic process that realigns social relations between teacher and student and among students, so that both teachers and students learn new speech. That is to say, to adopt the analogous terms used by Richard Rorty and Clifford Geertz, both teachers and students would learn to "speak differently," to "redescribe," to "translate." Under those conditions, Felman explains, knowledge

> is not a *substance* but a structural dynamic: it is not *contained* by any individual but comes about out of the mutual apprenticeship between two partially unconscious speeches which both say more than they know. Dialogue is thus the radical condition of learning and of knowledge, the analytically constitutive condition through which ignorance becomes structurally informative; knowledge is essentially, irreducibly dialogic. "No knowledge," writes Lacan, "can be supported or transported by one alone."[20]

Teachers and students learn new speech by interpreting each other's contribution to the conversation. They translate what Felman calls their own "texts"—what I have called here the language of the communities to which they belong—into others' "texts," the language of some other community. This learned ability to interpret and translate, Felman insists, cannot be generally or universally applied. It is specific to the languages of particular communities, to particular local "texts." College and university teaching must therefore somehow be tailored, or teachers must create conditions in which students can tailor it, to the local languages of the particular communities to which the teachers and students involved in any given case belong.

But just as teachers cannot generalize or universalize their "knowledge of the functioning of language, of symbolic structures," neither can teachers or students release themselves wholly (except, perhaps, Felman implies, through psychoanalysis) from the emotional heritage of local authority relationships constituted by their old speech, their old "texts," the languages that constitute the communities they come from. Membership in the communities we come from (and here Fish would certainly agree) can only be loosened, realigned, renegotiated; it cannot be canceled. You can take the boy out of Brooklyn, as the saying goes, but you can't take Brooklyn out of the boy.

Significantly for the potential pace of change in college and university education of the type described in this book (about which it would not do to raise one's hopes too high), the communities that are among the most difficult and painful to renegotiate membership in—because they provide the greatest comfort and security—are foundational communities of cognitive belief in "grounded" knowledge. "The chief instrument of cultural change," as Rorty puts it, is abandoning "old vocabularies" and acquiring "a talent for speaking differently," but this new speech "has to be constructed out of little pieces."[21] At the boundaries between the language communities they represent, students and teachers, like Latour's bird-naming mother and child, Perry's confused undergraduates, and Kuhn's scientists facing a theory crisis, whom we noticed in Chapter 7, learn new speech first by working painstakingly together to construct a transitional working language so that they can carry on their conversation and do the task that confronts them.

The example Felman chooses is an extreme one, but it is apt, and it has the advantage of presenting the process in microcosm. Her example is the boundary between the communities represented by psychoanalyst and analysand. Traditionally—that is, foundationally—a psychoanalyst is thought to bring a conceptual structure to bear on the analysand's emotional chaos or dysfunctional emotional structure. As Felman construes it, however, psychoanalysis is reacculturation. It is therefore an unusual but representative example of collaborative learning. Analyst and analysand are members of different communities: the analyst belongs to a professional discipline constituted by that community's "text," and the analysand belongs to one or more communities of the uncomfortably neurotic and socially dysfunctional constituted by the "texts," the familiar interpretive languages, of those communities. Together, the two form a tiny transitional community in which both learn new speech. They translate across the boundary that separates them by applying a "knowledge of the functioning of language, of symbolic structures," or, in Clifford Geertz's parlance, they display "the logic of [others'] ways of putting [things] in the locutions of" their own ways of putting things.[22]

Thinking of college and university teaching in this way, Felman argues, makes it possible for teaching to "subvert itself" sufficiently to negotiate temporary local release from the emotional legacy passed on by the hierarchical authority relationships inherent in family life and thus establish the new "condition" of knowledge that she calls for.[23]

Jean-François Lyotard's essay in Johnson's collection describes a classroom event that seems to illustrate this process, although it is certainly not a model to be emulated. The event involved a "fight" between two groups of students, similar to conflicts that many American college and university students and teachers experienced during the student strikes of the late sixties and early seventies. As a classroom teacher, Lyotard turned the "fight" into an exercise in nonfoundational learning. He did that by transforming two sets of vertical authority relations—the unselfaware compliance of the students in Lyotard's class and the unself-aware conformity of the platoon of striking students—into a horizontal conversation among peers.[24]

As Lyotard tells the tale, one group of students was dutifully engaged in rhetorical analysis following a lesson on "the operators in persuasive discourse." The other group, the strikers, was a "commando unit" of students who broke into their classroom "armed with clubs, shouting that [Lyotard and his students] were breaking the strike." A heated conversation ensued "between . . . the besiegers and the besieged." At a crucial moment in the conversation, Lyotard applied his "knowledge of the functioning of language, of symbolic structures" and of their "probable (and hidden) complexity." He asked the members of each group to display the logic of their own way of putting things in the locutions of the other group: he called for new speech. Specifically, he demanded that all the students—strikers and nonstrikers alike—distinguish between peaceably "study[ing] persuasive discourse, especially political discourse" in a classroom and forcibly "occupy[ing] the workplace [as strikers] and [thinking] together about the discourses which persuade or dissuade us from striking."

They could make this distinction, Lyotard suggested, if they "used certain words . . . a certain syntax . . . and certain names." Meanwhile he led both besieged and besieging students to see that the analysis involved in making this distinction would be complex and risky and that it could easily be misconstrued or trivialized ("Question: In your eyes how many 'Marxes' per sentence would it take for [the classroom students'] discourse to become one of active strikers?").

The result of the conversation, Lyotard reports, was that "most of the assailants backed off, admitting that we were as much 'out of it' as they were." That is, strikers and nonstrikers arrived at a consensus that went beyond the two first-order alternatives: agreement to act in concert (the strikers' demand) or a standoff. They agreed instead that, as a rhetorical gesture, both striking and talking about striking could, under different conditions, in different "situations," be equally effectual or equally ineffectual. The educationally significant issue was how language (for example, conversation among students, persuasive discourse, or political polemics) and paralinguistic symbolic structures (in this case, wielding clubs, shouting slogans, and disrupting classes) may all be part and parcel of the structure and condition of knowledge.

Because all of the students came to terms with this issue, the class turned out to be, in Lyotard's judgment, "worthwhile." Nonfoundationally speaking, the class involved an open-ended task that students accomplished collaboratively or interdependently in a way that brought them into a state of provisional consensus. The task was constructively open-ended because, although it seemed to offer a simple choice (to strike or not to strike), several pieces of the puzzle turned out to be inappropriately shaped for some of the spaces they were intended to fill ("How many Marxes per sentence would it take . . . ?").

It goes without saying, perhaps, that in offering this example I am not recommending siege by student strikers brandishing clubs as a preferred condition for teaching of any kind, much less collaborative learning. Nor do I want to suggest that nonfoundational teaching depends on serendipity. More typical of nonfoundational teaching at its best are carefully designed, replicable collaborative learning tasks undertaken by stable, well-organized consensus groups (as described in Chapter 2). But Lyotard's story does seem to illustrate several aspects of effective nonfoundational teaching, some of which we have not otherwise had occasion to discuss. For example, it illustrates Joan De Jean's observation that nonfoundational teaching may involve "a form of fiction-making" that selects or miniaturizes experience. It reorganizes social relations among students and between teachers and students by posing a task, staging an "experiential" scene, even extemporaneously "fictionalizing" an unforeseen event, as in Lyotard's story, in order to put serendipity to pedagogical use.[25]

The story also illustrates Angela Moger's comparison between the effects of teaching and narration. Both can be subject to productive misunderstanding. It may often matter less than we suppose whether students or audiences get precisely the point that teachers or narrators intend. Lyotard's class was "worthwhile," even though the strikers left with the grudging parting shot that they were all (themselves included) "out of it." " 'Lessons,' " Moger contends, "have as little to do with truth and falsehood as stories do . . . [and] instruction produces no greater awareness of how things 'really are' . . . than does fiction."[26]

And Lyotard's story can be read also as illustrating the teaching procedure that Fish recommends. Lyotard began by engaging the students in interpretation according to the rules and conventions of the diverse interpretive communities they were already members of. He asked them to apply familiar and available analytical terms (certain words, certain syntax, certain names) to the local "text"—in this case, the event—at hand. Then he brought them to a worthwhile conclusion by wittily guiding them to apply more sophisticated analytical tools to the event (in this case, *reductio ad absurdum*) in order to increase their awareness of the hidden complexities of language and their "situation."

Finally, Lyotard's story illuminates some perhaps unanticipated implications of Mary Louis Pratt's objection to traditional teaching in which teachers "feel that their teaching has been most successful when they have eliminated" their students' "unsolicited oppositional discourse, parody, resistance, [and] critique." Certainly the goal of traditional lecturing is, as Pratt puts it, to forge "an ad hoc community, homogeneous with respect to [the lecturer's] own words," to which oppositional discourse and parody are antithetical, with "a monologue that rings equally coherent, revealing, and true for all." And it is certainly possible to read Lyotard's story as suggesting that he allied himself with this traditional goal by striving to "homogenize" the community of students he engaged with.[27]

But Lyotard's translational response to the invading student strikers, the strikers' ultimate response to him, and the analysis of boundary or nonstandard discourse between teachers and students discussed in Chapter 4 all suggest that the case may be somewhat more complex. The issue may not be so much homogeneity gained (or not gained), but the manner in which it is striven for. Even for contact-zone pedagogy to work, teachers may sometimes need to find ways to minimize or eliminate students' oppositional discourse, parody, resistance, and critique. On the other hand, for contact-zone pedagogy to work the shears may sometimes have to cut both ways. Students may occasionally have to act collaboratively to construct for themselves the authority to eliminate or minimize teachers' unsolicited, oppositional discourse, parody, resistance, and critique, as we saw peer tutors doing in Chapter 5 and as the strikers do eventually in Lyotard's anecdote.

Lyotard's classroom story reminds us furthermore of the similarity between lessons and stories that Angela Moger points out. Moger suggests that both lessons and stories have a great deal to do with the ways in which communities construct knowledge. Both require linguistic flexibility and awareness of the hidden complexity of language and other symbolic structures. Both depend on the way certain people deploy certain words, certain syntax, certain texts. Both college and university classroom lessons and stories disrupt flawless discourses of knowledge in order to produce awareness of the constituting powers of language and the social systems governing meaning.

It might be said, then, that when we read these essays on college and university pedagogy that I have been discussing as exercises in proto-nonfoundational educational thinking, they turn out to have three things in common. First, and very much to the good, they describe college and university teaching as a process involving some sort of constructive sociolinguistic exercise on the part of both teachers and students that breaches community boundaries. Felman's and Lyotard's students learn new speech. De Jean, Fish, Graff, Moger, and Pratt all create conditions under which their students cannot avoid interpretation—or rather, conditions under which both teacher and students have to construe whatever they do as interpretation.

Second, however, most of them still tend to regard the new speech involved as "subject matter" or a body of expertise. Felman calls this expertise or subject matter "knowledge of the functioning of language, of symbolic structures." Fish calls it "the probable (and hidden) complexity" of "the workings of language." Felman construes it in psychoanalytical terms, Lyotard construes it in the terms of rhetorical analysis, De Jean and Moger construe it in terms of the literary analysis, Fish construes it in terms of "the authority of interpretive communities." Focusing on this element tends to blunt the edge of the authority-of-knowledge issue. The question left incompletely answered in every case is, How exactly are *students* to acquire the authority implicit in this linguistic flexibility?

And third, although in each case there is some awareness that college and university students are traveling across boundaries from countries where the languages familiar to them are always spoken into lands marked "No Familiar Language Spoken Here," every writer cited leaves somewhat vague or unspecified the social (as opposed to cognitive or "mental") nature of that journey. Only Graff specifies unequivocally that learning is some sort of "collective endeavor" or collaborative, constructive, sociolinguistic exercise, by observing that "reading books with comprehension, making arguments, writing papers, and making comments in a class discussion are *social* activities [that] involve entering into a cultural or disciplinary conversation."[28]

By recognizing the predicament that students find themselves in when they are plunged into a world composed of a multiplicity of communities rather than a single, familiar, coherent one, Barbara Johnson acknowledges the complexity of this conversation. She begins by asking a rhetorical question that brings to mind the resistance of science teachers to raising questions of scientific uncertainty alluded to in Chapter 9: Is not the way that college and university teachers

> ask *some* questions always correlative with [their] ways of teaching [students] *not to ask*—indeed, to be unconscious of—others? Does the educational system exist in order to promulgate knowledge, or is its main function rather to universalize a society's tacit agreement about what it has decided it does not and cannot know?[29]

To challenge that tacit agreement, Johnson says, college and university teachers have to displace "the One-ness of individual mastery."[30] They have to acknowledge that the sources of their own authority, like their students' ability to understand them, are diverse. Both involve a "plurality of forces and desires" represented by diverse genders, races, classes, and ethnic backgrounds and interests. In order to institutionalize this "plurality," as John Trimbur has argued, college and university teachers have to understand and respect the sociolinguistic ways in which diverse knowledge communities—their own and others'—are constructed and maintained.[31] Or, as Bruno Latour puts it, a student joins "a 'culture,' shares a 'paradigm,' or belongs to a 'society' " through an active process of "dissenting . . . from the outside," and by being "confronted by a choice about which group to belong to," a choice that involves "many little [and we might add, in some instances not so little] clashes between beliefs" maintained by those groups.[32]

College and university teachers therefore have to find ways in which students, who aspire to join the knowledge communities that their teachers represent, can take an active part in the intellectual negotiation by which beliefs are socially justified in those communities. They have to teach in ways appropriate to the source of their authority as represent-atives of the communities of socially justified belief of which they are responsible members. They have to help students acquire a sense of the authority of their own knowledge by exercising the craft of interde-pendence among themselves as student-peers. They have to help stu-dents develop the ability to interact socially over complex, intellectually demanding issues, thus integrating social and intellectual maturity. In-evitably, these implicitly conflicting needs involve college and university teachers in professional issues of the sort discussed in Chapter 8. And just as inevitably they lead them to collaborative learning.

Still another writer who has addressed educational issues in a non-foundational way is the cultural anthropologist Clifford Geertz. In a revealing controversy with Lionel Trilling about the premises of hu-manistic thought during the early 1970s, Geertz challenged a basic tenet of liberal humanism: empathy. In an essay written in response to Geertz, Trilling described empathy succinctly and characteristically in the pas-sage quoted early in this chapter. Traditionally, liberal humanists believe that they understand other cultures through "imaginative engagement" or "sympathetic imagination." Geertz challenged this foundational, lib-eral humanist assumption by arguing that empathic intuitive response is not a universal human experience. It is a socially constructed notion generated by a particular cultural community, the one we call the Western liberal humanist tradition.

Geertz shocked Trilling by rejecting as "magical" the belief that anyone can "perceive what [other people] perceive" by empathically "imagining [themselves] someone else . . . and then seeing what [they] thought." Rather than trying to see the experience of others "within the framework of their own" conceptions, "what the extolled 'empathy' in fact usually comes down to" Geertz claims, is "ethnocentric sentimentalism." At this stage in his argument, in fact, Geertz agrees with Fish's nonfoundational position at its most conservative. When we do try to place ourselves "inside" people of cultures other than our own and see things from their point of view, we inevitably wind up still seeing the world from our own point of view and calling it theirs.

Geertz does see value, however, in trying to get close to knowing how other peoples "really" see the world, and he explains how we can do that without "empathy." Instead of trying to perceive *as* others per-ceive, we can try to discover "what [people] perceive 'with'—or 'by means of' or 'through.'" That is, our goal is not to construct accounts of the sense *we* make of other persons and other groups of people. Our goal is (once again) to redescribe or "translate." We construct accounts of how other people make sense to themselves by discovering "the symbolic forms—words, images, institutions, behaviors—in terms of which . . . people actually [represent] themselves to themselves and to one another." In doing so we become, not Trilling's empathic liberal humanists, but Roth's citizens who maintain multiple allegiances.[33]

This alternative to "sympathetic imagination," transformed into classroom activities, can help students cope with what Geertz calls "the hallmark of modern consciousness . . . its enormous multiplicity" or "the radical variousness of the way we think now." This educational goal gives college and university teachers a clear direction. It is to integrate cultural life by

> making it possible for people inhabiting different worlds to have a genuine, and reciprocal, impact upon one another. If it is true that insofar as there is general consciousness it consists of the interplay of a disorderly crowd of not wholly commensurable visions, then the vitality of that consciousness depends upon creating the conditions under which such interplay will occur. And for that, the first step is surely to accept the depth of the differences; the second to understand what these differences are; and the third to construct some sort of vocabulary in which they can be publicly formulated.[34]

This book is addressed in one way or another to goals very much like these. The next chapter will suggest how they may possibly be met to some degree through curriculum design.

CHAPTER TWELVE

A Nonfoundational Curriculum

College and university education should help students renegotiate their membership in the knowledge communities they come from while it helps them reacculturate themselves into the academic communities they have chosen to join. The communities they have chosen to join are represented on campus by their teachers. What college and university teachers do when they design a curriculum, therefore, is choose the communities that they want their students to join.

How, then, should college and university teachers approach designing a curriculum that assumes a nonfoundational social constructionist understanding of knowledge and in which the goal is to induct students into knowledge communities where human interdependence is understood to be the norm? The answer is best described as a generalization of the discussion of collaborative learning tasks seen in Chapter 2. The point of departure in designing such a nonfoundational curriculum is not any knowledge community's common ground, a liberal education "core," or some canon of treasured texts. It is the notion of "knowledge communities" itself and the ways in which human beings negotiate and renegotiate knowledge within and among those communities. The goal would be to help students understand their academic studies—of mathematics, chemistry, sociology, English, whatever—*as* reacculturation, and specifically as reacculturation into communities in which knowledge is a construct of the community's constituting language or form of discourse. Along with this basic expertise in the workings of language and other symbolic systems, furthermore, would necessarily go basic expertise in how people live and work well together.

Such a curriculum would, first, help students recognize that they are already members in good standing of many communities of knowledgeable peers; second, help them discover which of their own and their classmates' beliefs have been socially justified, and in what ways; and third, help them explore the historical, sociolinguistic nature of knowledge.

In accordance with Stanley Fish's notion that teaching begins by identifying "knowledge with something that [students] are already doing" (discussed in Chapter 11), at each point in a curriculum of this kind teachers would select examples to be studied from the knowledge communities that students were currently members of as well as from the academic and professional disciplinary communities that teachers are members of. They would present this disciplinary subject matter and methodology as examples of how highly complex, self-aware communities of knowledgeable peers construct knowledge by justifying their beliefs socially and of how subject matter and methodology change when a community's consensus changes. These principles apply equally to courses in the sciences (discussed in Chapter 9) and courses in the humanities and social sciences.

The curriculum sketch that follows draws on my own understanding of knowledge as a sociolinguistic construct and of learning as a social, negotiated, consensual process. Its goal is to help students come to terms with cultural pluralism by demonstrating that knowledge is not a universal entity but a local one, constructed and maintained by local consensus and subject to endless conversation. The chapter ends with a nonfoundational critique of the nonfoundational curricular suggestions the chapter offers.

First, a curriculum based on a nonfoundational social constructionist understanding of knowledge would try to *help students recognize that they are already members in good standing of many communities of knowledgeable peers.* Students would consider the possibility that, as a consequence of joining new communities of college- and university-educated people, they may have to negotiate quite new relationships with the communities they come from.

To help students take these first steps in self-awareness, teachers would ask them to identify, in nonevaluative ways, their own beliefs and the beliefs of the overlapping and nested local, religious, ethnic, national, supranational, and special-interest communities they belong to. Protestant students from Kansas, Jewish students from Atlanta, Catholic students from Boston, Vietnamese from Michigan, Polish-Americans from Toledo, African-Americans from Chicago, Chicanos from Los Angeles; Southerners, Northerners, Easterners, Midwesterners, blacks and whites, women and men, middle class and poor; bridge addicts, hockey fans, oboe players, parents, police officers, balletomanes: people from potentially every conceivable community would become more aware of the beliefs held by the members of their own communities and the beliefs held by the members of other communities with whom, as it happens, they are being educated. They would try to discover what distinguishes beliefs of their own communities from those of other communities and in what respects, if any, the beliefs of most of those communities are nearly identical.

From the beginning, the curriculum would help students discover how a knowledge community defines and characterizes, and in some cases (as we noticed in Chapter 1) circumscribes, dominates, and suppresses, the lives of its members. It would provide linguistic tools that would help students diversify, individualize, and free themselves collaboratively. It would also help students learn how beliefs affect the ways in which community members and outsiders interact. The curriculum would help students make these discoveries in part through collaborative analysis and in part through self-conscious efforts to join the several disciplinary communities whose representatives are college and university teachers. Meanwhile it would give college and university teachers an opportunity to demonstrate the relationships that always exist between "popular culture" and the treasured texts of the Western or any other tradition.

It may not be easy at first to imagine undergraduate students undertaking any of this. The process may seem artificial, baroque in its complexity, and stressful. One reason it may seem so is that, in most colleges and universities today, conversation does not yet exist in which the analytical terms involved are the norm. Traditional academic study tends either to suppress or to sublimate the origins and extraacademic alliances of both students and teachers, in favor of the prevailing academic culture. This curriculum would not necessarily reverse that tendency. But it would understand communities of all kinds, academic and nonacademic, as similar in their constitution and goals.

Many colleges and universities have taken a step in this direction by finding a place on their campus and in their curriculum for peer tutoring (Chapter 5) and by including in the curriculum nontraditional cultures such as women's studies and ethnic studies: African-American, Italian-American, Hispano-American, Native American, and so on. Each of these nontraditional programs, besides being a protodiscipline with distinct community characteristics of its own, serves the valuable purpose of providing a cultural critical mass, a support group for community members, both students and faculty.

The most important difference between these nontraditional programs and the nonfoundational curriculum I am outlining here is the internal cultural coherence that the former provide. In most such programs currently, students learn to represent and speak for the community they belong to, primarily to other members of that community. Their admirable goal, as I pointed out in Chapter 11, is to provide new access to treasured texts and artifacts outside the Western cultural mainstream. But (again as pointed out in Chapter 11) these programs make the same cognitive assumptions that the Western liberal humanist curriculum makes. They assume that we understand other cultures, peoples different from ourselves, through empathy: imaginative engagement with other people, trying to "see the world as they see it."

The curriculum I am describing here, making nonfoundational assumptions of the sort that I attribute in Chapter 11 to Clifford Geertz, has a different goal. It creates conditions in which students learn to represent and speak for the communities they come from without immediate access to a familiar cultural critical mass for support. Unlike a women's studies or ethnic studies curriculum, its goals are not necessarily to provide students with the means to develop cultural identity by sharing familiar texts and artifacts with others like themselves and to defend themselves against prejudicial assaults by outsiders, however worthwhile these goals may be. Its goal is to help students examine their own and their peers' cultural attachments comparatively.

The process has some drawbacks. For example, membership in some communities (Little League, Girl Scouts, subscribers to *Field and Stream*) would be easier to speak for and analyze than membership in others (mothers, Secret Service agents, any religion, the Inuit nation). Membership in still other communities, antisocial in tendency (the KKK, child pornographers, crack dealers, inside traders) might be impossible for almost anyone to speak for and analyze.

But this goal of a nonfoundational curriculum is worth the effort, as Greg Sarris discovered in his work teaching Native American students in southern California and central Canada. Sarris uses fictional narratives chosen from American Indian literature to help his students "explore unexamined assumptions by which . . . [we] frame the texts and experiences of members of another culture." In doing this, he demonstrates in practical terms the educational value, as well as the difficulty, of trying to escape "the old and still pervasive misconception of critical thinking as something devoid of cultural and historical contexts," the "perceived split between life experience and critical thought."[1]

Besides being stressful, the introductory process that students will have undergone so far would be necessarily superficial. The second and third goals of a curriculum devised on nonfoundational social constructionist assumptions deepen the process considerably by considering some of the complexities of community composition and the relationships among communities. The *second goal* would be to *help students discover which of the beliefs that they and their classmates hold have been socially justified, and in what ways.* To achieve this goal, students would examine not only their own local communities but also the communities relevant to college and university education, both the academic disciplines such as chemistry, philosophy, and classics, and the larger, encompassing community of the college- or university-educated public, writers of standard written English, and so on. Studying the natural sciences as an interpretive, pragmatic intellectual tradition (discussed in Chapter 9) becomes especially relevant in meeting this goal.

Students would approach the justification of belief in three phases. In the first phase they would learn to distinguish between justified and unjustified beliefs. They would learn to distinguish beliefs that are justifiable in the terms of the subject community from those that are not. They would learn to ask if the members of that community hold any beliefs that remain unjustified, and, if so, why and how. The process would be something like the one Stanley Fish describes: shifting students' attention from what "texts" mean to what they "do," making the text "an *event*, something that *happens* to, and with the participation of, the reader."[2] "Texts," of course, can include anything from a slogan, a few sentences, a novel, an article in *Nature*, or Bach's partitas and Picasso's Blue Period paintings, to Boolean algebra, BASIC, or graphs representing results of research in the natural or social sciences.

For example, some ninety-nine percent of all Americans and Western Europeans believe that people have walked on the moon. What do we do to justify that belief, and by what assumptions? What does it do for us and to us as a community to justify that particular belief in that particular way? There may also be one percent or so of us who believe that people have never walked on the moon. Is that belief socially justifiable? If so, how? What assumptions are necessary in order to justify it? What does justifying it do for or to those who believe it? Moreover, by what processes do chemists justify their beliefs? Philosophers? Sociologists? Classicists? What, in each community, is regarded as evidence? Would a sociologist's criteria in examining evidence be accepted by a physicist? Do biologists, historians, geometricians, and English teachers all mean the same thing when they use the term "describe"? If not, why not, and what are the implications of their not doing so?

The second phase would generalize the first. Students would learn to distinguish what might be called genres of justification, typical ways in which members of various communities justify their beliefs. Can any belief be justified socially by explaining it logically? If so, by the logic of which community? What are the rules of logic as they are known in the West? Are "the universals of sound reasoning" really universal? If more than (or something other than) logic and sound reasoning are necessary for justifying beliefs socially in any community, what exactly is required and how does it work?

To return to our example, what would it take to convince the dissenting one percent that people really did walk on the moon? What would it take to convince the assenting ninety-nine percent that they did not? What part does metaphor play in justification, and how does that work? Which of the facts of the "hard sciences" depend for their conceptual-ization on metaphor? What role do terms such as "quark" and "charm" play in physicists' attempts to identify and characterize the "basic build-ing blocks" of nature? For that matter, what does that commonplace metaphor, "building blocks," do for those attempts, and to them?

In the third phase, students would learn and practice the techniques of discursive justification of belief and the critical analysis thereof as practiced in the large, encompassing community they are joining—the culture of people educated in the West or educated elsewhere according to Western educational principles and values. The point is not just that students would learn to write unified, coherent, readable prose, although that is certainly part of the point. They would learn, as Vincent Leitch puts it, that *"writing* produces all our knowledge." And since all writers are their own first readers, students would learn to read effectively in order to learn to write well and contribute in that way to the construction of knowledge. They would acquire an "active suspicion of all language formations," of every "system governing meaning," and of "the forms (in) which" they are taught.[3]

Here, the study of "the rhetoric of inquiry" might play a role. A collection of essays edited by John S. Nelson et al., entitled *The Rhetoric of the Human Sciences,* offers a number of persuasive examples of the use of rhetorical analysis for understanding the constituting languages of professional and academic communities: for example, Charles Bazerman on psychology, Philip J. Davis and Reuben Hersh on mathematics, Misia Landau on human paleontology, Allan Megill and Donald N. McCloskey on history, and Renato Rosaldo on anthropology.

An example of the kind of teaching that the second goal may yield is Albert D. Hutter's effort to help his students overcome "mistaken and confining assumptions, inculcated by their medical education." Hutter teaches M.D.s in training to become psychoanalysts. To help them begin to understand writing as constructing knowledge by learning to justify in writing their diagnoses and other beliefs they form about their patients, he teaches them not just to "write better" but also to "reconceptualize the nature of all writing."[4]

Another example of teaching relevant to the curriculum sketched here, seemingly at the other end of the professional spectrum from Hutter's but actually closely allied with it, is Susan Wells's work with technical writers in corporations that manufacture computers and large, complex machines. Hutter and Wells both want their students to understand the "mistaken and confining assumptions" involved in all attempts "to describe complex human behavior by 'objective' and 'complete' accounts." Wells's students write manuals that tell workers how to operate complicated machinery. She teaches them to become aware in doing so of the "authority claim" made in technical writing and to analyze the "interests" involved both in "producing knowledge [and] in our employment of it." Thus the interests of Hutter and Wells are also closely related to Sarris's attempt to overcome the "split between life experience and critical thought" perceived by his Native American undergraduates. In each case, the teacher leads students to examine their own and others' beliefs with the goal of discovering how community members justify those beliefs to each other.[5]

The *third curricular goal* of college and university education based on understanding knowledge as socially justified belief would be to *help students explore the historical, sociolinguistic nature of knowledge.* This goal would be approached in four phases. First, students would return to the question of what constitutes a knowledge community and examine it in greater detail. They would ask such questions as, What diverse sorts of social divisions might conceivably be described as knowledge communities? Is a Boy Scout troop a knowledge community? Is a family a knowledge community? What about the Mormon Church? Is the Woods Hole Marine Biological Laboratory a knowledge community? Is the Physics Department of Duke University one? The Democratic Party? A kindergarten class? All the readers of this (or any other) book? Some of those readers? Everyone who hasn't read it? They would also examine whatever tends to cement communities (especially knowledge communities), whatever tends to weaken or dissolve communities, and whatever characterizes a peer in any sort of community.

Second, students would examine the way people go about joining knowledge communities and the criteria that knowledge communities apply in defining a person as knowledgeable. They would learn to apply all kinds of knowledge communities questions such as those Thomas Kuhn has posed:

How does one elect and how is one elected to membership in a particular community, scientific or not? What is the process and what are the stages of socialization to the group? What does the group collectively see as its goals; what deviations, individual or collective, will it tolerate; and how does it control the impermissible aberration?[6]

To examine how knowledge communities come about would raise a further question crucial to change in knowledge: Once we are in a community of knowledgeable peers, how do we get out of it? *Can* we get out of a knowledge community once we have become a full-fledged member? Is renegotiating our membership a real alternative, and if so, how do we go about doing that? How do knowledge communities change? Do they in fact ever change? If knowledge is socially justified belief, and if the authority of knowledge is established by a community of assent, how do individuals "grow"? Does knowledge "grow"? If so, in what sense and how?

Third, students would consider how the heritage of the past contributes to the present composition of the community of college- or university-educated people and to the satisfactions that the community can provide. To what extent do the language and symbol systems of "the best that Western culture has to offer" constitute that community? To study that heritage for this purpose, students would undertake an archeological examination of the western cultural heritage of the sort implied in Bruno Latour's metaphorical use of the term "black box."

Latour adopts the "black box" as a metaphor for an understanding or concept that we have thoroughly learned or that a community accepts unquestioningly as established. A "black box" is an instrument that scientists regard as neutral relative to the results of an experiment. They do not know, and do not have to know, how the instrument works, what its history is, or how to fix it. For example, a dictionary is a "black box" to most people. So is a car, a telephone, and the color royal blue. A "black box," Latour says, is a routine, an enclosed, unexamined "premise . . . for all further reasonings in the matter" agreed upon by a certain community of knowledgeable peers. To follow the history of something "known" is therefore an "archeological" study. It is to dig down through strata of nested, overlaid, and overlapping "black boxes."[7]

Fourth and finally, students would consider the sense in which science, history, literature, and the arts are not a record of the work of "great" individuals (Rembrandt, Shakespeare, Woolf, Washington, Einstein, Faraday, Nightingale, Darwin, King). They would study the communities that those individuals belonged to, their society and culture, and their political, artistic, and intellectual cohorts. They would examine the role of "great" individuals in helping to create a consensus among members of those communities: ways of seeing, talking with, and hearing one another, ways of writing to and reading one another, and ways of acting in concert. Students would be led to describe the social construction of literary texts in many ways yet to be fully explored, some of which are represented, for example, in Jerome McGann's *Critique of Modern Textual Criticism*. Study of this nature is likely to result in new versions of such traditional academic fields as biography, history, and philology.

Humanists would also engage students in considering the contribution of the past to the composition of current communities by studying more carefully how literature communities are constituted and integrated over space and time. They would study how, with language and other symbol systems, communities transmit from place to place and from generation to generation their socially justified beliefs and their ways of socially justifying them that, as Kuhn puts it, "have withstood the test of group use."[8] And humanists would examine how humanistic texts and other cultural artifacts both reveal us to one another and hide us from one another.

This process would differ considerably from what is known as "sociology of literature," which is concerned with what Harry Levin called "literature as an institution." The sociology of literature is foundational in its phenomenological assumptions and is framed in subject-object terms, assuming as given the inner world of writers and the outer social world they inhabit. Its central issues are how literature "reflects" that world and how writers adapt to it or hope to change it.[9] Examining how literate communities are constituted and integrated would have more in common with a current approach described as the analysis of "narratives of socialization." These are, as Janet Carey Eldred puts it, texts "that chronicle a character's attempt to enter a new social (and discursive) arena," in the process dramatizing "the collision between competing discourse communities, their language conventions, and their inherent social logics."[10]

That is, a nonfoundational social constructionist study of literature of the sort sketched here would focus first on the *intratextual* communities of a text or other symbolic artifact, and of the language-constituted communities dramatized in it. It would identify the languages specific to those communities and the stories of fragments of stories that community members tell each other in order to explain who they are, what's going on, and how things hang together. It would identify changes in community membership that the text renders, how characters choose which communities to join or not to join, how communities choose individuals for membership (and decide to exclude others or eject current members), how members recognize potential new members, how communities reacculturate potential members into full-fledged membership, and what accounts for compatibility among communities, or their incompatibility.

Studies of this sort would also identify *extratextual* communities, membership in communities constituted by the text among those who read it, by virtue of reading and discussing it. Furthermore, some intratextual communities, rendered or implied within the text, would be found to be fictional extratextual communities, constituted by allusions to other texts. Illuminating parallels would be drawn between the way these fictional extratextual communities are constituted within the text and the way the text constitutes extratextual communities among its readers. And there would be a sense in which a text (or other symbolic artifact) "chooses" new members to join the extratextual communities it constitutes, through the nature of its language, its explicit narratives, and the already existing extratextual community of readers it constitutes.

The curriculum I have been sketching here is certainly incomplete and limited in many ways. For example, it does not promulgate the certainties and truths of Western intellectual and artistic accomplishment, and it does not confirm the unity of thought and knowledge. But criticism of that sort is based on foundational assumptions, in terms of which, of course, the whole project announced and carried forth in this book is flawed.

Even as a nonfoundational, social constructionist project, however, the curriculum I have outlined may be criticized from two quite different points of view. One of these is the conservative nonfoundational position perhaps best described, paraphrasing Richard Rorty, as "right-wing Kuhnian." This position is impeccably articulated by Stanley Fish.[11] Fish argues that because knowledge communities give rise to, determine, and control "the thoughts . . . [we] can think and the mental operations [we] can perform," we cannot analyze and understand what constitutes those communities or break through their boundaries and step outside them. All our beliefs are already inescapably "situated" in these historical, social, and ideational contexts. We cannot escape our acculturation.[12]

Any scheme that proposes to help us do that and calls itself "nonfoundational," such as the curriculum I have sketched here, Fish would say, is self-contradictory. It implies that people can leave communities into which they have been acculturated, or at least renegotiate their membership in them, by achieving a "perspective on [their] beliefs . . . from which those beliefs can be evaluated and compared with the similarly evaluated beliefs of others." It therefore manifests what Fish calls "theory hope," a wish to discover a foundational rationale the "consequences" of which are whatever it is one does or wants to do. We fail in these efforts to examine other community languages—other cultures—and to translate them into the languages of our own communities, Fish would explain, because we cannot avoid transforming what we examine or adopt: "The imported product will always have the form of its appropriation rather than the form it exhibits 'at home.' "[13]

Fish's argument identifies conceptual change exclusively with generational change. It is a position that at some level is difficult to gainsay (plus ça change . . .). As Max Planck said: "A new scientific truth does not triumph by convincing its opponents . . . , but rather because its opponents eventually die, and a new generation grows up that is familiar with it."[14]

However persuasive this conservative nonfoundational position may seem to be, it has the troubling disadvantage, as the social critic Roberto Unger puts it, of "justify[ing] the authority of existing institutional arrangements or of reigning modes of discourse."[15] It tends to deny the potential to effect change through education. It also masks self-contradiction of its own, as Fish has himself more recently begun tacitly to acknowledge.[16] The "situation" within which Fish believes everyone is unchangeably fixed is itself a social construct. It is some story or other that we tell ourselves about ourselves, about our knowledge, and about our past, present, and future. None of these stories is static. Like oral epic narratives, every such story is constantly undergoing change in the telling and retelling.

As we revise the stories we tell ourselves, moreover, they "enact possibilities." They help us, Unger says, "insert [ourselves] into a social world" other than one to which we are currently acculturated—into other "situations"—and to develop "our capacity to escape or to revise the social and imagination frameworks within which we deal with one another." By telling ourselves old stories, we remain what we are by describing ourselves as we have been. When we tell ourselves new stories, we redescribe who we are, what we are, and what we know, and thus how we learn. With new stories, we translate one "situation" into another, with the result, as Rorty puts it, of having "changed ourselves by internalizing a new self-description." At some point, even Copernicus and those who agreed with him had to become "Copernican" by telling a different story.[17]

To understand knowledge and learning nonfoundationally in this way and to explain collaborative learning as a kind of nonfoundational education is not, however, to adopt a social constructionist "theory" that "grounds" an educational "practice." It is to suggest that nonfoundational social construction and nonfoundational education are two practices related by common assumptions: that knowledge is a constructed, sociolinguistic entity and that learning is an interdependent social process. Social construction assumes that we construct and maintain knowledge not by examining the world but by negotiating with one another, within and among communities of knowledgeable peers. Similarly, a nonfoundational understanding of learning assumes that learning occurs among persons, not between persons and things. These statements do not adumbrate a theory. They provide new speech, new "texts"—language for describing and "speaking differently" about what college and university teachers do, a redescription that can suggest and energize ways of doing it differently.

The curriculum sketched here may also be criticized from a nonfoundational social constructionist point of view that is diametrically opposed to Fish's, namely, the one that Rorty has called the "left-wing Kuhnian" position.[18] From this position, of which Unger and Bruno Latour are perhaps the farthest "left," most attempts to make education nonfoundational that I have been discussing (including my own) share an assumption that Unger calls "modernist" and regards as obsolete. This assumption, Unger would argue, limits their long-run effectiveness.

The "modernist" assumption implicit in all these exercises in curricular speculation is revealed in their tendency to address cultural diversity as a problem in contextuality. Like Barbara Johnson's education in a "plurality of forces and desires" and Lyotard's "worthwhile" class (both discussed in Chapter 11), their purpose is to acknowledge "difference," resolve the differences that are resolvable, discover constructive ways to exploit tensions among other differences, and negotiate a truce among differences that defy resolution. All of them assume that human beings are "contextual beings": our mental and social lives are "shaped by institutional [and] imaginative assumptions" that are socially constructed and historical in nature.[19]

This is the process that the nonfoundational curriculum I have sketched recommends when it asks students to look at, in Unger's terms, "formative contexts," past and present, our own and others', locally and elsewhere: both people's institutional arrangements, such as economic and governmental structures, and their "explanatory or argumentative structure," such as religions, art, literature, music, research agendas, guiding concerns, and standards of sense, validity, or verification.[20] It also resembles the recommendations of most essayists in the Johnson and Nelson volumes (discussed in Chapter 11). The purpose of examining these "formative contexts" is to understand the "mental and social life" that we ourselves and other people are conditioned and limited by; they are the boundaries imposed by cultural conditions. Stanley Fish's belief in the unchangeable "situation" we inhabit is also contextual in this sense.

Traditional, foundational, humanist education assumes the value of understanding great works of the past, regarded as being deeper, richer, older, and more nuanced. "Modernist" educational thought, both foundational and nonfoundational, assumes that, with the skillful and appropriate application of interpretive techniques to significant texts and through "knowledge of the functioning of language, of symbolic structures," human beings—especially young ones—can destabilize, renegotiate, or abandon the contexts that have shaped them and replace them with contexts that seem to them, and perhaps to some others (such as their college and university teachers), more satisfactory.

Unger maintains that trying to cope with cultural diversity in this contextualist way alone, whether our assumptions are foundational or nonfoundational, falls short of our needs. It may even stand in the way of fulfilling those needs, because an exclusive concern with contexts evades what Unger regards as the central fact of human relations. Along with addressing "the problem of contextuality," we should also be addressing what he calls "the problem of solidarity" or what Latour calls "the powers of association."

Contextual and solidarian thought have a good deal in common. They share the nonfoundational assumption that we socially construct human identity, and hence human diversity. But contextual thought begins already a step removed from the direct impact of human relations. It addresses that impact displaced into conceptual and symbolic forms and institutional arrangements. In contrast, solidarian thought begins with the most immediate and direct impact of human relations: our ambivalence to one another, the "mutual longing and jeopardy," the "unlimited need and . . . unlimited danger" of social life. Unger's most important contribution to educational thought is probably this understanding of radical ambivalence in human relations. It underlies, for example, the difficulties discussed in Chapter 2 that students may encounter when they first begin collaborative learning and go through the two complex "phases of work," dependence and interdependence, involved in adaptation to group work. And it implicitly informs Latour's "performative" definition of power and the study of "associations" that he recommends.[21]

Unger elaborates his notion of social ambivalence in considerable detail, but the basic notion is easy to grasp because it is familiar to everyone. On the one hand, he reminds us, we all need one another's company, support, acceptance, recognition, engagement, and cooperation. Indeed, as Unger puts it, we crave the greater opportunity, the "enlarged possibility in self-expression and reconciliation," that we gain in association with one another. Each of us desires "acceptance and recognition, to be intimately assured that we have a place in the world, and to be freed by this assurance for a life of action and encounter."

On the other hand, in requiring the company of others, Unger reminds us, we submit to the threat of suppression, conformity, and constraint. Thus the inevitable counterpart and unremitting companion of our "unlimited need" for one another is our feeling of "unlimited danger" every time we try to fulfill that need. To satisfy our longing for acceptance, recognition, and freedom, "we must open ourselves to personal attachments and communal engagements whose terms we cannot predefine and whose course we cannot control," attachments and engagements that can lead to "a craven dependence" that may "submerge our individual selves under group identities and social roles." As liberating, productive, and satisfying as interdependence may be, therefore, it also tends to breed "domination and dependence." The freedom and self-realization that we gain in association with one another can always be compromised, and at worst crippled, by the "depersonalization [and] bondage" that results from entrenched, "ongoing, unaccountable, unreciprocal power."[22]

What we call individual "identity," and hence the differences among us, Unger argues, is in large part a product of the ways in which we manage—or fail to manage—to negotiate this ambivalence to interdependence. Like Fish, Felman, Geertz, Latour and others whose work I discussed in Chapter 11, for Unger the means we choose for negotiating that ambivalence is, to adopt Felman's phrase, our "knowledge of the functioning of language, of symbolic structures." But the nature of these linguistic constructs, Unger points out, is such that none of us can even "describe our situation and . . . reflect about ourselves unless we share in specific, historically conditioned traditions of discourse that none of us authored individually." Without this inherited language and without these inherited categories, he says, "the imagination cannot work."[23]

Because our language and categories are inherited, however, we continually feel our identity under threat. We "cannot easily prevent ourselves from becoming the unwitting reproducers" of a trite, conventional, oppressive "shared picture of the world." We risk confinement within this "collective script," and yet we cannot do without it. "If we stray too far or too quickly" from it, "we are left without a way to converse."[24]

The curriculum offered here does not address the educational implications of the deep social ambivalence that Unger contemplates. It does not address the full potential effect of that ambivalence on our primary tools for coping with it, language and other symbolic constructs. But the organization and constraints of collaborative learning, as described in Chapter 2 and Chapter 5, are designed to address them, however imperfectly. To explore the "problem of solidarity" collaboratively is to examine the emotional, social, economic, aesthetic, and political ways that, by trying to satisfy our "unlimited need" for one another, we may "aggravate" our sense of "unlimited danger." It is also to examine the emotional, social, economic, and political ways that, by trying to defend ourselves against the "unlimited danger" implicit in our need for one another, we may intensify that need. If students explore these forces collaboratively, therefore, they may help accomplish the "practical goal" that Rorty and Unger in common recommend: "human solidarity" based on "the imaginative ability to see strange people" both as "fellow sufferers" and as having the same right we have to life, liberty, and the pursuit of happiness.[25]

A step beyond the curriculum sketched here would guide students in reading our traditional treasured texts, as well as the texts in the newer "canon" currently being assembled, as episodes in that negotiation. To do that would be, once again, to read those treasured texts anew.

Architecture and Classroom Design

The British historian and philosopher of science, Nicholas Jardine, confirms the architectural historian Sophie Forgan's contention that the architectural design of most schools is based on "past assumptions about the practices and goals of the sciences." This relationship between educational assumptions, practices, and goals and the scenes of educational inquiry is most conspicuous in classrooms.

Classroom design is notoriously conservative. Twenty years ago, at the beginning of the study that resulted in this book, I attended a series of lectures on educational change prompted by the educational turbulence of the sixties. The lectures, sponsored by a local university, were delivered in a classroom roughly thirty feet by thirty feet designed as a raked theater, with desks fastened to the floor and facing an elevated podium. Three years or so ago the university that played host to those lectures received a large grant to refurbish its principal classroom building. On the advice, no doubt, of the most eminent architects, the university turned most of those classrooms into one version or another of a raked lecture hall with fixed desks facing a raised podium. This Appendix is devoted to resisting this traditional mindset in educational architecture.

Classroom Design

Collaborative learning does not exclude lecturing. It only changes the social context and the authority structure in which a lecture is delivered. Furthermore, collaborative learning can be successful in many classroom settings. But it will come as no surprise to readers of this book that, architecturally, collaborative learning has some ideal requirements, none of them characteristic of a lecture hall.

The ideal classroom for collaborative learning has a level floor, movable seats, chalkboards on three or four walls, controlled acoustics (acoustical-tiled ceilings and carpeted floors), and no central seminar table (or one that can be pushed well out of the way without threatening an advanced case of lumbago). An alternative is six to ten movable four- or five-sided tables of roughly card-table size.

For classrooms in which students will use computers collaboratively, designers have to make other adaptations. Architects have to realize that students learn through conversation with one another as well as through conversation with teachers and computer programmers (see Chapter 6). The conventional layout of computer work stations is a barrier to conversation and collaboration. The arrangement that computer advertisements usually show, for example, has machines set high on tables in long rows with breaks between tables only at the ends of the rows. Alternatively, they show a room with computers arranged against the walls, with or without a table for discussion in the middle of the room.

The arrangement of workstations in long rows is probably the worst possible arrangement for a computer classroom because it meets none of the requirements of collaborative learning. For conversation to take place conveniently, students and teachers have to be able to get around the room easily, and they have to be able to work easily on one another's machines. Arranging computers against the walls meets some of these requirements, but at a price. Students are seated back-to-back, so that they cannot face one another easily for conversation. Chalkboard space is almost entirely eliminated.

The best alternative is to organize computers in tight circles. In that case, either the monitors and keyboards are recessed into tabletops, set low enough to permit people to face one another over them, or are arranged around small tables on pedestals. In all three arrangements, students can face one another conveniently for conversation. Architects have to remember to allow enough room for handicapped students and students who are physically somewhat larger than average.

Laboratory Design

The conventional design of teaching laboratories, using long, uninterrupted lab benches, is an almost insuperable barrier to effective collaboration. Lab benches designed for collaborative learning would be round, pentagonal, or hexagonal, and they would be large enough to accommodate four to six students working on laboratory tasks.

Bench designs of this type can actually make some of the essential features of laboratories, such as access to sources of water, gas, and electricity and the placement of exhaust hoods in particular, easier and more economical to effect than traditional design. Furthermore, students facing across a circular bench can watch one another work and can talk easily about what they are doing. They can easily see, listen to, and talk with the lab instructor over the top of the bench, and the instructor can answer questions and instruct students in small lab groups assembled around each bench.

Notes

There is nothing very systematic about most of the reading that informs this book. Many readers will wonder how, for goodness' sake, I could possibly not have read this or that. Easy, I reply. But I regret not discovering, much less reading, everything relevant, and I welcome suggestions from my readers that will fill in the many blanks. Here, nevertheless, are citations for the sources to which I have referred.

Introduction

1. Oliver Wendell Holmes Society.
2. Kuhn 210.
3. Kuhn 210.
4. Newcomb "Student" 485. Until recently, studies of college and university education tended to confirm Newcomb's position inadvertently. Alexander Astin concluded in 1979, for example, that colleges might be able to reach a goal valued at the time, a high level of student satisfaction, by "finding ways to encourage greater personal contact between faculty and students" (223). But this conclusion implicitly contradicted one clear result of the study, that the key element in student satisfaction, "interpersonal self-esteem," increases only through peer relations (88, 223). Astin had not at that time studied substantive peer relations of the sort that occur in collaborative learning, did not index "peers," and indexed "relationships among students" only under *friendships*.

By 1993, the penny had dropped. Astin now regards "the peer group" as producing "some of the strongest and certainly the most widespread effects on student development" (351). And he recommends organizing students to "work together in small groups" where they "teach each other." His reason is that teaching of this sort "motivates students to become more active and more involved participants in the learning process," perhaps as a result of their tendency "to expend more effort [because] they know that their work is going to be scrutinized by peers" and to "learn course material in greater depth [because] they are involved in helping teach it to fellow students" (385, 427).

Remarkably, Astin also hazards a suggestion that could be read as adumbrating the argument pursued in this book: "the possibility" that college and university education "consists of something more than the content of what is taught and the particular form in which this content is packaged" (428).

5. Dewey 64.

6. Mason 33, 31.
7. Mason 16.
8. Perry *Forms* 213; Newcomb *College* 6.
9. Newcomb "Student" 486; *College* vii–viii.
10. Johnson, Johnson, and Smith.
11. Mason 139.
12. The most useful guide to answering this question is Wiener on evaluating teachers' skill organizing their students to learn collaboratively.
13. *Scenes* 99–103, 119–20.

Chapter One
Collaboration, Conversation, and Reacculturation

1. I have adapted Trimbur's story from the Introduction of Bruffee, *A Short Course in Writing*, 3rd ed., 7–8.

Chapter Two
Consensus Groups: A Basic Model of Classroom Collaboration

1. For a more thorough survey of this research see "Developing a New Group Service: Strategies and Skills" in Gitterman and Shulman.
2. This and the next two paragraphs are loosely based on Bennis and Shepard.
3. Rorty *Contingency* 11–12.
4. Hawkes, 141; Hawkes explains this task in helpful detail.
5. Arons 61–32, 171.
6. Vygotsky, *Mind* 84–87.
7. Edited version republished by permission of Peter Hawkes.
8. Thomas 15, 73.

Chapter Three
Writing and Collaboration

1. Latour and Woolgar 48. See also Latour and Bastide, and Knorr-Cetina, chapter 5 ("The Scientist as a Literary Reasoner, Or the Transformation of Laboratory Reason," 94ff), and Bazerman. My point here is hardly to deprecate the role of talk in constructing knowledge, as should be clear from this book's emphasis on direct as well as indirect conversation. To "make the rationale behind laboratory moves apparent," as Knorr-Cetina puts it, "we must rely on talk" (21).
2. See, for example, Latour and Woolgar, Knorr-Cetina, and Callon.
3. Latour and Woolgar 51 and 273, emphasis theirs.
4. Latour and Woolgar 173. Knorr-Cetina's analysis (94ff) characterizes this "reasoning" process in detail.
5. The way of teaching writing described in this chapter is set out in detail in Bruffee, *A Short Course in Writing*, 4th ed.
6. See Hunter, *passim*.

Chapter Four
Toward Reconstructing American Classrooms:
Interdependent Students, Interdependent World

1. For a general discussion of negotiation see Fisher, Ury, and Patton, and Fisher and Brown. Although we know a lot about how negotiation works in political, legal, and economic situations, we are only beginning to learn (from studies such as those of Latour and Knorr-Cetina) how it works in epistemological or educational ones. Perhaps more to the point, as Fisher and Ury put it, we normally think of negotiation in any context as "positional bargaining." The craft of interdependence, involving what Fisher calls "principled negotiation," is a good deal more complex than that. It almost goes without saying that nothing like principled negotiation has yet been systematically applied to learning and to constructing knowledge.

2. Pratt 34, her emphasis.

3. Pratt 38.

4. On Roland Barthes, see Steven Ungar, "The Professor of Desire," in B. Johnson 81–97.

5. Dewey 64–65.

6. Dewey 55–56.

7. Dewey 56.

8. Kuhn 209–10.

9. Rorty *Philosophy* 187, his emphasis.

10. On support groups see, for example, Evans.

11. Knorr-Cetina 131. In this passage Knorr-Cetina describes the process of enrollment in translation (or transition) communities, and the "process of conversion" involved, as it occurs in scientific research.

12. Perry *Forms* 214.

13. Kuhn 203.

14. Perry *Forms* 65.

Chapter Five
Peer Tutoring and Institutional Change

1. The late Robert L. Hess, author of the document, was President of Brooklyn College.

2. See Roswell for discussion of some of these institutional constraints as they apply to peer tutoring.

3. From "A Way of Learning," an essay by Hung Chan, in *Writing Center: Points of View—Essays by Undergraduate Peer Tutors of the Brooklyn College Writing Center, A Center for Collaborative Learning,* lithographed booklet (Brooklyn, NY: Brooklyn College Writing Center, 1977).

4. From a log entry by Gail Olmstead, a peer tutor at the Brooklyn College Writing Center. Adapted from "A Course for Writing Peer Tutors," in Bruffee, *A Short Course in Writing,* 4th ed., 297.

5. See Bruffee, "A Course for Writing Tutors," *A Short Course in Writing,* 4th ed., 293–318.

6. The *Times* reporter whose comments I found insightful and encouraging was Edward B. Fiske.

7. See Sophie Bloom, David Johnson, Sharan, and Slavin.

8. I had also been helping them negotiate Bennis and Shepard's phase 2 of group work. See Chapter 2.

9. Passages from Hung Chan's log, in Bruffee, *A Short Course in Writing*, 4th ed., 296. Chan cites Axline.

Chapter Six
Mime and Supermime:
Collaborative Learning and Instructional Technology

1. Ward 425, their emphasis.

2. Comstock 371, 146.

3. Annenberg 6.

4. Fred W. Bornhauser.

5. See Evans.

6. On mutual evaluation, see "Peer Review" in Bruffee, *A Short Course in Writing*, 4th ed., 169–87. See also Wiener, whose suggestions for evaluating collaborative learning could be readily adapted to instructing students on how to evaluate each other, either in classrooms or in "distance learning."

7. Donald A. Sutton, quoted in *The Chronicle of Higher Education,* September 25, 1991, A22.

8. Bechtel 219–20.

9. Bechtel 221–22.

Chapter Seven
Education as Conversation

1. Kuhn 210.

2. Oakeshott 199.

3. Brann 42. I do not want to be misunderstood. St. John's does the right sort of thing, in my view. I disagree with the justification offered for doing it.

4. Fish *Is There a Text?* 14.

5. Geertz *Interpretation* 360.

6. Rorty *Philosophy* 170.

7. Lewin 58.

8. Vygotsky, *Mind* 56.

9. Vygotsky 56, his emphasis.

10. Vygotsky 56.

11. Vygotsky 30.

12. Vygotsky 27, his emphasis. Vygotsky's example, 25.

13. Vygotsky 24–26, his emphasis.

14. Vygotsky 57, his emphasis.

15. Kuhn's example, Suppe 473–82; Latour's example, Latour *Science* 198–200, his emphasis.

16. Perry *Forms* 121.

17. Kuhn 199–203.
18. Rorty *Philosophy* 320.
19. Pratt 34.
20. Rorty *Philosophy* 320, 339.
21. Perry *Forms* 21.
22. Perry *Forms* 167.
23. Rorty *Philosophy* 320.
24. Perry *Forms* 162.

Chapter Eight
Anatomy of a Profession:
The Authority of College and University Teachers

1. See Larson *Rise* 181, Leggatt 159, and Becher *passim*.
2. Larson "In the Matter" 25–26.
3. See Chapter 10, note 21.
4. Knorr-Cetina 13.
5. Rigden.
6. Kuhn 199–203, 209–10.
7. Welker 10 and 142, note 39. Welker refers to reports and reforms funded by the Holmes Group and the Carnegie Corporation. His study is about primary and secondary education, but in college and university education the individualistic bias implied in the medical (and legal) metaphor is if anything more deeply ingrained.
8. On negotiation, see Chapter 4, note 1.
9. On margins see, for example, Wallis and Collins.
10. See Chapter 12, note 14.
11. Feynman 75.

Chapter Nine
Science in the Postmodern World

1. Latour and Woolgar 75. For Knorr-Cetina's evidence, see her Chapter 5; she summarizes arguments in support of understanding science as an interpretive enterprise, 138 ff.
2. Jardine *Scenes* 166.
3. Rorty *Philosophy* 175.
4. Jardine *Scenes* 5, 155. To make this point Jardine focuses ingeniously on the questions of science rather than its doctrines. But in doing so he uses some foundational terms that he has trouble disciplining to the demands of an otherwise impeccably nonfoundational social constructionist argument. See Chapter 10.
5. Tobias *They're Not Dumb* 8, her emphasis.
6. Tobias 17.
7. Tobias 59–61.
8. Tobias 21.
9. Rigden.

10. Tobias 9; she quotes Sharon Traweek, *Beamtimes and Lifetimes: The World of High Energy Physics* (Cambridge: Harvard UP, 1988).

11. Tobias 14: "Of the [college] freshmen who switched out of science and engineering [in 1973, 1981, and 1983] only 31 percent did so because they found the course work too difficult; 43 percent [did so because they] found other fields more interesting." Tobias quotes Richard C. Atkinson, "Supply and Demand for Scientists and Engineers: A National Crisis in the Making," Presidential Address, AAAS National Meeting, New Orleans, February 18, 1990, p. 18.

12. Tobias 19, 21–24.

13. Tobias 37, 22.

14. Tobias 52.

15. Tobias 37, 51.

16. Knorr-Cetina 87; for the "crisis of legitimacy," see for example "The Limits of Scientific Inquiry," *Daedalus,* Spring 1978.

17. Geertz *Local* 30.

18. Geertz *Local* 21, 19; Tobias 8.

19. Tobias 27.

20. Tobias 64–65, 37; her emphasis.

21. Tobias 41.

22. Tobias 57.

23. Tobias 30.

24. Successful collaborative learning in college and university science courses requires teachers to devise tasks that represent what actually happens in scientific work and to organize students to do those tasks collaboratively. In place of tasks socially organized in vertical or hierarchical ways, teachers substitute tasks that induce students to think interdependently. Arnold B. Arons's *Guide to Introductory Physics Teaching,* suggests what tasks of this kind might look like. When teachers guide students working together to see or experience physical phenomena, part of the students' work should be to "suggest, try, argue, and interpret [what happens] in their own words, carefully avoiding any, so far undefined, technical vocabulary" and then write out "full verbal descriptions." The goal is to lead students "into participating in the invention of the concept," doing an end run around "polished and seemingly inevitable end results" by understanding how scientific principles "were originally achieved" or "how something came to be known" (Arons 62, 225, 15, 172, 175). That is, the goal is to reproduce in the students' work the immediate and displaced conversation (the talking and writing) about what they do and what they experience that is involved (as Chapter 3 points out) in all scientific investigation. Most of the tasks that Arons suggests, and tasks designed on the same principles in any science, are eminently adaptable to the two basic kinds of collaborative learning tasks described in Chapter 2.

Chapter Ten
The Procrustean Bed of Cognitive Thought

1. Abercrombie 19. Her research is described in Chapter 1.

2. Abercrombie 23, 65 and *passim.*

3. Abercrombie 65.

4. Perry *Forms* 211, 5 (Perry is quoting Henry Adams), 214.

5. Perry *Forms* 214.

6. Perry *Forms* 65–66.

7. Perry *Forms* 108, 121, 162.

8. Perry *Forms* 171.

9. Perry *Forms* 21. Cf. on student experience, p. 188, and ch. 11, n. 32.

10. Kuhn 201–2; Perry *Forms* 167.

11. Rorty *Philosophy* 320.

12. I have used Bruner's autobiographical record for this account, rather than the original research reports or his more recent publications, because it narrates the process of his research and interpretive thought.

13. Bruner 149–50.

14. Latour *Science* 200.

15. Vygotsky *Mind* 24.

16. Bruner 170.

17. Bruner 158.

18. Bruner 171–72.

19. Bruner 172, his emphasis.

20. Bruner 171.

21. Freud 55, 47. The three heroic virtues of post-Cartesian thought implied in this paragraph—constancy, bravery, and plenitude—supplement the one alluded to in Chapter 8: being in touch with eternal verities. See also Chapter 11, note 18.

22. Latour and Woolgar 281.

23. Latour and Woolgar 281.

24. Latour and Woolgar 273.

25. Latour *Science* 201.

26. Knorr-Cetina 22–23, 52, 135, 5. Confusing generation and construction is especially unfortunate because Knorr-Cetina clearly understands as indistinguishable "group consensus formation" and the way scientific knowledge is "selectively constructed and reconstructed" (14).

27. Jardine *Scenes* 155–67.

28. Jardine *Scenes* 2–3, 77.

29. Jardine *Scenes* 62, 77. See also remarks about Jardine in Chapter 9.

30. Jardine *Scenes* 236.

31. Jardine *Scenes* 77.

32. Latour and Woolgar 259, note 9.

Chapter Eleven
A Plurality of Forces, Desires, and
Not Wholly Commensurable Visions

1. Roth 21.

2. Trilling 212.

3. Roth 21.

4. Fish *Is There a Text?* 342, 14.

5. Fish *Is There a Text?* 318.

6. Fish *Is There a Text?* 22.

7. Fish *Is There a Text?* 22, 315.
8. Fish *Is There a Text?* 316.
9. Fish *Is There a Text?* 66.
10. Fish *Is There a Text?* 371.
11. Fish *Is There a Text?* 326, 359.
12. Fish *Is There a Text?* 171–72, 314.
13. Fish *Is There a Text?* 66, 22; Kuhn 210.
14. Pratt 40; Graff 51.
15. See Chapter 10, note 21, and Chapter 11, note 18.
16. William R. Schroeder in Nelson *Theory* 10; Lawrence Grossberg in Nelson *Theory* 191, 177; Susan Wells in Nelson *Theory* 265; Paul DeMan in B. Johnson 3–4; Shoshana Felman in B. Johnson 27; Michael Ryan in B. Johnson 53–54; Johnson in B. Johnson 181; Jane Gallop in B. Johnson 126.
17. Penley in Nelson *Theory* 139, 141; Terdiman in B. Johnson 206, 221, 223; Leitch in Nelson *Theory* 54, his emphasis; Mohanty in Nelson *Theory* 155.
18. Johnson in B. Johnson 181; Felman in B. Johnson 29, Felman's emphasis. Felman's remarks about authority relations between teachers and students in the cognitive tradition suggest two more traits of the heroic myth: the radical interdependence of hero and antagonist and the conspiracy of silence between them. See p. 164 and Chapter 10, note 21. The effort to deconstruct the traditional heroic stereotype by creating a new "condition of knowledge" using "knowledge of the function of language" turns up in literary as well as philosophical texts. Several important modern authors, such as Conrad, Fitzgerald, Ford, Mann, Nabokov, and Warren, dramatize it. This fiction revives and radically alters what Terdiman calls the "dead genre" of the *roman d'education* by focusing in a distinctively modernist way on "the exteriorized interchange between a hero and an objective world of social meaning" (B. Johnson 199n). See Bruffee, *Elegiac Romance*. Other writers, such as Henry James and Virginia Woolf, undertake the effort in other ways.
19. Felman in B. Johnson 31.
20. Felman in B. Johnson 33, Felman's emphasis (she quotes Lacan from *Scilicet* I, 59).
21. Rorty *Contingency* 7.
22. Geertz *Local* 10.
23. Felman in B. Johnson 39.
24. Lyotard's illustrative classroom event, B. Johnson 74.
25. Joan De Jean in B. Johnson 102.
26. Angela Moger in B. Johnson 135.
27. Pratt 39.
28. Graff 51, his emphasis.
29. Johnson in B. Johnson 173.
30. Johnson in B. Johnson 181.
31. Trimbur "Consensus and Difference."
32. Latour *Science* 201. Cf. on student experience, pp. 158, 160, 165.
33. Geertz *Local* 36–54, 58, 59, 119.
34. Geertz *Local* 161.

Chapter Twelve
A Nonfoundational Curriculum

1. Sarris 169, 171; see also Pratt *passim*.
2. Fish *Is There a Text?* 25, his emphasis.
3. Nelson *Theory* 53–54, Leitch's emphasis.
4. Nelson *Theory* 222.
5. Nelson *Theory* 222, 262; Sarris 171.
6. Kuhn 209.
7. Latour *Science* 204.
8. Kuhn 196.
9. Laurenson 15; see Harry Levin, "Toward a Sociology of the Novel," in *Refractions: Essays in Comparative Literature* (New York: Oxford UP, 1966).
10. Eldred and Mortensen 513; Eldred 686.
11. Rorty, "Science as Solidarity" 41.
12. Fish "Anti-Foundationalism" 73, 65.
13. Fish "Being Interdisciplinary" 19.
14. Kuhn 151. Kuhn quotes Max Planck, *Scientific Autobiography and Other Papers*, trans. F. Gaynor (New York, 1949), 33–34.
15. Unger 88.
16. Until 1989, Fish argued that we cannot "simultaneously operate within a practice and be self-consciously in touch with the conditions that enable it . . . Once the conditions enabling a practice become the object of analytic attention . . . [we] are engaging in another practice ("Being Interdisciplinary," 20). But that is a move we cannot make, Fish implies, because it entails changing interpretive communities. In *Is There a Text in This Class?* for example, Fish denies the possibility of reacculturating students into communities new to them, because all knowledge is "situated": "a perspective that is not culturally determined" is just "unavailable" ("Being Interdisciplinary" 19). You can't get there from here.

In a 1989 footnote, however, Fish tacitly admits the possibility of reacculturation by acknowledging that "an analytical perspective on a practice does not insulate one from experiencing the practice in all its fullness, that is, in the same way one would experience it were the analytical perspective unavailable." His example, suggested by Stephen Booth, is "knowing while watching a horror movie that certain devices are being used to frighten us and yet being frightened nevertheless" ("Being Interdisciplinary" 21n). In fact, as I explain here, the teaching procedure that Fish sketches in *Is There a Text in This Class?* is designed specifically and precisely for reacculturating students from communities in which "analytical perspective" is "unavailable" to communities in which it prevails.
17. Unger 293, 22; Rorty *Contingency* xvi, *Philosophy* 386.
18. Rorty "Science as Solidarity," 41.
19. Unger 7.
20. Unger 5.
21. Unger 20; Latour "Powers," see especially 276–77.
22. Unger 95, 20.
23. Unger 20–21.
24. Unger 99, 20.
25. Rorty *Contingency* xvi.

Glossary

This book uses some terms that may be unfamiliar to some of its readers. The terms have to do mainly with the way we think about knowledge and learning. This glossary is intended to help readers through what may sometimes seem to be a thicket of jargon. It defines and comments on unfamiliar terms, and it places them in familiar contexts. Its purpose is to offer readers another way to approach what the book has to say. Words set in **boldface** are also referred to elsewhere in the Glossary.

Abnormal Discourse. See **Nonstandard discourse**.

Authority is "clout." The authority of college and university teachers refers to their "right to teach," their say-so, their reliability as a source of knowledge or expertise. The *authority of knowledge* refers to our belief that that knowledge is reliable, justified, "true," or authoritative. The way college and university teachers teach and their authority to teach are related to their understanding of the authority of knowledge.

This book contrasts two ways of understanding the authority of knowledge: **foundational** and **nonfoundational**. (See pp. 49–50, 126–28.)

Boundary discourse. See **Nonstandard discourse**.

Community of knowledgeable peers. See **Knowledge community**.

A **Consensus**, my *American Heritage* dictionary says, is a "collective opinion, general agreement, or accord." What the members of a knowledge or discourse community "know" is therefore what the members of the community agree to. But this definition does not indicate the measure of dissent that may be part of an actual everyday consensus (the loyal opposition: grudging assent, willingness to go along, trade-offs, agreements to disagree, recorded objections; or alternatively, the disloyal opposition: passive, covert, or overt resistance, walkouts, sabotage). As used in talking about collaborative learning and the nonfoundational social construction of knowledge, *consensus* implies the potential for all that happening, as well as the need to agree on methods and procedures and the historical and changing nature of knowledge understood as a social construct. (See pp. 45–47, 49–50, 78–79, 113, 184–85.)

Constructing knowledge refers to the way in which those who make **nonfoundational** assumptions think knowledge comes about. Members of a knowledge **community** construct knowledge in the language that constitutes that community by justifying beliefs that they mutually hold. But they do not justify those beliefs by testing them against a "foundation"—either a presumed mental structure or a presumed reality. They justify them socially in conversation with one another. The **authority** of knowledge is constructed similarly. A community persuades outsiders (members of other knowledge communities) to accept one or more of the community's beliefs, justified in the way the community justifies them. (See pp. 49–53, 115–23.)

Discourse community. See **Knowledge community**.

Foundational and **nonfoundational** refer to two different ways of thinking about knowledge. Most of us think about knowledge in the traditional, foundational way that refers to learning as "cognition." We read about the "cognitive sciences," school teachers tell us that our children have (or don't have) well-developed "cognitive skills," and so on.

The cognitive understanding of knowledge is *foundational* because it assumes that there is a ground, a base, an idea, a theory, a structure, a framework—a foundation—beneath or behind knowledge on which all knowledge is built. It is a Platonic formula that supposes that knowledge has two foundations. One is an "outer" entity that we usually call external reality, objective facts, or the world around us. Philosophers call it *res extensa*. We "see" this "reality" reflected in a second major cognitive entity, the philosopher's *res cognitans*. This is the mental image-gathering piece that we commonly call the subjective self, our inner world, or "the mind's eye."

A *nonfoundational* understanding of knowledge is an alternative to this traditional, cognitive, foundational idea. It assumes that knowledge has no foundations, internal or external. People construct what we call knowledge out of the various languages available to us: spoken languages (English, French, Chinese), mathematical and computer symbol systems (algebra, calculus, COBOL), and unspoken or **paralinguistic**, language-like, symbol systems (gestures, touch, music, art, dance). Knowledge is therefore not universal and absolute. It is local and historically changing. We construct it and reconstruct it, time after time, and build it up in layers. Other foundational entities, such as reality, objective facts, subjective selves, minds, and inner worlds, are understood to be social constructs as well.

Some nonfoundational ways of understanding knowledge (such as some branches of the philosophical and literary critical school of thought called "deconstruction") explore in great detail how knowledge is constructed and reconstructed in written texts. But they barely raise the question, How were those texts and their languages constructed in the first place? Who constructs knowledge and how?

The school of thought called *nonfoundational social construction* answers those questions by saying that knowledge is a community project. People construct knowledge working together in groups, interdependently. All knowledge is therefore the "property" not of an individual person but of some community or other, the community that constructed it in the language spoken by the members of that community.

Inevitably, these two ways of talking about knowledge and teaching—foundational and nonfoundational—strike us in quite different ways. The foundational, cognitive way seems as native and natural to most of us as the water we drink and the air we breathe. The nonfoundational way seems alien and absurd. How can we possibly talk at all about knowing, learning, and teaching, without talking about what we take in from outside us when we learn, and about what goes on inside us when we learn it? Yet it is quite possible to do exactly that, and this book is about the implications for college and university education when we do. (See pp. 98–99, 128–31 and Chapters 10 and 11 *passim*.)

Foundational education and **nonfoundational education** differ in much the same way that the nonfoundational and foundational understandings of knowledge differ. *Foundational education* assumes that an education is something we "give" people. Teachers help students to "assimilate," "absorb" or "synthesize" knowledge. They ask students to perform in a way that the teacher has determined ahead of time and to arrive at predetermined answers—answers that the disciplinary community to which the teacher belongs has decided are correct.

In contrast, *nonfoundational education* assumes that education is **reacculturation**. Teachers help students construct or reconstruct knowledge socially. They trust students to perform in ways that the teacher has not necessarily determined ahead of time and to arrive at answers that may or may not agree with those that the disciplinary community has decided are correct. Collaborative learning is one kind of nonfoundational teaching. (See also pp. 66–72, 172–78, 191–209.)

Interpretive community. See **Knowledge community**.

Knowledgeable peers are status equals within an institution or interpretive community. Every community member regards every other community member as knowledgeable and as fluent in the language that constitutes the community. For example, to understand "the law" is to understand the language that lawyers are fluent in—not only the language of written laws and statutes, but the language in which lawyers think and carry on the day-to-day practice of their profession. Similarly, to understand the numbers racket is to understand the language that numbers runners are fluent in—the language in which they think and carry on their day-to-day practice.

Knowledge community, community of knowledgeable peers, discourse community, and **interpretive community** are, roughly speaking, synonyms. They all designate a group of people with similar interests and goals who constitute themselves with a characteristic "language." This language may be a temporary ad hoc expedient or it may be entrenched. Also, it may be highly distinguished from other languages and easily recognizable by outsiders (Chinese, legalese, computer programmers' jargon), or it may be distinguished only subtly from everyday speech and hard to pin down (the Biblical "shibboleth," the manners of an upper class Englishman or the posture of a military officer in mufti). Some knowledge communities are organized in the form of institutions such as colleges and universities, churches and temples, or major league baseball teams. Others are informally organized: reading or writing groups, prayer meetings, sandlot ball games.

Glossary

In any case, the characteristic language of a knowledge community reveals one salient condition of knowledge community membership: the need to identify other members and the ability to do so unequivocally. That condition in turn implies another not always acknowledged one: the interdependence of community members. We depend on one another for our identity; some would say we even depend on one another for what we call our "self."

Each phrase in the title of this glossary note emphasizes a different aspect of knowledge community membership. *Knowledge community* stresses what Thomas Kuhn calls a community's "common property" (Kuhn 210). *Community of knowledgeable peers* stresses the status equality of the community's members: that they are, roughly speaking, equally knowledge-able. *Discourse community* stresses the constitutive and constructive nature of the language spoken by community members: their normal discourse. *Interpretive community* stresses the process by which community members construct knowledge. (See pp. 130–31, 192–93.)

Nonfoundational. See **Foundational**.

Nonfoundational teaching, nonfoundational education. See **Foundational education**.

Nonstandard discourse, abnormal discourse, and **boundary discourse** are roughly synonymous terms that refer to conversation that occurs at the boundaries of **knowledge communities**. This conversation is a negotiation between those who know and accept a community's values and conventions and those who do not. Nonstandard discourse, Rorty says, "is what happens when someone joins in the discourse who is ignorant of [the community's] conventions or who sets them aside." It can result in "anything from nonsense to intellectual revolution, and there is no discipline which describes it, any more than there is a discipline devoted to the study of the unpredictable, or of 'creativity' " (*Philosophy* 320).

Each of these terms stresses a different aspect of a conversation that may go on between people who "don't speak the same language." *Nonstandard discourse* stresses the differences between the criteria or standards of judgment—what is acceptable and unacceptable—of one community and another. *Abnormal discourse* stresses the "local foundationalism" of socially constructed knowledge: the sense we have that the knowledge and mores we and the other members of our community ascribe to are "natural" and "normal" and the shock and disbelief with which we tend to greet the knowledge or mores of another community. *Boundary discourse* stresses the negotiative nature of the conversation that may occur between members of different knowledge communities. (See pp. 45–47, 122–25, 136–38, 140–41.)

Normal discourse is the language with which each community constitutes itself and by which community members recognize one another. When we "speak the same language," normal discourse is the language we speak. More narrowly, normal discourse is the linguistic and paralinguistic symbol system with which an institutionalized knowledge community socially justifies its beliefs. Knowledge constructed in the normal discourse of a disciplinary community or subcommunity is, as Clifford Geertz puts it, "local." Its locality may be bound geographically by region or institution (the Joffrey Ballet Company, the Woods Hole Oceanographic Institute, most Yankees fans) or it may be spread thinly throughout the world and maintained by letter, phone, radio, or journal publication (astrophysicists, readers of *The Times Literary Supplement*, airline pilots and air traffic controllers). In either case, the language distinguishes and defines that particular community of knowledgeable peers.

The normal discourse of a knowledge community is what is or can be said in that community's language by members of the community speaking or writing to other members of the community. It is conversation, as Richard Rorty puts it, "conducted within an agreed-upon set of conventions about what counts as a relevant contribution, what counts as answering a question, what counts as having a good argument for that answer or a good criticism of it." It is "the sort of statement which can be agreed to be true by all participants whom the other participants count as 'rational' " (*Philosophy* 320). (See pp. 113, 120–21.)

A **Paralinguistic symbol system** is a system of expression that can be "read" as having an organization and coherence that is language-like. Some kinds of paralinguistic symbol systems are languages of sound (tone of voice, whistles and sirens, music), shape (sculpture and painting, costume and dress, tool design), and gesture (facial expression, physical stance, hand gestures, dance). For example, lumped together under the term "professional style," paralinguistic symbol systems account for many of the differences that outsiders could notice between the members of different professional communities. They distinguish, say, people attending a convention of geologists, dentists, or electrical engineers from the people attending a convention of French teachers, interior decorators, or eye surgeons. (See pp. 162–63, 184–85.)

Reacculturation is switching membership from one culture to another. It is always a complex, in most cases incomplete, and usually painful process. Reacculturation involves giving up, modifying, or renegotiating the language, values, knowledge, mores, and so on that are constructed, established, and maintained by the community one is coming from, and becoming fluent instead in the language and so on of another community.

This book defines learning as reacculturation and defines college and university teaching as helping students reacculturate themselves and one another into the community that the teacher represents. We are acculturated first into the minuscule community we join when we are born, the community of infant and mother. In the narrowest sense of acculturation, everything we learn after that is reacculturation. For example, Robert Fulghum may overstate the case somewhat when he says that everything he really needs to know he learned in kindergarten, but it is nevertheless certain that most of us take a major reacculturative step as little children when we first go to school.

In the broader sense intended in this book, however, most of our education up to the time we enter a college or university is primary acculturation. The indispensable task—and duty—of school teachers is to initiate children and adolescents into the prevailing culture we hold in common: the alphabet, Arabic numerals, waiting your turn, crossing the street on green, imagining something new, adding and subtracting, standard English spelling, standard English syntax, fractions, the events and battlegrounds of the American Revolution, Euclidian geometry, the Gettysburg Address.

The purpose of college or university education, this book assumes, is to help students renegotiate their membership in that prevailing common culture. It offers them the opportunity to join interpretive communities constituted by diverse, uncommon, and often dissenting languages: fractals, Old Norse, textual criticism, linguistics, the causes of the American Revolution, the effects of the Civil War, deconstruction, set theory, field theory, Plato's *Republic*, *Ulysses*, Georgia O'Keeffe, Mary Wollstonecraft, Bach's cello sonatas, John Cage.

Cooperation is an element in the prevailing culture that school teachers initiate children and adolescents into. And cooperation among students, overt or covert, is essential to primary and secondary education and to college and university education, because both acculturation and reacculturation are, as Chapter 1 points out, extremely difficult for individuals to accomplish working alone.

But there are two differences between primary or secondary education and college or university education. These differences are attributable to how much the people undergoing acculturation have already been acculturated. The first difference is that school children still have to learn the mores of cooperation—the craft of interdependence—whereas (most) college and university students do not. The second difference is that the answers to most of the questions school children address are so broadly agreed upon that there is usually little dispute about those answers or the best way to arrive at them. For college and university students, both the answers and the methods are, or should be, up for grabs. To put the case concisely in the terms used in this book, primary and secondary school education is, and should be, mostly **foundational**; college and university education is, or should be, mostly **nonfoundational**. (See pp. 15–21, 22–23, 115–16, 120–21, 159–61, 176–78.)

A **transition community** is an ad hoc community that people organize in order to **reacculturate** themselves. The transition group supports them while they renegotiate their membership in a knowledge community they already belong to and negotiate new membership in a community they don't yet belong to. Also called a "support group." (See also pp. 75–77.)

Translation is a term used in this book mostly in its common sense of rendering a statement written or spoken first in language A into language B. But the book also uses *translation* to denote what happens during negotiation at the boundaries of **knowledge communities**. In that sense, the word retains some of its root or etymological meaning of displacement or movement from one place to another. So in this book *translation* may sometimes also imply change of context, emphasis, or identity. It may even carry more distant implications such as transformation through metaphor or analogy, or, in a social context, representation, delegation, or enrollment in a new community. In stretching the term in this way I follow Michel Callon and Bruno Latour. (See also pp. 23–24, 75–77, 159–61.)

Works Cited

The most interesting recent research on collaboration in learning has been done by David and Roger Johnson, Shlomo Sharan, and Robert Slavin. The most concise compendia are those of Anne S. Goodsell and David Johnson, *Cooperative Learning*. The standard history of American college and university education is that of Frederick Rudolph.

Abercrombie, M.L.J. *The Anatomy of Judgment*. Harmondsworth, England: Penguin, 1969; New York: Hutchinson, 1960.

Annenberg: Research Communications, Ltd. *Executive Summary: Student Uses of the Annenberg/CPB Telecourses in the Fall of 1984*. Washington, D.C.: Annenberg/CPB Project, 1988.

Arons, Arnold B. *A Guide to Introductory Physics Teaching*. New York: Wiley, 1990.

Astin, Alexander W. *Four Critical Years: Effects of College on Beliefs, Attitudes and Knowledge*. San Francisco: Jossey-Bass, 1979.

———. *What Matters in College? Four Critical Years Revisited*. San Francisco: Jossey-Bass, 1993.

Axline, Virginia Mae. *Dibs, In Search of Self*. New York: Ballantine, 1964.

Bazerman, Charles. *Shaping Written Knowledge: The Genre and Activity of the Experimental Article in Science*. Madison: U Wisconsin P, 1988.

Becher, Tony. "Professional Education in a Comparative Context." In Torstendahl.

Bechtel, Joan M. "Conversation, A New Paradigm for Librarianship?" *College and Research Libraries* 47 (1986): 219–24.

Bellah, Robert N., et al. *Habits of the Heart: Individualism and Commitment in American Life*. Berkeley: U California P, 1985.

Bennis, Warren G., and Herbert A. Shepard, "A Theory of Group Development." *Human Relations* 9 (1956): 415–37.

Bloom, Allan David. *The Closing of the American Mind*. New York: Simon and Schuster, 1987.

Bloom, Sophie. *Peer and Cross-Age Tutoring in the Schools: An Individualized Supplement to Group Instruction*. Washington, D.C.: Department of Health, Education, and Welfare, Education Division, National Institute of Education, 1976.

Bloor, David. *Wittgenstein: A Social Theory of Knowledge*. New York: Columbia UP, 1985.

Works Cited

Borrensen, C. Robert. "Success in Introductory Statistics with Small Groups." *College Teaching* 38 (1990): 26–28.

Bouton, Clark, and Russell Y. Garth, eds. *Learning in Groups*. San Francisco: Jossey-Bass, 1983.

Brann, Eva T. H. "St. John's Educational Policy for a 'Living Community.'" *Change*, Sept.–Oct. 1992: 36–43.

Bruffee, Kenneth A. *Elegiac Romance: Cultural Change and Loss of the Hero in Modern Fiction*. Ithaca: Cornell UP, 1983.

———. *A Short Course in Writing*. 3rd ed., Boston: Little, Brown, 1985. 4th ed., New York: Harper/Collins, 1992.

———. "Social Construction, Language, and the Authority of Knowledge: A Bibliographical Essay." *College English* 48 (1986): 773–90; and discussion in "Comment and Response," *College English* 49 (1987): 707–16.

Bruner, Jerome S. *Acts of Meaning*. Cambridge: Harvard UP, 1990.

———. *Actual Minds, Possible Worlds*. Cambridge: Harvard UP, 1986.

———. *In Search of Mind: Essays in Autobiography*. New York: Harper, 1983.

———. "Life as Narrative." *Social Research* 54 (1987): 11–32.

Burrage, Michael, and Rolf Torstendahl, eds. *Professions in Theory and History: Rethinking the Study of the Professions*. London: Sage, 1990.

Callon, Michel. "Some Elements of a Sociology of Translation: Domestication of the Scallops and the Fishermen of St. Brieuc Bay." In Law.

Chickering, Arthur. *Commuting Versus Resident Students: Overcoming the Educational Inequities of Living Off Campus*. San Francisco: Jossey-Bass, 1974.

Coleman, James S. *Youth: Transition to Adulthood*. Report of the Panel on Youth of the President's Science Advisory Committee. James S. Coleman, Chair. Washington, D.C.: Office of Science and Technology, 1973.

Collins, H. M., and T. J. Pinch. *Frames of Meaning: The Social Construction of Extraordinary Science*. London: Routledge, 1982.

Comstock, George, Steven Chaffee, Natan Katzman, Maxwell McCombs, and Donald Roberts. *Television and Human Behavior*. New York: Columbia UP, 1978.

Coulter, Jeff. *The Social Construction of Mind: Studies in Ethnomethodology and Linguistic Philosophy*. London: Macmillan, 1979.

Culler, Jonathan D. *Ferdinand de Saussure*. 2nd ed. Ithaca: Cornell UP, 1986.

Dewey, John. *Experience and Education*. New York: Collier, 1963; first published in 1938.

Eldred, Janet Carey. "Narratives of Socialization: Literacy in the Short Story." *College English* 53 (1991): 686–700.

Eldred, Janet Carey, and Peter Mortensen. "Reading Literacy Narratives." *College English* 54 (1992): 512–39.

Elsasser, Nan, and Vera P. John-Steiner. "An Interactionist Approach to Advancing Literacy." *Harvard Educational Review* 47 (1977): 355–69.

Evans, Glen. *The Family Circle Guide to Self-Help*. New York: Ballantine, 1979.

Feynman, Richard P., and Ralph Leighton. *"Surely You're Joking, Mr. Feynman!": Adventures of a Curious Character*. Ed. Edward Hutchings. New York: Bantam, 1984.

Fish, Stanley. "Anti-Foundationalism, Theory Hope, and the Teaching of Composition." *The Current in Criticism: Essays on the Present and Future of Literacy*

Theory. Ed. Clayton Koelb and Virgil Lokke. West Lafayette, Ind.: Purdue UP, 1987.

———. "Being Interdisciplinary Is So Very Hard to Do." *Profession 89.* New York: Modern Language Association, 1989.

———. "Consequences." *Against Theory: Literary Studies and the New Pragmatism.* Ed. W.J.T. Mitchell. Chicago: U Chicago P, 1985.

———. *Is There a Text in This Class? The Authority of Interpretive Communities.* Cambridge: Harvard UP, 1980.

Fisher, Roger, and Scott Brown. *Getting Together: Building a Relationship That Gets to Yes.* New York: Houghton Mifflin, 1988.

Fisher, Roger, William Ury, and Bruce Patton. *Getting to Yes: Negotiating Agreement without Giving In.* 2nd ed. New York: Penguin, 1991.

Forgan, Sophie. "The Architecture of Science and the Idea of a University." *Studies in History and Philosophy of Science* 20 (1989): 405–34.

———. "Context, Image and Function: A Preliminary Inquiry into the Architecture of Scientific Societies." *British Journal for the History of Science* 19 (1986): 89–113.

Freire, Paulo. *Pedagogy of the Oppressed.* Trans. Myra Bergman Ramos. New York: Herder, 1972.

Freud, Sigmund. *The Future of an Illusion.* Trans. W. D. Robson-Scott, ed. James Strachey. Garden City, N.Y.: Anchor, 1964.

Fulghum, Robert. *All I Really Need to Know I Learned in Kindergarten: Uncommon Thoughts on Common Things.* New York: Random House, 1988.

Geertz, Clifford. *The Interpretation of Cultures: Selected Essays.* New York: Basic Books, 1973.

———. *Local Knowledge: Further Essays in Interpretive Anthropology.* New York: Basic Books, 1983.

Gere, Anne Ruggles. *Writing Groups: History, Theory, and Implications.* Carbondale: Southern Illinois UP, 1987.

Gergen, Kenneth J. "The Social Constructionist Movement in Modern Psychology." *The American Psychologist* 40 (1985): 265–75.

———. *Toward Transformation in Social Knowledge.* New York: Springer-Verlag, 1982.

Gitterman, Alex, and Lawrence Shulman, eds. *Mutual Aid Groups, Vulnerable Populations, and the Life Cycle.* New York: Columbia UP, 1993. Also *Mutual Aid Groups and the Life Cycle,* Itasca, IL: Peacock, 1986.

Glidden, Jock, and Joanne Gainen Kurfuss. "Small-Group Discussion in Philosophy 101." *College Teaching* 38 (1990): 3–8.

Goffman, Erving. *The Presentation of the Self in Everyday Life.* Garden City, N.Y.: Doubleday, 1959.

Goodsell, Anne S., Michelle R. Maher, and Vincent Tinto. *Collaborative Learning: A Sourcebook for Higher Education.* University Park, Pa.: National Center on Postsecondary Teaching, Learning, and Assessment, 1992.

Graff, Gerald. "Disliking Books at an Early Age." *Lingua Franca,* Sept.–Oct. 1992: 45–51. Excerpted from *Beyond the Culture Wars: How Teaching the Conflicts Can Revitalize American Education.* New York: Norton, 1992.

Harre, Rom. *Personal Being: A Theory for Individual Psychology.* Cambridge: Harvard UP, 1984.

Works Cited

———. *Physical Being: A Theory for a Corporeal Psychology.* Oxford: Blackwell, 1991.

———. *The Social Construction of Emotions.* Oxford: Blackwell, 1986.

Hawkes, Peter. "Collaborative Learning and American Literature." *College Teaching* 39 (1991): 140–44.

Herzog, Don. *Without Foundations: Justification in Political Theory.* Ithaca: Cornell UP, 1985.

Hesse, Mary. "Texts without Types and Lumps without Laws." *New Literary History* 17 (1985): 31–48.

Hirsch, E. D. *Cultural Literacy: What Every American Needs To Know.* Boston: Houghton Mifflin, 1987.

Holt, Mara Dawn. "Collaborative Learning from 1911–1986: A Socio-Historical Analysis." Diss. U Texas, 1988.

Hunter, Kathryn Montgomery. *Doctors' Stories: The Narrative Structure of Medical Knowledge.* Princeton: Princeton UP, 1991.

Ignatieff, Michael. *The Needs of Strangers.* New York: Viking, 1985.

Jardine, Nicholas. *The Fortunes of Inquiry.* Oxford: Clarendon, 1986.

———. *The Scenes of Inquiry: On the Reality of Questions in the Sciences.* Oxford: Clarendon, 1991.

Johnson, Barbara, ed. *The Pedagogical Imperative: Teaching as a Literary Genre. Yale French Studies* 63 (1982).

Johnson, David W., et al. *Circles of Learning: Cooperation in the Classroom.* Alexandria, Va.: Association for Supervision and Curriculum Development, 1984.

———. "Effects of Cooperative, Competitive, and Individualistic Goal Structures on Achievement: A Meta-Analysis." *Psychological Bulletin* 89 (1981): 47–62.

Johnson, David W., Roger T. Johnson, and Karl A. Smith. *Cooperative Learning: Increasing College Faculty Instructional Productivity.* ASHE-ERIC Higher Education Report No. 4. Washington, D.C.: George Washington University, School of Education and Human Development, 1991.

Kail, Harvey, and John Trimbur. "The Politics of Peer Tutoring." *WPA: Writing Program Administration* 11 (1987): 5–12.

Kent, Thomas. "On the Very Idea of a Discourse Community." *College Composition and Communication* 42 (1991): 425–45.

Knorr-Cetina, Karen D. *The Manufacture of Knowledge: An Essay on the Constructivist and Contextual Nature of Science.* Oxford: Pergamon, 1981.

Kuhn, Thomas S. "Second Thoughts on Paradigms." In Suppe.

———. *The Structure of Scientific Revolutions.* 2nd ed. Chicago: U Chicago P, 1970.

Larson, Magali Sarfatti. "In the Matter of Experts and Professionals, Or How Impossible It Is to Leave Nothing Unsaid." In Torstendahl.

———. *The Rise of Professionalism: A Sociological Analysis.* Berkeley: U California P, 1977.

Latour, Bruno. "Clothing the Naked Truth." *Dismantling Truth: Reality in the Post-Modern World.* Ed. Hilary Lawson and Lisa Appignanesi. London: Weidenfeld and Nicolson, 1989.

———. "Mixing Humans and Non-Humans Together: The Sociology of a Door-Closer." *Social Problems* 35 (1988): 298–310.

———. *The Pasteurization of France*. Trans. A. Sheridan. Cambridge, Mass.: Harvard UP, 1988.

———. "Post-Modern? No, Simply Amodern! Steps toward an Anthropology of Science." *Studies in History and Philosophy of Science* 21 (1990): 145–71.

———. "The Powers of Association." In Law.

———. *Science in Action: How to Follow Scientists and Engineers Through Society*. Cambridge: Harvard UP, 1987.

———. "Visualization and Cognition: Thinking with Hands and Eyes." *Knowledge and Society: Studies in the Sociology of Culture Past and Present* 6 (1986): 1–40.

Latour, Bruno, and Françoise Bastide. "Writing Science—Fact and Fiction: The Analysis of the Process of Reality Construction Through the Application of Socio-Semiotic Methods to Scientific Texts." *Mapping the Dynamics of Science and Technology: Sociology of Science in the Real World*. Ed. Michel Callon, John Law, and Arie Rip. London: Macmillan, 1986.

Latour, Bruno, and Steve Woolgar. *Laboratory Life: The Construction of Scientific Facts*. Princeton: Princeton UP, 1986.

Laurenson, Diana T., and Alan Swingewood. *The Sociology of Literature*. New York: Schocken, 1972.

Law, John, ed. *Power, Action and Belief: A New Sociology of Science?* London: Routledge, 1986.

Leggatt, T. "Teaching as a Profession." *Professions and Professionalization*. Ed. J. A. Jackson. Cambridge: Cambridge UP, 1970.

Lewin, Kurt, and Paul Grabbe. "Conduct, Knowledge, and the Acceptance of New Values." *Resolving Social Conflicts: Selected Papers on Group Dynamics*. Ed. Kurt Lewin. New York: Harper, 1948. Reprinted from *Journal of Social Issues* 1 (1945): 53–64.

Loche, David. *Science as Writing*. New Haven: Yale UP, 1993.

Mason, Edwin. *Collaborative Learning*. London: Ward Lock Educational, 1970; New York: Agathon, 1971; Introduction by Ronald Gross.

McGann, Jerome J. *A Critique of Modern Textual Criticism*. Chicago: U Chicago P, 1983.

Nelson, Cary, ed. *Theory in the Classroom*. Urbana: U of Illinois P, 1986.

Nelson, John S., Allan Megill, and Donald N. McCloskey, eds. *The Rhetoric of the Human Sciences: Language and Argument in Scholarship and Public Affairs*. Madison: U Wisconsin P, 1987.

Newcomb, Theodore M., and Everett K. Wilson, eds. *College Peer Groups: Problems and Prospects for Research*. Chicago: Aldine, 1966.

———. "Student Peer-Group Influence." In Ed. Nevitt Sanford, *The American College: A Psychological and Social Interpretation of the Higher Learning*. New York: Wiley, 1962.

Oakeshott, Michael. "The Voice of Poetry in the Conversation of Mankind." *Rationalism in Politics*. New York: Basic Books, 1962.

Oliver Wendell Holmes Society. *Program Guide to the New Pathway, September 4, 1985*. Foreword by Gordon T. Moore. Cambridge: Harvard Medical School, 1985. See also "Can We Make a Better Doctor?" *NOVA* 1521. Boston: WGBH Educational Foundation, 1988.

Perry, William G., Jr. "Examsmanship and the Liberal Arts: A Study in Educational Epistemology." *Examining in Harvard College: A Collection of Essays by Members of the Harvard Faculty.* Cambridge: Harvard UP, 1963.

———. *Forms of Intellectual and Ethical Development in the College Years: A Scheme.* New York: Holt, 1968.

Pratt, Mary Louise. "Arts of the Contact Zone." *Profession 91.* New York: Modern Language Association, 1991: 33–40.

Rau, William, and Barbara Sherman Heyl. "Humanizing the College Classroom: Collaborative Learning and Social Organization among Students." *Teaching Sociology* 18 (1990): 141–55.

Reither, James A., and Douglas Vipond. "Writing as Collaboration." *College English* 51 (1989): 855–67.

Rigden, John S., and Sheila Tobias. "Point of View: Too Often College-Level Science Is Dull as Well as Difficult." *Chronicle of Higher Education,* March 27, 1991: A52.

Rodriguez, Richard. *Hunger of Memory: The Education of Richard Rodriguez.* New York: Bantam, 1983.

Rorty, Richard. *Contingency, Irony, and Solidarity.* Cambridge: Cambridge UP, 1989.

———. *Philosophy and the Mirror of Nature.* Princeton: Princeton UP, 1979.

———. "Science as Solidarity." In Nelson, *Rhetoric.*

Roswell, Barbara. "The Tutor's Audience Is Always a Fiction: The Construction of Authority in Writing Center Conferences." Diss. University of Pennsylvania, 1992.

Roth, Philip. "The Man in the Middle." *New York Times,* October 10, 1992: 21. Abridged from a speech before the New Jersey Historical Society, Oct. 5, 1992.

Rudolph, Frederick. *The American College and University: A History.* New York: Knopf, 1962.

Sarris, Greg. "Storytelling in the Classroom: Crossing Vexed Chasms." *College English* 52 (1990): 169–85.

Sennett, Richard, and Jonathan Cobb. *The Hidden Injuries of Class.* New York: Knopf, 1972.

Sharan, Shlomo. "Cooperative Learning in Small Groups: Recent Methods and Effects on Achievement, Attitudes, and Ethnic Relations." *Review of Educational Research* 50 (1980): 241–71.

———, ed. *Cooperative Learning: Theory and Research.* New York: Praeger, 1990.

Sharan, Shlomo, and Hana Sachar. *Languages and Learning in the Cooperative Classroom.* New York: Praeger, 1990.

Slavin, Robert E. *Cooperative Learning.* New York: Longman, 1983.

———. *Learning to Cooperate, Cooperating to Learn.* New York: Plenum, 1985.

Sprague, Elmer. "Using the 'Group Method' in Teaching Introductory Philosophy Courses." *APA Newsletter on Teaching Philosophy* 4 (1984): n.p.

Steffens, Henry. "Collaborative Learning in a History Seminar." *The History Teacher* 21 (1983): 1–14.

Stillinger, Jack. *Multiple Authorship and the Myth of Solitary Genius.* Oxford: Oxford UP, 1992.

Works Cited

Suppe, Frederick, ed. *The Structure of Scientific Theories.* 2nd ed. Urbana: U Illinois P, 1977.

Thomas, Lewis. *The Lives of a Cell: Notes of a Biology Watcher.* New York: Bantam, 1975.

Tobias, Sheila. *Overcoming Math Anxiety.* New York: Norton, 1978.

———. *They're Not Dumb, They're Different: Stalking the Second Tier.* Tucson, Ariz.: Research Corporation, 1990.

Torstendahl, Rolf, and Michael Burrage, eds. *The Formation of Professions: Knowledge, State and Strategy.* London: Sage, 1990.

Toulmin, Stephen. "The Inwardness of Mental Life." *Critical Inquiry,* Autumn, 1979: 1–16.

Trilling, Lionel. "Why We Read Jane Austen." *The Last Decade: Essays and Reviews, 1965–75.* Ed. Diana Trilling. New York: Harcourt, 1979; reprinted from *TLS* 5 March 1976: 50–52.

Trimbur, John. "Collaborative Learning and Teaching Writing." *Perspectives on Recent Research and Scholarship in Composition.* Ed. Ben W. McClelland and Timothy R. Donovan. New York: Modern Language Association, 1985.

———. "Consensus and Difference in Collaborative Learning." *College English* 51 (1989): 602–16.

Trimbur, John, and Lundy A. Braun. "Laboratory Life and the Determination of Authorship." *New Visions of Collaborative Writing.* Ed. Janis Forman. Portsmouth, N.H.: Boynton/Cook-Heinemann, 1992.

Unger, Roberto Mangabeira. *Passion: An Essay on Personality.* New York: Free Press, 1984.

Vollmer, Howard M., and Donald L. Mills, eds. *Professionalization.* Englewood Cliffs, N.J.: Prentice-Hall, 1966.

Vygotsky, L. S. *Mind in Society: The Development of Higher Psychological Processes.* Ed. Michael Cole, Vera John-Steiner, Sylvia Scribner, and Ellen Souberman. Cambridge: Harvard UP, 1978.

———. *Thought and Action.* Ed. and trans. Eugenia Hanfmann and Gertrude Vakar. Cambridge: Harvard UP, 1962.

Wallis, Roy, ed. *On the Margins of Science: The Social Construction of Rejected Knowledge.* Sociological Review Monograph No. 27. Keele, England: U Keele P, 1979.

Ward, Scott, and Daniel Wackman. "Family and Media Influences on Adolescent Consumer Learning." *American Behavioral Scientist* 14 (1971): 415–27.

Welker, Robert. *The Teacher as Expert: A Theoretical and Historical Examination.* Albany: State U of New York P, 1992.

Wertsch, James V. *Vygotsky and the Social Formation of Mind.* Cambridge: Harvard UP, 1985.

Whitehead, Alfred North. *Science in the Modern World.* New York: Mentor, 1948; first published in 1925.

Wiener, Harvey S. "Collaborative Learning in the Classroom: A Guide to Evaluation." *College English* 48 (1986): 52–61; reprinted in Goodsell.

Winnicott, D. W. *The Child and the Family: First Relationships.* Ed. Janet Hardenberg. London: Tavistock, 1957.

Index

Abel, Reuben, ix
Abercrombie, M.L.J., 24–25, 56–57, 75–77,
153, 155–57, 165; implications, 170–71
Academic disciplines, 1, 3–4, 135–36, 193;
contrasted with public professions, 126–
27, 131–35; expertise, language, and
values of, 29, 33, 35–36, 63–64, 74, 77,
101, 126–27, 128–31, 148–49, 223–25;
nondisciplinary language and, 77–78,
survival of, 131–32, 137–39, 175; and
teaching, 7–8, 44, 49–50, 136, 139–41,
178, 195. *See also* Knowledge
communities
American Council of Learned Societies, 8
Annenburg School for Communication,
102
Apprenticeship, 4, 7, 132, 182
Arons, Arnold B., 38, 216
Astin, Alexander, 211
Atkinson, Richard C., 216
Authority, accepting and granting, by
peers, 4, 21, 24, 29, 33–34, 107–8, 186–
87; resistance to, 26, 43–44
Authority, dependence on, 8, 39, 43, 70,
183, 188
Authority, teachers', viii–ix, 7–8, 10, 27,
29–31, 39, 43, 65, 82, 94–95, 126–27,
132–33, 178–79, 181–82; as exercised in
collaborative learning (*see* Collaborative
learning, authority in); as exercised in
traditional teaching, 66–69, 72–73, 128–
30. *See also* Knowledge, authority of

Barthes, Roland, 69
Bazerman, Charles, 196
Bechtel, Joan M., 109–10
Bennett, William, 8
"Bert and Ernestine," 59–60

Bloom, Alan, 8
Booth, Stephen, 219
Brooklyn College, City University of New
York, 15
Bruner, Jerome, 116, 122–23, 161–65, 171

California, University of, at Berkeley, 25,
153
Callon, Michel, 144, 226
Chickering, Arthur, 159
City College, City University of New
York, 16
City University of New York, 15, 177
Cobb, Jonathan. *See* Sennett, Richard
Cognition. *See* Knowledge, foundational
Cognitive myth, 157, 160–61, 164–65, 170–
71, 180, 181–82, 217, 218
Cold fusion, 138–39
Coleman, James S., 5–6
Collaborative learning: architecture of,
110, 207–9; assumptions of, 3–4, 8–9,
18, 130–31, 175–76, 200–202; authority
in, viii–ix, 4, 7, 26–27, 44–50, 70–72, 73–
74, 131, 140–41, 188–89; conformity in,
29, 33, 90–91, 121–22, 192–94; consensus
in, 24–25, 28, 35–36, 41, 45–47, 49–50,
78–79, 106–7, 184–85; conversation in,
22–23, 25, 48, 63, 73, 85; dissent in, 32–
34, 36–37, 42, 45–46, 107, 188;
evaluation in, 34, 44–50, 60–61, 91, 106,
211, 214; evaluation in traditional
teaching contrasted, 67–69, 87, 129;
evaluation of, 185, 200–202, 211, 212;
exemplified, 15–21, 22–23, 24–25, 116,
117–18, 159–60; group composition in,
32–35; history of, 5–6, 24–26, 155–57,
172–76; institutionalization of, 79, 80–92,
93–96, 152–53, 172–76, 191–92; language

Index

Index

Index

Knowledge, foundational *(cont'd.)*
of, 156, 158–59, 161, 165–71, 176–77,
179, 180; "local," 120, 183, 192–94, 224–
25; objectivist and subjectivist, 54, 69–
70, 98–99, 156, 164, 180, 222; research
limited by, 6–7, 155–71; teaching limited
by, 35–36, 66–69, 72–73, 144–45, 153,
170–71, 178–79, 180–81. *See also*
Cognitive myth
Knowledge, nonfoundational, 3, 63–65,
103–4, 109–10, 113, 115–23, 130–31, 140,
149–51, 163–65, 200–205, 221–23;
language of, 9, 36, 54–55, 147–48, 162–
63, 165–70, 172, 177; as "locally"
foundational, 120, 183, 192–94, 224–25;
in science, 142–43, 144, 145; in teaching,
7–8, 64–65, 104–5, 119–21, 140–41, 144,
145, 158, 176–78. *See also* Collaborative
learning
Knowledge, social construction of, 51, 55,
63–64, 113–15, 122, 130–31, 142–43, 150,
162–63, 224–25; college and university
education and, 3, 8–9, 38, 40–41, 49–50,
64–65, 95–96, 121–25, 144, 151–53, 156–
57, 160, 176–78, 182–84, 195–96;
interpretation as, 52–53, 116, 131, 145,
176–78, 223–24
Knowledge communities, 3–4, 47, 130–31,
175, 176, 191–93, 223–24; boundaries of,
17–18, 22–24, 120–21, 122–23, 135–41,
174–75, 183, 199–200, 224; boundaries
of, in education, 22–24, 64–65, 75–77,
85, 123–24, 158, 160–61, 177, 184–85,
188; conformity in, 19, 33, 121, 192–94,
203–4; constitution of, 3, 16–19, 26, 27,
54–55, 75–77, 91, 103–4, 116, 118–25,
130–31, 140, 163, 165, 177, 183, 191,
197–202; languages of, 18–19, 22–24, 32–
33, 52–53, 63, 64–65, 101, 114, 118–21,
122, 126–27, 130–31, 134, 135–36, 141,
150–51, 153, 162–64, 196, 199–200, 204;
margins of, 136–39; in sciences, 51, 52–
53, 60, 63, 68, 74, 122–23, 138–39, 141,
142–43, 145, 150, 175, 201; relations
among, 47, 50, 119–23; survival of, 131–
32. *See also* Collaborative learning,
conformity in; Negotiation; Translation
Kuhn, Thomas S., 64, 119, 124, 160;
knowledge as community property in,
3, 114–15, 131, 176, 179, 197–98; "left-

wing Kuhnianism," 202–5; "paradigms"
in, 116; translation in, 76, 122, 123, 183;
"right wing Kuhnianism," 175, 200–202

Lacan, Jacques, 181, 182
Lafayette College, 110
Landau, Misia, 196
Language, social construction of, 17–21,
22–24, 54–55, 57, 78–79, 118–21, 151,
165–71, 182–84, 184–85
Larson, Magali Sarfatti, 126
Latour, Bruno, 131, 167–68, 183, 188;
"black boxes" in, 118, 198; on language,
119–21, 123, 162, 183–204, 226; on
"powers of association," 203
Latour, Bruno, and Steve Woolgar, 51, 52–
53, 56, 142, 145, 153, 166–67; on
limitations of cognitive thought, 170–71
Lecture, 9, 30–31, 67, 105, 153, 207
Leitch, Vincent, 181, 196
Levin, Harry, 199
Lewin, Kurt, 19, 116
Liberal education, 17, 81, 151–52, 178,
189–90, 191–92; as reacculturation, 76,
135–36, 139–41
Liberal humanism, limitations of, 173–74,
189–90, 194
Libraries, conversation and, 109–10
Literacy, 17, 18
Literature: foundational readings of, 173–
74, 193–94, 199; nonfoundational social
constructionist readings of, 151, 199–
200; social construction of, 166–67, 176–
78, 186–87, 198–99; sociology of, 199.
See also Narration
Lyotard, Jean-François, 184–87, 202

McCloskey, Donald N., 196
McGann, Jerome, 199
Maimon, Elaine, 44
Marshall, Thurgood, 173
"Mary," 22–24, 27, 53, 60, 85, 96, 103–4,
121
Mason, Edwin, ix, 4–5, 7
Mathematics, 25–26, 37–38, 88, 136, 143;
languages of, 73, 130, 149–51
Megill, Alan, 196
Mind Extension University, 109
Modern Language Association, 8
Moger, Angela, 186, 187
Mohanty, S. P., 181

Index

Multicultural issues, 124, 172–76, 188, 189–90, 193–94

Narration, knowledge as, 115–16, 118–19, 120–21, 186, 187, 199–200, 201. *See also* Literature
National Association of Scholars, 8
Negotiation, 117–18, 120–21, 204, 213; boundary conversation and, 23, 63–65, 78, 124, 135–40, 158, 173–74, 183–84; college and university education defined as, 63, 65–66; knowledge and, 9, 63–65, 161–63, 177, 200–202. *See also* Collaborative learning, negotiation in; Knowledge communities, boundaries of, in education
Nelson, Cary, 180
Nelson, John S., 196
New Pathways. *See* Harvard University Medical School
New School, ix
Newcomb, Theodore, 4, 6, 90
Nietzsche, Friedrich, 130
Nintendo, 104
Nonfoundational. *See* Knowledge, nonfoundational
Nonstandard discourse. *See* Knowledge communities, boundaries of, in education
Normal discourse. *See* Knowledge communities, languages of

Oakeshott, Michael, 55, 110, 113–14
Ohmann, Richard, viii

Peer group, influence of, 5–6, 23–24, 57–58, 79, 108, 157, 160, 211. *See also* Collaborative learning, authority in, resistance to, stress in, coping with; Interdependence
Peer review, 48, 53, 61–62, 68, 89, 108. *See also* Collaborative learning, evaluation in
Peer tutoring, 80–97; institutional impact of, 81; outcome of, 82, 88–92, 93–94; "politics" of, 86, 93; "training" for, 85–87, 94–95; types of, 83–85; tutors' authority in, 85–87. *See also* PSI
Peers: knowledgeable, 50–51, 56, 130, 157, 192–93, 223–24; rigor in defining, 7, 82–83, 197–98

Penley, Constance, 181
Perry William G., Jr., 6, 19, 58, 76, 79, 121–22, 123, 124, 157–61, 165, 171, 177, 183
Piaget, Jean, 157
Plagiarism, 27, 66
Planck, Max, 137, 201
Plato, 128, 180, 222
Plenary. *See* Collaborative learning, plenary discussion in
Post-Cartesian thought, 128. *See also* Knowledge, foundational
Pratt, Mary Louise, 65, 123, 180, 186–87
Professions academic, contrasted with public professions, 126, 132–34, 139
PSI, 69–70, 83
Psychoanalysis, 183–84, 196–97

Queens College, City University of New York, 16
Quine, W.V.O., 142–43, 151

Rau, William, 5
Reacculturation, education as, vii, 3, 26, 74, 131, 139–40, 173, 174, 176–78, 191–92, 201, 225–26; exemplified, 15–21, 22–23, 116, 117–18, 120–21, 159–60, 184–85. *See also* Collaborative learning, reacculturation through
Reading, 16–17, 18–19, 20, 22–24, 27, 40–41, 61–62, 80, 188; solitude and, 54. *See also* Conversation, indirect or displaced
Recitation, 9, 31, 67–69
Recorder. *See* Collaborative learning, recorder's role in
Research, educational, 6–7
Rigden, John S., 145
Rocky Horror Picture Show, 103
Rodriguez, Richard, 173, 174, 175
Rogerian psychology, 69
Rorty, Richard, 35–36, 64, 165, 168, 200, 201, 202, 205, 225; on learning as change in human relations, 18, 74; on social justification of belief, 50–51, 115–16, 130, 131, 176; on nonstandard discourse, 123–24, 161, 182, 183, 224; on normal discourse, 225
Rosaldo, Renato, 196
Roth, Philip, 173, 174, 190
Ryan, Michael, 180